THE ROUGH GUIDE TO

TENERIFE

INCLUDING LA GOMERA

Forthcoming titles include

The Algarve • The Bahamas • Cambodia
Caribbean Islands • Costa Brava
New York Restaurants • South America • Zanzibar

Forthcoming reference guides include

Children's Books • Online Travel • Videogaming
Weather

CANCELLED

D0715216

WEST DUNBARTONSHIRE
LIBRARIES

C030139912

CBS	22/03/2002
916.4'9'048	5.99
	CL

Penguin Books Canada Ltd, 10 Alcorn Avenue,
Toronto, Ontario, Canada M4V 1E4
Penguin Books (NZ) Ltd,
182–190 Wairau Road, Auckland 10, New Zealand

Typeset in Bembo and Helvetica to an original design by Henry Iles.
Printed in Spain by Graphy Cems.

No part of this book may be reproduced in any form
without permission from the publisher except for the
quotation of brief passages in reviews.

© Christian Williams
368pp, includes index
A catalogue record for this book is available from the British Library.

ISBN 1-85828-665-4

The publishers and authors have done their best to ensure
the accuracy and currency of all the information in
The Rough Guide to Tenerife, however, they
can accept no responsibility for any loss, injury or
inconvenience sustained by any traveller as a result of
information or advice contained in the guide.

THE ROUGH GUIDE TO

TENERIFE

INCLUDING LA GOMERA

by Christian Williams

ROUGH
GUIDES

We set out to do something different when the first Rough Guide was published in 1982. Mark Ellingham, just out of university, was travelling in Greece. He brought along the popular guides of the day, but found they were all lacking in some way. They were either strong on ruins and museums but went on for pages without mentioning a beach or taverna. Or they were so conscious of the need to save money that they lost sight of Greece's cultural and historical significance. Also, none of the books told him anything about Greece's contemporary life – its politics, its culture, its people, and how they lived.

So with no job in prospect, Mark decided to write his own guidebook, one which aimed to provide practical information that was second to none, detailing the best beaches and the hottest clubs and restaurants, while also giving hard-hitting accounts of every sight, both famous and obscure, and providing up-to-the-minute information on contemporary culture. It was a guide that encouraged independent travellers to find the best of Greece, and was a great success, getting shortlisted for the Thomas Cook travel guide award, and encouraging Mark, along with three friends, to expand the series.

The Rough Guide list grew rapidly and the letters flooded in, indicating a much broader readership than had been anticipated, but one which uniformly appreciated the Rough Guide mix of practical detail and humour, irreverence and enthusiasm. Things haven't changed. The same four friends who began the series are still the caretakers of the Rough Guide mission today: to provide the most reliable, up-to-date and entertaining information to independent-minded travellers of all ages, on all budgets.

We now publish more than 150 titles and have offices in London and New York. The travel guides are written and researched by a dedicated team of more than 100 authors, based in Britain, Europe, the USA and Australia. We have also created a unique series of phrasebooks to accompany the travel series, along with an acclaimed series of music guides, and a best-selling pocket guide to the Internet and World Wide Web. We also publish comprehensive travel information on our Web site: **www.roughguides.com**

Help us update

We've gone to a lot of trouble to ensure that this Rough Guide is as up to date and accurate as possible. However, things do change. All suggestions, comments and corrections are much appreciated, and we'll send a copy of the next edition (or any other Rough Guide if you prefer) for the best letters.

Please mark letters "Rough Guide Tenerife Update" and send to:

Rough Guides, 62–70 Shorts Gardens, London, WC2H 9AH, or Rough Guides, 4th Floor, 345 Hudson St, New York NY 10014.

Or send email to: mail@roughguides.co.uk
Online updates about this book can be found on Rough Guides' Web site (see opposite)

The author

As a toddler Christian fell into the Atlantic off the coast of Tenerife, years later he rode his first bicycle there. So having written a Mountain Bike Guide to Edinburgh and the Tweed Valley it seemed to make sense to head to Tenerife. Christian is currently working on a Rough Guide to the US Rockies, where he currently resides.

Acknowledgements

The author would like to thank those people on Tenerife who helped to make the book as accurate as possible and for all the others for knowing how to throw a good party. Thanks in particular to Bicisport in Los Cristianos for storing my gear, to Monika for my German, Raymond for commas, Heather for companionship and Christmas for the wanderlust.
At Rough Guides, thanks to Martin Duford for suggesting I was the right man for the job, Paul Gray and Andrew Tomicic for their deft use of the red pen in the early stages, and to Judith Bamber for picking up the editorial reigns for the hardest part of the project and guiding me through to the end.

CONTENTS

CONTENTS

●

MAP LIST

Maps at back of book

MAP SYMBOLS

▬▬▬	Motorway	ⓘ	Information office
▬▬▬	Road	⊠	Post office
- - - - -	Footpath	@	Internet access
▬▬▬	Waterway	⌂	Refuge
♦	Point of interest	⚠	Campsite
⚓	Harbour	◉	Accommodation
⌘	Church (regional maps)	▣	Places to eat and drink
♛	Castle	⊼	Picnic area
☨	Lighthouse	▬┼	Church (town maps)
▲	Peak	⊞	Cemetery
☼	Viewpoint		Dry creek
⊥	Gardens		Beach
⚑	Golf course		National park
★	Bus stop		Park
✈	Airport		Scrubland
⊞	Hospital		

Introduction

Despite its predictably sunny weather and the wide variety of landscapes that attract millions of tourists every year, Tenerife has a bit of an image problem, thanks largely to the attentions of the package tourism industry. As a result the entire island is commonly, though rather mistakenly, assumed to be just a playground for the hordes of rowdy, booze-fuelled holiday-makers looking for sun, sea and often sex in the island's large resorts, particularly Playa de las Américas. And though most visitors largely content themselves with lazy days on the beach, there are plenty of opportunities to be more active and go surfing, windsurfing, sailing, diving or deep-sea fishing.

Tenerife first established itself as a holiday destination over a century ago when it became a fashionable place for the aristocracy of Europe to spend the winter months. Since then, but particularly in the last fifty years, during which time **mass-tourism** has become a major global industry, the numbers of holiday-makers have vastly increased. Today the island gets over four million annual visitors who, together with the thousands of northern Europeans settling here, have significantly changed the personality of the island.

Though commonly viewed by independent travellers as an aesthetic and social curse that has distorted the cultural landscape and cloaked vast areas in concrete, mass tourism has also guaranteed plentiful and excellent services in the resorts towns and **cheap flights** to the island. And if the resort honey-pots aren't to your taste, you'll find that it's easy to leave the mass of holiday-makers behind. Despite the compactness of the island that puts most areas of the island within an easy **day trip** of its resorts you won't find many other foreigners in the island's vibrant, unpretentious and distinctly Canarian urban centres and only a small stream of hikers in its **mountainous regions**. Here it's easy to find great quiet **hiking trails**, a couple of good **climbing areas**, as well as some quiet (though hilly) backroads and dirt roads for **cycling** and **mountain biking**. And for those wanting to get even further from the humdrum, there's the option of heading out to hike or bike on the strikingly precipitous and laid-back nearby island of **La Gomera**.

Around the islands

For a small island, only 86km long and 56km wide, **Tenerife** has a startling range and number of distinct **ecological zones** arising from the island's mountainous topography which is dominated by a huge and barren volcanic backbone centre on **Mount Teide**. The island's mountains stand in the way of prevailing cool northerly trade winds, forcing them to condense as cloud and bringing moisture to the island and keeping its **northern** side damp and green, while having little effect on the **southern** side – which is left to bake in the sun.

At the northeast end of the island the capital and largest city, **Santa Cruz**, is at the heart of a large sprawling urban area that also encompasses the old university town **La Laguna**, and houses around half of the island's population of 650,000. Preventing the expansion of this urban area further north is the steep, wildly rugged, forested and impenetrable **Anaga** region where modern infrastructure has only recently arrived to its remote villages which remain great gateways for quiet **hikes** through the area's mist-smothered laurel forests or along its beautiful unspoilt rocky coastline.

There are more good hikes through the thick forest of Canarian pines on the **north** side of the island. This is at its thickest on the old volcanic ridges surrounding the island's most verdant region, the heavily populated, fertile, terraced and thickly planted **Orotava valley**, where the island's first resort, the stylish **Puerto de la Cruz**, became fashionable over a century ago.

Further **west** along the coast pines give way to the deforested dry, rocky and steep-sided **Teno** massif, an ancient volcanic area. And though there's more good hiking here, the area is best known for the presence of the giant cliffs **Los Gigantes**, from which a quiet neighbouring resort has taken its name.

Like the African continent only 300km to the east, the island's **southern side** is dry and dusty. Only a few hardy shrubs and cacti can take hold in this sun-baked desert, although the ubiquitous sunshine has resulted in the construction, from scratch, of the lion's share of Tenerife's big resorts. Lining the coasts of the south and attracting thousands of tourists are **Playa de Las Américas**, **Los Cristianos** and the **Costa del Silencio** – strings of hotels, restaurants and bars, many of which line the island's major (artificial) beaches.

A much more stunning and memorable island landscape, though equally barren, is that around its **central volcanic plateau**. The massive 3,718m volcano **Mount Teide**, the highest point on Spanish territory and symbol of the island, is at the centre of this region and surrounded by **Las Cañadas**, a vast beautiful tree-less volcanic wasteland containing gnarled and twisted lava contortions which are protected as a national park.

There's another national park on Tenerife's closest neighbour in the Canarian archipelago, the small round and much less visited island of **La Gomera**, 28km away. But in complete contrast to Tenerife's national park the **Parque Nacional de Garajonay**, a UNESCO world heritage site, is a haven for the world's premium remaining deep green and misty laurel forest. Also in contrast to Tenerife, the resorts in La Gomera are remarkably small-scale.

Climate and when to go

For islands at this latitude, level with Morocco 300km to the west, their climate is generally **milder** than you'd expect – mainly thanks to the northeast **trade winds** – but also because of the cool **Canary current** in the surrounding Atlantic ocean. As a result the **variation around the islands** is marked and since there is only relatively minimal seasonal change the choice of where to go tends to be as important as when.

Winds and currents have the greatest effect on climate on the **north** side of the island, where northern slopes catch cool trade winds, forming a cloud base that results in less sunshine, more rain and cooler temperatures than at the southern end of the island. The only wind that affects the **south** is an occasional hot, dry, gentle and dusty *Calima* blowing from the Sahara – sometimes for days at a time. The climatic table below summarises variation around the island using data from the coastal resorts of Puerto Cruz in the north and Los Cristianos in the south. This pattern of variation also exists on **La Gomera** which, though tending to be a little cooler all round than Tenerife, also has a colder, wetter north and sunnier, drier south. Moving **inland** from the coast to higher ground on both islands, temperatures become progressively cooler, with Mount Teide often experiencing freezing temperatures and occasionally snow cover.

So, holiday-makers intent on spending time on **sunny beaches** would do best to stay in the **south** of either island at any time of year, while those seeking an **active holiday** in the **summer**, would be best off in the **cooler north**. Spring (March–May) is a particularly pleasant time for outdoor activities since many endemic species flower at this time.

Thus, with remarkably little variation year round in the weather conditions in the Canaries, the peak times for tourists to visit reflect the weather conditions back home rather than on the islands. Thus, the **busiest times to visit** – and in contrast to resorts on the Spanish mainland – are from mid-December to February, when many northern Europeans are keen to escape long and dreary winters. The islands are also popular at Easter and during summer holidays (June–Sept) when the nightlife in the resorts gets particularly busy and numbers are further bolstered by visitors from the Spanish mainland, arriving to escape the heat of their plains. There's a slight **low season** between these times (March, May, Oct & Nov) – with the notable exception of the **carnival** period (Feb or March), when Santa Cruz is at its busiest; an excellent time to catch the island's native nightlife in full swing.

TENERIFE CLIMATE CHART

The figures below give the average daily temperature (by day/night; °C), water temperature (°C), number of hours of sunshine per day (hrs) and average monthly rainfall (mm) across Tenerife. Statistics for north and south La Gomera are comparable.

Los Cristianos (south of the island)

	°C	°C	hrs	mm
Jan	21/15	19	6	22
Feb	21/15	19	7	17
March	22/16	19	7	13
April	23/16	19	8	9
May	24/17	20	10	2
June	27/19	20	11	0
July	29/21	22	11	0
Aug	30/21	23	11	0
Sept	28/21	22	9	2
Oct	26/20	22	7	12
Nov	24/18	21	7	23
Dec	22/16	20	6	26

Puerto Cruz (north of the island)

	°C	°C	hrs	mm
Jan	19/13	19	5	88
Feb	19/13	19	6	82
March	20/14	19	7	55
April	21/14	19	8	48
May	22/16	20	9	26
June	23/18	20	10	13
July	24/19	22	11	7
Aug	26/20	23	10	11
Sept	26/20	22	8	19
Oct	24/18	22	6	48
Nov	22/17	21	6	97
Dec	20/14	20	5	105

BASICS

Getting there

With regular, inexpensive flights from almost all their international airports, it could hardly be easier to get from the UK and Ireland to Tenerife. The majority of flights to Tenerife are charters serving the needs of the package-holiday industry, but there are some scheduled flights available. There are no direct flights, however – and few package deals – from North America, Australia or New Zealand, though there are good deals from each to London, Madrid and Barcelona, from where you can easily get onward connections to the Canary Islands. If you're not pushed for time, it may be worth trying for a cheap flight to southern Spain, from where you can catch the weekly ferry from Cádiz to Santa Cruz de Tenerife.

Good weather year round means that there's really no off-season in the Canaries, though **fares** do go up, and accommodation is harder to find, from May to September and over Christmas and the New Year.

FLIGHTS AND PACKAGE DEALS

Most people fly to Tenerife (though rarely La Gomera) as part of a **package deal**. The variety of deals available ranges from simply self-catering apartments – usually the cheapest option – to luxury hotels. Though most of the accommodation on offer is concentrated in vast, rather soulless hotel or apartment blocks, package holidays do represent good value for money and can offer access to sports facilities and provide entertainment for children that would be hard to organize independently.

There is generally little to be saved by getting a **flight-only** deal – except for those travelling alone, who will be faced with exorbitant single-occupancy supplements on most package deals. Of course, you will have the extra hassle of organizing your own accommodation, but this may well be worth it to avoid the brasher complexes and to gain more flexibility in touring around the island. The cost of a **scheduled flight** out of the UK is likely to be double that of the best charter deals, most of which fly out of the London airports. Monarch, who fly out of Luton, have the best deals, starting from as little as £170 return, while British Airways fly from Gatwick and Go fly from Stansted, both for around £200.

You can often cut costs by going through a specialist **flight agent** – either a consolidator, who buys up blocks of tickets from the airlines and sells them at a discount, or a discount agent, who in addition to dealing with discounted flights may also offer special student and youth fares and a range of other travel-related services such as travel insurance, rail passes, car rentals, tours and the like. Don't automatically assume that tickets purchased through a travel specialist will be cheapest, however – once you get a quote, check with the **airlines** and you may turn up an even better deal. As tour operators rely on flight availability to sell more profitable package holidays, flight-only deals are kept artificially high until the last minute. This means that if you try to buy a seat on a charter flight as little as a couple of weeks in advance you are often looking at around £300 return in high season

– but you should be able to get something for closer to £100 if you can book a day or two before travelling.

From the **Spanish mainland** there are three airlines that fly direct to Tenerife. The Mallorca-based Spanair has scheduled flights to Tenerife from Madrid, Barcelona, Santiago de Compostela and Palma de Mallorca; Air Europa flies to Tenerife from numerous airports including Madrid, Barcelona, Alicante and Malaga; while Iberia flies from eight mainland destinations, which can be linked with the company's UK services via Heathrow, Gatwick and Manchester. Ticket **prices** can be as low as €120 return outside the busiest summer months. The standard fare is, however, much closer to that of a one-year open return ticket with Air Europa which costs around €310 from Madrid and €390 from Barcelona.

The Internet is a good place to find some of the best deals around. Sites such as Ⓦ**www.cheapflights.com**, to which numerous travel agents send in their best flight prices, and Ⓦ**www.centralholidays.com** are an invaluable resource, as is Teletext, which can be accessed via the Internet at Ⓦ**www.teletext.co.uk**. In addition, newspaper travel sections and magazines such as *Time Out* and *TNT* are a good source of information on cheap deals.

AIRLINES

Britain
Air 2000 Ⓣ01293/596620, Ⓦwww.air2000.com
British Airways Ⓣ 0845/773 3377, in Republic of Ireland Ⓦwww.britishairways.com
Go Ⓣ0870/607 6543, Ⓦwww.go-fly.com

Monarch Airlines Ⓣ08700/405040, Ⓦwww.fly-crown.com

North America
American Airlines Ⓣ1-800/433-7300, Ⓦwww.aa.com

British Airways
 ☎ 1-800/247-9297,
Ⓦ www.british-airways.com
Continental Airlines
☎ 1-800/231-0856,
Ⓦ www.continental.com
Iberia ☎ 1-800/772-4642,
Ⓦ www.iberia.com
United ☎ 1-800/538-2929,
Ⓦ www.aul.com

Australia and New Zealand

Garuda Australia ☎ 13/1223 or
☎ 02/9334 9900, New Zealand
☎ 09/366 1862,
Ⓦ www.garuda-indonesia.com

Qantas Australia ☎ 13/1313,
New Zealand ☎ 09/357 8900
or ☎ 0800/808767,
Ⓦ www.qantas.com.au
United Airlines Australia
☎ 13/1777, New Zealand
☎ 09/379 3800,
Ⓦ www.ual.com

Spain

Air Europa
Ⓦ www.easyspain.com
Iberia ☎ 902/400 500,
Ⓦ www.iberia.com
Spanair ☎ 902/131 410,
Ⓦ www.spanair.com

TRAVEL AGENTS

Britain and Ireland
Joe Walsh Tours Dublin
☎ 01/872 2555 or 676 3053,
Cork ☎ 021/277959,
Ⓦ www.joewalshtours.ie.
General budget fares agent.
North South Travel ☎ & Ⓕ
01245/608291,
Ⓦwww.northsouthtravel.co.uk.
Friendly, competitive travel
agency, offering discounted
fares – profits are used to
support projects in the
developing world, especially

the promotion of sustainable
tourism.
STA Travel ☎ 0870/160 6070.
Low-cost flights for all, with
particularly good deals for
students and under-26s.
Thomas Cook
☎ 08705/666222,
Ⓦ www.thomascook.co.uk.
Long-established firm offering
package holidays and
scheduled flights.
Usit Campus ☎ 0870/240 1010,
Ⓦ www.usitcampus.co.uk.

GETTING THERE

Student and youth travel specialist, offering discounted flights.

Usit Now Belfast ☎ 028/9032 7111, Dublin ☎ 01/602 8117, ⓦ www.usitnow.ie. Student and youth travel specialist, offering discounted flights.

North America

Council Travel ☎ 1-800/226 8624, ⓦ www.counciltravel.com. Student/budget travel specialist.

STA Travel ☎ 1-800/777-0112 or ☎ 1-800/781-4040, ⓦ www.sta-travel.com. Independent-travel specialist.

Travac ☎ 1-800/872-8800, ⓦ www.thetravelsite.com. Consolidator and charter broker.

Travel Cuts Canada ☎ 1-800/667 2887, US ☎ 416/979 2406. Canada-based student-travel outfit.

Australia and New Zealand

STA Travel Australia ☎ 13/1776 or ☎ 1300/360960, New Zealand ☎ 09/3090458 or ☎ 09/366 6673, ⓦ www.statravel.com.au. Independent travel specialists.

Thomas Cook Australia ☎ 13/1771 or 1-800/801002, New Zealand ☎ 09/379 3920, ⓦ www.thomascook.com.au. Scheduled flights, plus insurance, fly-drives and so on.

Usit Beyond New Zealand ☎ 09/379 4224 or ☎ 0800/788336, ⓦ www.usitbeyond.co.nz. Student- and youth-travel specialist.

FERRIES

From the Spanish mainland, the quickest option is clearly to fly, since there is only one weekly ferry and the sea-crossing takes two days. But if you're in southern Spain anyway, or can get a cheap flight there and are not pushed for time, it's an option worth considering. Trasmediterránea's (☎ 902/454 645, ⓦ www.trasmediterranea.es) weekly **ferry**

GETTING THERE

crosses from Cádiz to Santa Cruz de Tenerife. Single fares start from around €181 for foot passengers for the most basic cabin options and include all meals; cars travel from €160 and motorcycles from €60. Bookings for cars generally need to be made at least a month in advance and can be done through Trasmediterránea representatives outside Spain.

Visas and red tape

The rules governing entry to Tenerife are the same as those governing the rest of Spain. Most EU citizens, as well as those from Norway and Iceland, can visit Spain for up to ninety days with just their national identity card or passport. Currently, citizens of the US, Canada, Australia and New Zealand can also enter for up to ninety days with just a passport, but visa requirements do change and it is always advisable to check the situation before leaving home.

EU nationals wishing to stay longer than ninety days need to apply for a **permiso de residencia** (EU residence permit) in Spain. The initial residence permit is valid for one year, after which you'll need an extension. Applications for both are made at the closest police station to where you intend to live and need to be accompanied by proof of sufficient funds (currently €30 per day) for your intended stay, or proof of employment either in the form of a contract (*contrato de trabajo*) or tax-office registration details if you're self-employed. Non-EU nationals can usually get ninety-day extensions to their visa, again by applying to a police station and showing proof of funds. Longer stays require a special visa. Contact your Spanish embassy or consulate for current information.

SPANISH EMBASSIES ABROAD

Australia 15 Arkana St, Yarralumla, ACT 2600 ℡ 02/6273 3555.

Britain 20 Draycott Place, London SW3 2RZ ℡ 020/7581 5921.

Canada 74 Stanley Ave, Ottawa, Ontario K1M 1P4 ℡ 613/747 2252.

Ireland 17a Merlyn Park, Ballsbridge, Dublin 4 ℡ 01/269 1640.

New Zealand No Spanish representation.

USA 2375 Pennsylvania Ave NW, Washington DC 20009 ℡ 202/728–2330.

FOREIGN EMBASSIES AND CONSULATES IN SPAIN

Australia Embassy: Plz. Del Descubridor Diego de Ordás, 3, Madrid ℡ 914/419 300 or 914/425 362.

Canada Embassy: C/Núñez de Balboa 35, 28001, Madrid ℡ 914/314 300, ℻ 914/312 367.

Ireland Honorary Consul: C/Castillo 8, 4°A, Santa Cruz de Tenerife ℡ 922/245 671, ℻ 922/249 957. Embassy: Pº de la Castellana 36 Madrid ℡ 915/763 500, ℻ 914/351 677.

New Zealand Embassy: Plaza de la Lealtad, 2, 3º, Madrid ☎915/230 226 or 915/230 171.

South-Africa Consulate: C/Franchy Rosa 5, 6º 35007, Las Palmas de Gran Canaria ☎928/226 004, ℱ928/226 015.

Britain Consulate: Plaza de Weyler, Santa Cruz de Tenerife ☎922/286 863, ℱ922/289 903). Embassy: C/de Fernando el Santo 16, Madrid ☎913/190 200.

USA Honorary Consul: Los Martínez de Escober, 3, Oficina 7, Las Palmas de Gran Canaria ☎928/271 259. Embassy: C/Serrano, 75, Madrid ☎915/872 200, ℱ915/872 303.

Information, maps and Web sites

The Spanish National Tourist Office (SNTO) produces and gives away a number of maps and pamphlets on the Canaries. Most of what they have available can be picked up at tourist offices on Tenerife and La Gomera along with a number of local maps, pamphlets and accommodation listings unavailable elsewhere. Most major towns have a tourist office, but the main and best-stocked offices on Tenerife are at Reina Sofía airport and in Santa Cruz de Tenerife, while San Sebastian has the best office on La Gomera.

SNTO OFFICES ABROAD

Australia 203 Castlereagh St, Suite 214 PO Box L6S5, Sydney, NSW ⓣ02/9264 7966.

Canada 102 Bloor St West, 14th Floor Toronto, Ontario ⓣ1416/9613131.

Netherlands Laan Van Meerdervoort 8, 2517 AJ Den Haag ⓣ170/346 69 00.

Britain 22–23 Manchester Square, London WIM SAP ⓣ020/7486 8077.

USA 666 5th Avenue New York, NY 10103 8383 ⓣ212/265 8822; Wiltshire Boulevard, Suite 960, Beverly Hills, Los Angeles, California 90211 ⓣ213/658 7188; Water Tower Place, Suite 915 East 845 North Michigan Ave, Chicago, Illinois 60611 ⓣ312/642 1992;1221 Brickeil Avenue, Miami Florida 33131 ⓣ305/358 1992.

USEFUL WEB SITES

The official glossy **Web sites** of Tenerife (ⓦwww.webtenerife .com/index_en.htm), La Gomera (*www.la-gomera.net*), and the national parks of the two islands (ⓦwww.vanaga.es/parques/) may help to orient travellers, but give little help with travel practicalities. Luckily a handful of commercial sites help fill this gap – the best are listed below.

www.ecanarias.com One of the slickest and most useful sites, particularly for the mass of listings information in its yellow pages section and its facility for booking cars and accommodation – mostly studio, apartments and houses – online (via email).

www.abcanarias.com/touristg uide.html Contains a good search engine facility for finding accommodation on both Tenerife and La Gomera.

www.canary-isles.com Though a little under-developed in many areas and having a broader focus than just visitor needs, this isn't a bad resource for visitors to Tenerife and includes a useful weekly magazine, with a what's on guide.

www.tenerife-holidays.com Similar to the last, this is more focused on the interests and requirements of holidaymakers.

www.bjerkholt.com/tenerife/ welcome/ A small, insider's guide to Tenerife that includes listings sections contributed to by viewers.

www.tizz.com/spain/ For more specific interests and needs than the last check the general Spain Web site where there's an excellent, annotated, Canarian links section.

MAPS

The **maps** in this book, together with the city maps handed out by the various tourist offices should satisfy the needs of most travellers. If you do want to buy a good general map before you leave, try and get hold of one by *Freytag & Berndt* who publish some of the best glossy fold-outs available depicting Tenerife at a scale of 1:75,000 and La Gomera at 1:35,000. The latter is good enough for **hiking**, but the former only just about acceptable. If you intend to explore off the beaten track then you're best getting hold of the 1:25,000 scale topographical maps produced by the *Servico Geografico del Ejército* (*Cartografia Militar de España*). These tend to be fairly up to date, though they often miss off some current trails and include some trails that are no longer in existence. Bookshops on both Tenerife and La

Gomera (particularly in Valle Gran Rey) should stock most good maps; but for the *Servico Geografico* maps, you'll need to head for the military offices (*Capitaña*) on Weyler Square in Santa Cruz (Mon–Fri 9am–12pm).

MAP OUTLETS ABROAD

Britain and Ireland

Hodges Figgis Bookshop, 56–58 Dawson St, Dublin 2 ℡ 01/677 4754, Ⓦ www.hodgesfiggis.com.

John Smith and Sons, 26 Colquhoun Ave, Glasgow G52 4PJ ℡ 0141/552 3377, Ⓦ www.johnsmith.co.uk.

Stanfords, 12–14 Long Acre, London WC2E 9LP ℡ 020/7836 1321, Ⓦ www.stanfords.co.uk.

North America

Map Link Inc., 30 S La Patera Lane, Unit 5, Santa Barbara, CA 93117 ℡ 805/692-6777, Ⓦ www.maplink.com.

Travel Books & Language Center, 4437 Wisconsin Ave, Washington, DC 20016 ℡ 604/737-1122, Ⓦ www.bookweb.org /bookstore/travellers.

World Wide Books and Maps, 1247 Granville St, Vancouver V6Z 1G3 ℡ 604/687-3320, Ⓦ www.worldofmaps.com.

Australia and New Zealand

Perth Map Centre, 1/884 Hay St, Perth ℡ 08/9322 5733, Ⓦ www.perthmap.com.au.

Mapland, 372 Little Bourke St, Melbourne ℡ 03/9670 4383, Ⓦ www.mapland.com.au.

Mapworld, 173 Gloucester St, Christchurch ℡ 03/374 5399, Ⓕ 03/374 5633, Ⓦ www.mapworld.co.nz.

INFORMATION, MAPS AND WEB SITES

Health and insurance

Tenerife is home to numerous medical facilities and English-speaking doctors and dentists (and even some pharmacists), keeping the hassle of seeking medical attention on the island to a minimum.

For minor complaints go to a **pharmacy** (*farmacia*). You'll find one in virtually every village, marked by a large green cross and open during normal shop hours (Mon–Fri 9am–1pm & 4pm–8pm, Sat 9am–1pm). Additionally, pharmacies in each area have a rota to provide 24-hour emergency cover, details of which are usually posted on any pharmacy door. Pharmacists are highly trained and able to dispense many drugs available only on prescription in many other countries. In more serious cases you can get the address of an English-speaking **doctor** or **dentist** from your embassy or consulate, or with luck from a *farmacia*, the local police or tourist information.

In a medical **emergency** call ☎ 061 for an amublance

The **Cruz Roja** (Red Cross) runs a national ambulance service, and numbers for local branches are usually given in a blue square on the information sheet in public telephones; alternatively call ☏061. If an emergency arises as the result of an accident with someone else the police also need to be informed. In most cases ambulances will take you to one of the island's major hospitals – in Santa Cruz, La Orotava or Playa de Las Américas.

TRAVEL INSURANCE

Even though EU health care privileges apply in Tenerife, you'd do well to take out an **insurance policy** before travelling to cover against theft, loss and illness or injury. Before buying a new policy, however, it's worth checking whether you are already covered: some all-risks home insurance policies, for example, may cover your possessions against loss or theft when overseas, and many private medical schemes such as BUPA and PPP provide cover when abroad, including baggage loss, cancellation or curtailment and cash replacement as well as sickness or accident. In Canada, provincial health plans usually provide partial cover for medical mishaps overseas, while holders of official student/teacher/youth cards in Canada and the US are entitled to meagre accident coverage and hospital in-patient benefits. Students will often find that their student health coverage extends during the vacations and for one term beyond the date of last enrolment. Some bank and credit cards include certain levels of medical or other insurance and you may automatically get travel insurance if you use a major credit card to pay for your trip.

After exhausting the possibilities above, you might want to contact a specialist travel insurance company, or consider the travel insurance deal we offer (see below). A typical travel insurance policy usually provides cover for the loss of baggage, tickets and – up to a certain limit – cash or cheques, as well as cancellation or curtailment of your journey. Most of them exclude so-called dangerous sports unless an extra premium is paid: in Tenerife this can mean scuba-diving, whitewater rafting, windsurfing and trekking, though probably not kayaking or jeep safaris. Many policies can be chopped and changed to exclude coverage you don't need – for example, sickness and accident benefits can

ROUGH GUIDE TRAVEL INSURANCE

Rough Guides offers its own travel insurance, customized for our readers by a leading UK broker and backed by a Lloyds underwriter. It's available for anyone, of any nationality, travelling anywhere in the world.

There are two main Rough Guide insurance plans: Essential, for basic, no-frills cover; and Premier – with more generous and extensive benefits. Alternatively, you can take out annual multi-trip insurance, which covers you for any number of trips throughout the year (with a maximum of 60 days for any one trip). Unlike many policies, the Rough Guides schemes are calculated by the day, so if you're travelling for 27 days rather than a month, that's all you pay for. If you intend to be away for the whole year, the Adventurer policy will cover you for 365 days. Each plan can be supplemented with a "Hazardous Activities Premium" if you plan to indulge in sports considered dangerous, such as skiing, scuba-diving or trekking. Rough Guides also does good deals for older travellers, and will insure you up to any age, at prices comparable to SAGA's.

For a policy quote, call the Rough Guide Insurance Line on UK freefone ⓣ 0800/015 0906; US freefone ⓣ 1-866/220 5588, or, if you're calling from elsewhere ⓣ +44 1243/621046. Alternatively, get an online quote and buy your cover at ⓦ www.roughguides.com/insurance.

often be excluded or included at will. If you do take medical coverage, ascertain whether benefits will be paid as treatment proceeds or only after return home, and whether there is a 24-hour medical emergency number. When securing baggage cover, make sure that the per-article limit – typically under £500 – will cover your most valuable possession. If you need to make a claim, you should keep receipts for medicines and medical treatment, and in the event you have anything stolen, you must obtain an official statement from the police.

Costs, money and banks

With a flat-rate 4.5 percent sales tax, Tenerife and La Gomera are two of the cheapest destinations in western Europe. Even in the resort areas, where costs are bumped up way over the odds, luxury goods and gifts are priced well below the European average.

CURRENCY

Spain is one of twelve European Union countries who have changed over to a single currency, the **euro** (€). The transition period, which began on January 1, 1999, is however lengthy: euro notes and coins are not scheduled to be issued until January 1, 2002, with pesetas remaining in place for cash transactions, at a fixed rate of 166.386 pesetas to 1 euro, until they are scrapped entirely at the end of February, 2002.

Even before euro cash appears in 2002, you can opt to pay in euros with a credit card and you can get travellers' cheques in euros – you should not be charged commission for changing them in any of the twelve countries in the euro zone (also known as "Euroland"), nor for changing from any of the old Euroland currencies to any other (French francs to pesetas, for example).

When the new currency takes over completely, prices are likely to be rounded off – and if decimalization in the UK is anything to go by, rounded up. All prices in this book are given in euros only.

Euro notes will be issued in **denominations** of 5, 10, 20, 50, 100, 200 and 500 euros, and coins in denominations of 1, 2, 5, 10, 20 and 50 cents and 1 and 2 euros.

COSTS

High season runs for much of the year, with Christmas and New Year proving to be especially expensive times for booking accommodation, so there's little to be saved by travelling outside the summer months. The cheapest way to visit the islands is by travelling independently and camping. This way you can probably get by on €12 per day. For a little more comfort – staying in a reasonable pension, eating out once a day and travelling by public transport – you're looking at €30–€36, and around €60–€70 to upgrade to a three-star hotel, add a modest lunch and a rental car. Prices in La Gomera tend to be a little more modest across the board than those in Tenerife. Travelling alone to either island will drive costs up by around a third.

BANKS AND EXCHANGE

The Canary Islands has a surfeit of **banks**, many with **ATMs**. Banking hours are generally Monday to Friday 9am to 2pm and Saturday 9am to 1pm – except between late May and September when banks close on Saturday, and during the Carnival period (February or March) when banks close at midday. Outside these times, it's usually possible to change cash at larger hotels, exchange booths, and in resort areas often with real-estate or travel agents. Though hotel rates are usually poorer rates, exchange booths and agents sometimes give better rates than the banks – though you should check these carefully.

Bringing large amounts of **cash** into Tenerife is not really recommended, not only for security reasons, but also because the rate of exchange on cash is generally not as good as that offered on travellers' cheques, or on ATM withdrawals. Travellers from the UK are likely to get the best rate of exchange on cash from English bar owners who often need to change money for their UK holidays. **Travellers' cheques** are one of the safest and easiest ways to carry money around. Sometimes these attract commission, but it usually doesn't take much hunting around to find a bank or exchange facility where these are low or non-existent.

Credit cards are widely accepted on Tenerife and are the most practical means by which to make larger purchases, such as accommodation or car rental. Credit and debit cards can also be used in the many ATMs (*cajeros* *automaticos*) – check the display for the appropriate sign – or to obtain over-the-counter cash advances in many banks. Check with your bank before travelling about restrictions and charges.

It is also worth bearing in mind that you can **wire money** from another country to a local bank, though the prohibitive cost and hassle involved makes this an emergency-only option. Get advice from your bank on how to set up a transfer. Costs for the service are about €24 plus whatever your bank charges and funds take a week to clear. Western Union and American Express can also arrange transfers to offices on the island. These transfers typically take less time and attract a 4 to 5 per cent charge.

Getting around

Getting around the relatively small island of Tenerife is quite straightforward. An excellent island-wide bus service is supplemented by plentiful and fairly cheap taxis. But for added flexibility and to enable exploration off the beaten track renting a car or a bicycle is both practical and inexpensive. **Those wanting to be guided around island sights will find plenty of bus tours and boat trips to choose from, too.**

BUSES

Operated by the public bus company, TITSA, local **buses** (generally referred to as *guagua*, rather than *autobus*) offer an extensive and inexpensive service all over the island. **Fares** are low – Los Cristianos to Reina Sofía airport, for example, costs €3 – and can be made around a third cheaper by purchasing a **Bono-Bus card**, a pre-paid ticket which is fed into a machine on the bus and, once you've told the driver your destination, your fare is deducted from it. The cards, which usually cost €12, can be bought from newsagents and news-stands.

Timetables are generally clearly laid out and attached to the main bus stops – for intermediate stops the exact times of arrival and departure are rarely given so you are advised to err well on the side of caution when estimating the time of arrival, since buses rarely arrive late. Stops are marked with either the destination of the bus (*destino*) or the origin or the bus (*desede*). Most routes don't run late into the evening or during the night – and some don't run on Saturdays either. If you plan to use the bus network extensively, it's well worth picking up a copy of the excellent bus-route map and timetable, available from major bus stations, some kiosks and most tourist information centres. Alternatively, you can call the 24-hour information service in both English and Spanish ☏ 922/531 300, or check the Web site ⓦ www.titsa.com.

If you're not interested in exploring the island under your own steam, you might be attracted to one of the many **bus tours** of Tenerife. Other than a circular tour of the island (for around €15), bus-tour itineraries typically include the mountain village of Masca and the Parque Nacional del Teide or Santa Cruz. Those with little time might also consider a bus trip around La Gomera (€42), offered in the southern resorts. Note that bus trips that seem extraordinarily cheap, typically around €3, are thinly disguised outings to the restaurants and gift shops that subsidize them – the true cost of these trips lies in numerous hours of hard-sell along the way.

TAXIS

Though **taxis** are usually frustratingly absent at peak times at the airport, in the island's major towns and resorts there are always plenty of taxis available. The minimum charge for a ride is €2, with surcharges added for luggage, travel between 10pm and 6am or on Sundays, and journeys to the airports or docks. Fares will also vary according to traffic conditions, but you can expect to pay €15 from Los Cristianos or Playa de Las Américas to Reina Sofía airport, and €54 from Puerto de la Cruz. A green light on top of a taxi denotes a vacant cab, the numbers beside denoting the kind of fare: #1 for a city, #2 and #3 for outside. Taxi drivers should always use their meters, though on shorter journeys in the resorts some don't bother: these journeys should never cost more than about €3.

CARS

Cars are particularly practical for exploring upland areas – including the national park – which are poorly served by the bus network. Travelling under your own steam also allows frequent stops at various points of interest and viewpoints along the way. And though the roads are often steep, twisting and tiring to drive, they are at least relatively quiet– whereas driving around towns, particularly Santa Cruz tends to be a hectic experience and finding a parking space on the narrow roads of most larger towns and resorts is often a tricky matter.

While the local minimum driving age is 18, to rent a car you need to be over 21 (though some operators won't rent to anyone under 25) and have had your licence for over a year. EU licences (either pink or pink and green) are accepted as are most other foreign licences, though the latter officially need to be accompanied by an International Driving Permit, available from automobile clubs in the country of issue. Most operators also require a €30 deposit or a credit-card number and sometimes an island address as well.

Rental rates for a car usually start at around €20 per day for a small hatchback, and all operators offer substantial discounts for rentals of a week or more. You can also save money by using smaller local operators, though the cars of some are in poor condition. If using international companies – such as Hertz or Avis – try to book in advance to take advantage of discounted rates that may be enabled by membership of an automobile club like the AA. In addition, if you are booking a holiday through a travel agent, you may also want to consider a fly-drive deal. Rental usually includes tax, unlimited mileage and full insurance (including collision damage waiver), but these details should be double-checked with any operator – particularly smaller ones who sometimes build odd exclusions like axle damage into contracts. Most operators will not allow you to island-hop with their car and don't include petrol in prices – lead-free petrol (*sin plomo*) costs around €0.55/litre.

CAR RENTAL COMPANIES

- -

Auto Reisen Reina Sofia airport ℡ 922/392 216 or 922/392 255.

Avis Reina Sofia airport ℡ 922/392 056, Los Rodeos airport ℡ 922/258 713; also

Los Cristianos ☎ 922/753 544, El Duque ☎ 922/714 414, Playa de las Américas ☎ 922/791 001, Puerto de la Cruz ☎ 922/384 698 and Santa Cruz ☎ 922/241 294.

OrCar Reina Sofia airport ☎ 922/392 216, (F) 922/392 255.

Hertz Tenerife: Reina Sofia airport ☎ 922/759 319, Los

Rodeos airport ☎ 922/251 917; also Playa de las Américas ☎ 922/792 320, Puerta de la Cruz ☎ 922/384 719 and Torviscas ☎ 922/797 565. La Gomera: San Sebastian ☎ 922/870 461 and Valle Gran Rey ☎ 922/805 954.

Cicar Central reservations ☎ 928/597 019.

CYCLING

The terrain on both Tenerife and La Gomera is generally mountainous and many of the narrow roads are very busy, so neither is ideal for leisurely **cycle touring**. It is, however, well suited to more exciting and satisfying **day rides** – particularly on dirt roads by mountain bike. With the exception of areas within the national park, all hiking trails on **Tenerife** are open to mountain bikes – though many, particularly in the Anaga, are too steep and uneven for such use. The roads of **La Gomera**, though quieter than those on Tenerife, almost always involve extremely tough climbs over the 800-metre passes that separate most major towns. Mountain bikers will, however, be pleased to find that once they've climbed to the high ground of the national park at the centre of the island its trails are open to bikers.

Most carriers **flying** to Tenerife from the UK have no objections to taking bicycles, providing they are packed in a box or bag – available from most bike shops. To pack a bike in a bag, wheels and handlebars often need to be taken off and other luggage packed around it – with practice this is no more than a ten-minute job. Bagged bikes are also allowed in the hold of **buses** on both islands. This means you have the option of cutting out particularly busy parts of a route or even shuttling up to the national park to descend back to the coast – but the bag will need to fold down to a reasonable size to enable this.

For a private **shuttle service** contact Diga Sports on Tenerife (see p.177) or Bike Station on La Gomera (see p.259). Both companies will transport bikes to pretty much anywhere on either island, leaving riders to make their own way back. They also offer **tours** and **bike rental**, as do Fun Factory El Cabezo in El Médano (see p.197) and Mountain Bike Active in Puerto de la Cruz (see p.115). Renting a quality front-suspension mountain bike will set you back around €13 per day, €60 per week.

Accommodation

Despite the vast amount of accommodation on Tenerife, most of what is on offer is in bland hotel and apartment complexes and given over to package tours. Few places are available to the independent traveller, and those that do offer room will usually do so for considerably more than the pre-booked package rates. This leaves independent travellers with a relatively small stock of options, ranging from small family-run pensions and smaller hotels in the main towns and resorts to a couple of campsites and some attractive self-catering properties – often pleasant old renovated houses – in the countryside. The situation in La Gomera is slightly different to that in Tenerife. Here, independent travel is the norm and numerous pensions and small, simple and inexpensive apartment blocks have emerged to meet demand.

ACCOMMODATION PRICE CODES

Throughout the *Guide*, accommodation has been graded according to price, based on the cost of the cheapest double room in high season – but excluding the time around Christmas and New Year, when rates can rocket. In the case of apartments that sleep more than two, the price for the smallest available unit, as described in the body text, is given; price codes have been included where apartments are available by the night, and then refer to the cheapest two-person apartment. Where singles – which are usually more than half the price of doubles – are available, this has also been mentioned. Travellers wanting to stay a week or more may find that nightly rate can be reduced a little.

❶ up to €12		❺ €48– €60	
❷ €12–€24		❻ €60– €84	
❸ €24–€36		❼ €84– €120	
❹ €36–€48		❽ over €120	

HOTELS AND PENSIONS

Both hotels and pensions are graded by island authorities, using a star system to describe the level of facilities. **Pensions**, marked with a large P sign, and sometimes also called Hostales or Hotel-Residencia are graded with up to three stars. An establishment with one star will typically have rooms sharing a bathroom, while those with two or three stars often have en-suite facilities. The difference between a three star pension and a one star **hotel** (usually ❸) is often academic, both are likely to be family-run and in old houses – and in some cases the pension may even be a good deal smarter. In two star hotels (up to ❹) you are guaranteed to have your own bathroom. While the quality of a three star hotel (up to ❻) can vary dramatically, it is likely to be a little smarter over all and will usually have its own small pool. You can expect both four (up to ❼) and five (up to ❽) star hotels to have extremely good facilities, particularly with regard to sports. But to earn five stars a hotel needs to be a mini-village in its own right – including a variety of restaurants, bars, salons, pools as well as lush gardens and extravagant architecture.

APARTMENTS AND APARTHOTELS

Almost half the beds in Tenerife are in **apartment blocks**, but as with hotels a large proportion of these are reserved for package holidays sold abroad and will not take in people applying either in person or by phone. Independent travellers will still find plenty of smaller apartment blocks to choose from, however, as well as a selection of apartments offered by agencies managing properties on behalf of absentee owners, particularly in Puerto de la Cruz, Las Américas and Los Cristianos (see p.101 & p.151).

The size and quality of apartments can vary tremendously and it's well worth having a look at a unit before you commit yourself to staying in one. Some apartments are described as studios, which means they are one room affairs where the living room has a kitchenette tagged onto the side and converts into a bedroom at night. Otherwise apartments usually have at least one separate bedroom – though often four-person apartments will require two people on a sofa bed in the living-room, which can be a bit of an awkward and cramped set-up.

Aparthotels, as the name suggests, are a hybrid of hotels and apartment complexes – generally an apartment block with hotel facilities such as restaurants and room service.

CASAS RURALES

If you are heading to Tenerife or La Gomera with the intention of "getting away from it all" or spending a lot of time hiking, then the idea of renting a refurbished rural house – **casas rurales** – is a tempting one. It is in finding this kind of accommodation that the Internet comes into its own – with several self-catering specialists offering detailed information about properties on their Web sites. Typically a week of house rental will cost from £200 for one bedroom and from £300 for two.

CAMPING

Despite the ideal weather conditions, **camping** has not really taken off on either Tenerife or La Gomera, which between them have only three commercial sites. Two of these are in southern Tenerife – one near the airport (see p.191), the other near Las Galletas (see p.183) – the last is in La Gomera, on the edge of its national park (see p.264).

In addition, camping in the national parks of both islands is allowed with prior permission, and you can also camp in seventeen mountain recreation zones on Tenerife. The facilities at these campsites are fairly basic, but usually include pit-toilets, drinking water and fireplaces. Many of these sites are within the band of Canarian pines, which starts at over 800m, so it can be quite cold, particularly in winter, and heavy morning dews are to be expected. Perhaps for this reason, these sites are hardly used – outside of weekends – though it may also be a consequence of the rather involved process required to get **permission to camp**. This must be gained at least three days in advance by faxing the Island administration (*Cabildo Insular*; ⓕ922/239 191; ⓦwww.cabtfe.es). On receipt of your request, they will fax you back an application form (in Spanish) and details of site locations, you then need to fax back the completed form so that a final fax, containing your permit – that needs to be taken to the site itself – can be sent to you.

Those looking to camp off the official sites will generally find both Tenerife and La Gomera relatively hospitable, with several places popularly used. Though this is generally not with the agreement of local authorities, there is often little done to move people on. In Tenerife there are almost permanent tented camps on the beach Playa de Benijo in the Anaga (p.89), and La Gomera has a long history of free camping on its beaches, particularly near Valle Gran Rey (p.249) and Playa del Santiago (p.267).

ACCOMMODATION

Food and drink

The wide range of food and drink on Tenerife reflects the large number of immigrant groups that have made the island their home. Canarian food has traditionally based itself around simple dishes such as stews, grilled meat and seafood, with occasional influences from South America or the Spanish mainland in evidence. However, the large number of expatriate restaurants opening in resorts has meant that on the island as a whole a huge variety of cuisines is represented – from English and Italian to Swiss and Chinese.

Each restaurant listed in the *Guide* has been categorized as either inexpensive (under €6), moderate (€6– €10) and expensive (above €10) – indicating the price of an average main course.

CAFÉS, BARS AND SNACKS

The Canaries share in the Spanish **café culture**, with both cafés and bars well patronized throughout the day by customers dropping by for a coffee. An intimidating variety of coffees is offered, of which *cafe solo* – generally a slightly bitter espresso, served black, is the simplest. If you want it white ask for *café cortado*, or for a really milky coffee (around half hot milk), ask for *cafe con leche*. Other variations on the theme include *cortado con leche condesada*, where a layer of condensed milk sits below a black coffee and *cortado leche leche*, a white coffee with condensed milk. Most coffees come in a small cup as standard, so grande should be specified if you want a large cup. Iced coffee, *café con hielo*, is also frequently available, as is coffee laced with a shot of brandy, cognac or whisky (all known as *carajillo*).

Food is served in cafés and bars, as well as restaurants, though the nature of each overlaps considerably. Exactly what they serve varies according to the whim of the owner, but typically cafés specialize in baked goods and include *Pasteleria* (cake shops) and *Zumeria* (juice bars), while bars variously described as *tascas*, *bodegas*, *cervecerias* and *tabernas* have a greater range of not only alcoholic drinks but also savoury snacks, including tapas or raciones.

Tapas, the tiny portions of meat, seafood and salad dishes, were traditionally offered free with drinks, but today you can expect to pay €1.50–3 a dish. **Raciones** are simply bigger plates of the same, enough for a light meal. Most bars will only have a selection of half a dozen tapas dishes, freshly made and laid out under a glass counter at the bar. The actual contents of the tapas can vary considerably and of course many are considered specialities of a particular bar. Bear in mind that it's often 20 percent cheaper to eat at the bar rather than at a table – and up to 30 percent more expensive out on a terrace. Some bars, calling themselves *areperas*, also serve deep-fried crispy pockets of cornmeal dough stuffed with fillings like chicken, cheese or ham. Originally a South American dish, **arepas** usually cost around €2 and make for a filling snack.

Occasionally cafés and bars offer more substantial simple meals, particularly for lunch between about 2pm and 4pm.

These can include hearty Canarian **soups** such as water-cress soup (*potaje de berros*), vegetable soup (*sopa de verdura*) or a thick, hearty meat potato and noodle soup known as *Rancho canario*, and the similar, but thicker **stew** *Puchero Canario*. And in many of the more traditional bars and restaurants soups and stews come accompanied by a bowl of the uniquely Canarian **gofio** – a finely ground mixture of roasted wheat, maize or barley. The origins of this powder have been traced back to Guanche goatherds who used to take a pouch of it to the hills with them, to later eat it as little dough balls made using either milk or water. Now this Canarian staple, regularly offered up in place of bread, is still used to make some traditional Canarian foods, such as the unappealing but filling **escaldón**, a dish made by pour-ing broth containing boiled meat or fish over *gofio* and nor-mally served in a clay dish. Sometimes classier places will add mint, onion, potatoes and chillies to brighten up the dish.

RESTAURANTS

Canarian **restaurants** tend to serve simple meals (from around €6 per main dish) and can broadly be divided into those by the coast serving mainly fish and seafood, and inland establishments which tend to specialize in meat dish-es. Wherever you chose to go, eating out is good value and even the island's top restaurants you're unlikely to spend much more than €24 a head, including wine.

Fish and **seafood restaurants** will typically have a large range – including tuna, bream, eel, pollack, comber, sea perch, hake and numerous shellfish, particularly lobster – though availability will often depend on the luck of the local catch and the season. A traditional Canarian fish dish is *zarzuela*, a stew that typically takes at least half an hour to prepare. Fish and seafood paellas are also common on the islands. Specialities at **upland restaurants** include the rich *conejo en salemorejo* – marinated rabbit in a garlicky sauce – and goat (*cabra*) – particularly in January and February when local kids are slaughtered.

Both fish and meat is generally served grilled and most frequently with *papas arrugadas*, unpeeled new potatoes boiled dry in salt water. Occasionally vegetables – or a pitiful side salad – are served along with the potatoes, but the presence of *mojo* can virtually be guaranteed. Mojo is a garlic dressing that comes in two varieties: *rojo* (red) or *verde* (green). *Rojo* tends to be a spicy chilli, oil and vinegar mix, while *verde* is milder and contains coriander. To many Canarians the quality of its *mojo* is the measure of a restaurant.

Eating in traditional Canarian bars and restaurants is not an easy task for **vegetarians**. While there's usually something to eat, it usually involves egg-based staples, such as omelettes, and most vegetable dishes are generally off-limits, as pieces of fish and meat are often added to make them more interesting. Consequently a useful phrase is: *Soy vegetariano. Hay algo sin carne?* ("I'm a vegetarian. Is there anything without meat?") – to which you should add *y sin mariscos* ("and without seafood") and *y sin jamon* ("and without ham") to be safe.

DRINKING

Although the island's **tap water** is safe to drink, it's often heavily chlorinated and unpalatable, making the inexpensive *agua mineral* (mineral water), that comes either sparkling (*con gas*) or still (*sin gas*), a worthwhile investment.

Bars, restaurants and many cafés serve **alcohol**. The most popular drink is generally light **beer**, usually lager, served in bottles (*cerveza*) or on tap (*caña* is a small beer, *jarra* a larger measure – generally 400ml). The most popular local brewery is Dorada, who recently began brewing the distinctive Volcán, which is brewed using *gofio*. It's also worth sampling the local **wine**. Famous in the sixteenth century for its sweet heavy malmsey (*malvaiser*), Tenerife has re-established itself as a producer of respected dry white wines, having introduced new grapes to the island in the mid-1980s. Wines from the Tacoronte area are considered the best developed – try the *Viña Norte*, characterized by its strong character and fruity flavour; while wines of El Sauzal, like the *Viñatigo*, are known for their crisp, dry freshness. Another distinctively local drink is the Gomeran liqueur **Gomerón** – a mix of white rum and locally produced palm honey (*Miél de Palma*) – the result of a lengthy bleeding and boiling process that results in a sweet dark treacle.

Communications and the media

Both Tenerife and La Gomera have a well-developed communications network. Ubiquitous phone booths and the presence of Internet cafés in all major towns and resorts compensate for the rather slow postal service. Regular deliveries of international newspapers also mean that you need never lose touch with news abroad, while a number of Canarian and expatriate-run papers can keep you abreast of local issues.

PHONES

Most hotels add surcharges to calls made from rooms, so the cheapest way to call home is to use one of the many **payphones** out on the streets. Various companies offer **phone cards** that can be used from any payphone, and while some work out cheaper than feeding in coins, it's worth checking to see if the card provider charges a connection fee – with some cards you will end up paying €3 just to speak to an answerphone.

DIALLING CODES

To **call Tenerife or La Gomera from abroad** use the international access code (00 34 from the UK, Ireland and New Zealand; 011 34 from North America; 0011 64 from Australia), together with the nine-digit local number.

To make **local or national calls on Tenerife and La Gomera** you need to use all nine digits of the phone number.

To **call abroad from Tenerife or La Gomera**, dial 00 followed by the country code (44 for the UK, 353 for Ireland, 1 for the US and Canada, 61 for Australia, 64 for New Zealand) and then the number (minus the initial zero if you are calling the UK, Ireland or New Zealand).

POST

The **postal system** in the Canary Islands is quite slow, and it usually takes at least ten days for a postcard or letter to reach the UK or mainland Europe (outside Spain). As well as the post offices, most of the shops selling postcards will also be able to sell you **stamps** (*segells*). A letter or card up to 20g in weight is charged at €0.42 to EU destinations, €0.70 outside. A full list of rates, including those for registered mail (*certificado*), and the express mail (*urgente*) service can be found at ⓦ www.correos.es.

Most **post offices** are open Mon–Fri 8.30am–2.30pm & Sat 9.30am–1pm.

Other useful facilities offered by some post offices include a **fax service** (both sending and receiving) and a **poste restante** service. Mail using the latter should be clearly marked with your surname in capital letters and underlined, followed by your first name, and addressed to

"Lista de Correos", with the town, postcode and island name to which you want the parcel sent. Unless specified otherwise, the parcel will then be sent to the given town's main post office, where it will be held for a maximum of three weeks. American Express also offers a poste restante service for card or cheque holders with its representatives in Santa Cruz and Los Américas. A passport or identity card must always be shown to pick up any mail.

INTERNET AND EMAIL

Every major town and resort on both Tenerife and La Gomera has at least one café with **Internet connections** where half an hour on-line usually costs around €4. Those wanting to plug their own equipment into the local telephone system should be aware that phone jacks are American style. If using a hotel network, it is always worth enquiring into the compatibility of their system, since in rare cases these can damage your modem. If you are looking for a local server, then one of the best places for advice is a local Internet café.

NEWSPAPERS

Newspapers from all over western Europe reach Tenerife within a day of publication. A big ex-pat presence on the island means that local news – particularly that of interest to resident foreign communities – and tourist-oriented listings fill the column inches of several German- and English-language newspapers. Ones to look out for (all free from tourist information and some bars) are *Island Connections* (Ⓦ www.ic-web.com) *Tenerife News* (Ⓦ www.tennew.com), *The Western Sun*, *The Weekly Canarian* and *Here and Now*.

For local news and listings in Spanish, try the Tenerife-based Diario de Avisos or the online newspaper provided by Canarias7 (Ⓦ www.canarias7.es).

Festivals, events and public holidays

A look at the festival calendar, with over three hundred annual entries, shows Canary Islanders to be partial to a party or two. Both local and island festivals are mostly of Catholic origin and are certainly enthusiastically observed, although most of the population is not otherwise passionately religious. The largest island festival is without doubt Carnival, celebrated around February or March. Other major events include the vast processions and intricate street decorations of Corpus Christi in May or June and a succession of Romeriás, harvest festivals throughout the summer.

In addition to these and other major, island-wide festivities, most villages have several local fiestas, including those in honour of their patron saints. These **local festivities** typically involve parading statues of the saints while setting off rockets to clear their path of demons. Processions tend to be solemn, and the low profile of visitors appreciated, but the mood of evening celebrations is much more boisterous, with live folk music and dancing inevitably included in the programme of events. Some locals, mostly those performing in some way, will usually arrive dressed in folk costumes – women in striped skirts, embroidered lace tops and head scarves; men in linen shirts, red vests and knee-length trousers wrapped with a cummerbund. Traditional instruments, particularly the *tambor*, a goatskin drum of Berber origin and the *timple* a small string instrument, are also brought out to accompany castanets and traditional dances.

Most towns will have a **public holiday** around the time of their fiesta. Where these or island-wide public holidays fall near a weekend, extra days are also taken off to make a long weekend. Should a holiday fall on a Sunday, then Monday is usually taken off in lieu. While banks will not be open on public holidays most shops rarely close for more than a day at a time – though they will often implement shorter hours than usual.

CALENDAR

January 1 New Year's Day. A Spanish public holiday, New Year's Day is traditionally greeted by fireworks and the eating of a grape at every chime.

January 6 Epiphany. A Canarian public holiday, and welcomed in by processions in major towns the day before. This, rather than Christmas Day, is traditionally the day of present giving among islanders.

January 20 Fiesta de San Sebastián (La Gomera).

February/March Carnival. The biggest event of the year. Festivities begin in Santa Cruz (see p.78), which is stormed by hundreds of thousands of costumed partygoers. From there it moves to other large towns on the island, most spectacularly in Puerto de la Cruz (see p.99).

March 19 Día de San Juan. Public holiday.

Late March/early April Easter week (*santa semana*), with Maundy Thursday (*Jueves Santo*) and Good Friday (*Viernes Santo*) both public holidays. Elaborate processions take place on both days in La Laguna, one a silent procession of brotherhoods and fraternities.

April 25 Fiesta de San Marcos in Icod (Tenerife) and Agulo (La Gomera).

May 1 Labour day. Public holiday.

May 3 Festival celebrating the founding of Santa Cruz with a procession and lots of traditional festivities such as harvest festivals, stock shows and Canarian wrestling.

May Numerous *Romeriás* (harvest festivals) take place in the Orotava valley, the main one is in La Orotava. Dates vary, but most are in the second half of May.

May 30 Canary Island's day. Public holiday with folkdances on the plazas of Santa Cruz.

May/June Corpus Christi. On the Thursday that follows the eighth Sunday after Easter, Corpus Christi is celebrated all over the island. Major events are held in La Laguna and, a week later, in La Orotava – where streets are covered in floral carpets. These carpets are worth examining a couple of days before the festival, to avoid the need to jostle through hordes, and to actually see the artists at work.

June 13–29 Los Piques celebrated in Agulo (La Gomera), a festival that includes quarrels in the whistling language El Silbo (see box on p.245).

June 23 & 24 Fiesta de San Juan. Herds of goats from the surrounding area are driven to be bathed in the harbour at Puerto de la Cruz.

First Sunday of July Romería de San Benito Abad, La Laguna. Celebrations include a major religious procession.

July 15 Fiestas del Gran Poder de Díos in Puerto de la Cruz.

July 16 Fiesta Virgen del Carmen (patron saint of fishermen and sailors) The largest celebrations are in Santa Cruz and Puerto de la Cruz on Tenerife, and in Valle Gran Rey and Playa de Santiago on La Gomera. Celebrations usually include a procession of boats.

July 25 Public holiday in honour of St James the Apostle, the patron saint of Spain. The Virgin of Candelaria, the patron saint of the archipelago, is removed from the altar of the church in the eponymous town to be paraded in fine robes adorned with gold and surrounded by folk dances and offerings of flowers and produce. Major celebrations also take place in Santa Cruz, where citizens are also celebrating the anniversary of the defeat of Nelson and his British fleet (see p.72).

August 15 Fiesta Virgen de la Candelaria (the patron of the archipelago) and also the date of *Beñasmen*, a Guanche harvest festival – which explains the flowers, greenery, sheep and goats that are paraded behind the statue of the virgin. Most of the night is spent singing and dancing in the church square in honour of both events.

August (dates vary) Romería de San Roque in Garachico, one of the largest and most spectacular harvest and folk festivals on Tenerife.

September 6 Fiesta de Cristobel Colón. Anniversary of the departure of Columbus from La Gomera on his first voyage to the Americas (San Sebastián).

September 7 Fiesta de la Virgen del Socorro (Güimar). Involves a large procession from the church to the sea in honour of the town's patron saint.

September 7–15 Fiesta del Santísimo Cristo La Laguna. A lengthy religious festival that includes a procession behind a fifteenth century Gothic carving of Christ on the Cross, given to the island's conquerour, Alonso de Lugo.

October 5 Bajada de la Virgen de Guadalupe (San Sebastián, La Gomera). Observed only every five years (the next in 2003).

October 12 Día de la Hispanidad (National Day). Anniversary of Columbus's discovery of the new world. Public holiday.

November 1 All Saints Day. Public holiday with fiestas in many towns around Tenerife.

November 29 Fiesta del Vino. Evening wine festival in Icod and Puerto de la Cruz to celebrate the grape harvest. Children run with strings of tins and other metallic junk making as much noise as possible – to emulate the sound of barrels rolling out. The highlight of the festivities is kamikaze sledding (sleds were once used to transport the grape harvest) on the streets, with Icod's course the steepest and most dangerous. New wines are served, with roast chestnuts and grilled sardines as appetisers.

December 6 Día de la Constitución. Public holiday to celebrate the Spanish political constitution.

December 8 Feast of the Immaculate Conception. Public holiday.

December 25 Christmas Day (*Navidad*). Public holiday.

Sports and activities

A s mountainous islands in the Atlantic, both Tenerife and La Gomera offer a great range of environments in which to pursue a variety of both sea and land-based sports, most of which are made possible year-round thanks to the archipelago's consistently fine weather. And in addition to the natural attractions provided by the waves, winds and mountains, there's a boom in the popularity of golf on Tenerife.

WATER SPORTS

Neither Tenerife nor La Gomera have many natural **beaches** along their rocky coastlines, but to satisfy the tourist appetite, a few have been made on Tenerife using imported sand from the Sahara. The beaches of the popular southern resorts Las Américas and Los Cristianos tend to be crowded affairs with neat, cramped rows of sun loungers and sunshades. Various **water sports** are offered off these beaches – mostly motorized sports such as jet-skiing or motorboating, or at least being towed by a motorized craft on water skis, a huge inflatable banana or attached to a parachute.

A variety of barriers alongside the island's artificial beaches, there to prevent the sands being washed away, have reduced the sea to a rather dull and wave-free lapping mass. Elsewhere along the coast though, the sea has a very different personality, with powerful swells, huge Atlantic rollers and strong currents, particularly in the north, where swimming is often treacherous and the appearance of red flags common. For safer swimming, resorts in this part of the island generally provide man-made bathing pools, many of which are only accessible at low tide – including the unique pools in Garachico, which have been hollowed out of lava flows.

SURFING AND BODYBOARDING

Away from the protected artificial beaches the tempestuous conditions of the sea attract thrill-seeking local **surfers** and **bodyboarders**, who happily dodge scattered rocky outcrops. Those keen to try to ride waves should first talk to local surfers as they know the whereabouts of rocks and undercurrents. Playa Benijo, in the Anaga region, is one of the main surfing centres on the island and a friendly community waits here for the right conditions in the bay. The more accessible Playa de Troya in Las Americas is another popular spot, while the surf off the pebble beach in Las Galletas and in El Médano is more suitable for beginners. El Médano is much more renowned as premium **windsurfing** territory, however, and international competitions are regularly held here. Well-known around the windsurfing world, the conditions here are usually too hard for beginners, who would be better off learning in the calmer conditions of Las Américas.

SNORKELLING AND SCUBA-DIVING

It's also possible to go **snorkelling** alongside the rocky island shores, or **scuba-diving** further out to sea. And although the local underwater scenery and wildlife do not provide world-class dive sites, there are plenty of fish – barracudas, grouper, rays, sharks and even turtles – and competition between the many island dive schools has made it relatively inexpensive (around €240) to do the basic PADI or CMAS dive courses. Visibility around the islands is usually around 25m and the island's best dive sites include the spectacular underwater cliffs (60m) just south of Los Cristianos, the so-called Stingray City near Las Galletas, the massive tuna shoals near Los Gigantes and a DC3 aeroplane wreck near Puerto de la Cruz.

SAILING AND BOAT TRIPS

The windsurfing school in Las Américas also teaches **sailing**, but if you already have experience then it's possible to rent from a variety of sail **boats**, including luxury yachts, from outfits in the resort's harbour, Puerto Colón. CCB Yacht Charters (☏922/794 404) charge €271 a day for a yacht carrying up to eight people, and with a crew the charge rises to €723; reservations are usually required at least six weeks in advance. Other boats, particularly motorboats, requiring less experience, commitment or advance reservation are available from €60 per day.

Those who'd rather be guided around the seas will also find a massive array of **boat trips**, starting from Las Américas, Los Cristianos or Los Gigantes. Most of these head out into the Gomeran channel in search of whales and dolphins, while others stop to enable passengers to swim or snorkel along the coast. Some trips are specifically **fishing trips** (starting at about €48 per person for five hours), with deep-sea game fishing particularly popular and marlin, tuna and swordfish abundant. However, most local fishermen spend their time fishing off the seashore (which doesn't require a permit), and there are plenty of bait and tackle shops on the island to furnish you with the necessary equipment. The north coast of the Teno range is one of the best places to fish.

HIKING

Possessing incredibly varied terrain and ecological landscapes, Tenerife and La Gomera are both great year-round **hiking** venues. The obvious place to head for **on Tenerife** is the lunar landscapes of the Parque Nacional del Teide, although there are plenty of good, well-marked hikes elsewhere too – particularly in the wildly rugged Anaga and Teno regions or in the densely forested Orotava valley. While on neighbouring **La Gomera** the most enticing area is at the centre of the island among the ancient laurel forest of the Parque Nacional de Garajonay. But, again, you can find first-class hiking along almost any of the island's steep-sided gorges or ridges.

If you are heading to La Gomera to go hiking, consider the escorted hiking tours of Wilderness Walks (℡01227/779 199; ⓦwww.wildernesswalks.com) who run trips for all abilities, costing from around £425 per week (excluding flights).

Most of the hiking on Tenerife will not start from the front door of your accommodation and will involve making use of the dependable bus network (see p.21) or renting a car. Puerto de la Cruz is traditionally the resort of choice for hikers, being well-connected by buses and served by a good range of accommodation (and operators offering guided hiking trips), as well as being on the north side of the island where much of the best hiking is. However, for those wanting to stay in less of a resort environment, Santa Cruz can also make a good base. Alternatively, if you want to mix hiking with the nightlife, beaches and sunshine of the southern resorts, then Los Cristianos makes a good base, well connected as it is to the local bus network.

Maps and hiking guides are available at bookshops in the island's main towns and resorts, but to save time, it's worth picking up information before you head out to Tenerife (see p.12). Two UK publishers produce particularly useful hiking companions: Sunflower Guides publish two books on Tenerife and one on La Gomera, while Discovery Walking Guides publish folded pamphlets in poly-pockets with good, clear, annotated island maps, as well as books that reprint portions of their map with the addition of further route-finding information.

CLIMBING

Climbers visiting Tenerife looking for good rock will find over a hundred climbing routes on a marvellous rough rock-climbing medium – with lots of pinch grips, pockets and incut edges. And while few routes are of international quality, the island's fair weather nevertheless makes it a worthwhile winter destination. Some of the best climbs are in Las Cañadas, in the Parque Nacional del Teide, particularly around Los Roques – and the nearby La Catedral is the island's main traditional climbing area. The smooth open faces of a quarry-like gorge near Arico also contain interest and problems, though there are easier routes here too.

The only climbing **shop** on the island is Na Maste, C/Maquinez 15, Puerto de la Cruz – opposite Futuro Parque Maritimo. As this is remote from the climbing areas, climbers should aim to be self-sufficient in their equipment

needs before they arrive on the island. The recently revised
climbing guide: *Rock Climbs in Majorca, Ibiza and Tenerife*
by Chris Craggs (Cicerone Press) should also be considered
an essential part of your luggage.

GOLF

Thanks in part to relentless promotion by the island's tourist
board, Tenerife has begun to emerge as a popular **golfing**
destination. Of course the island's pleasant climate would
encourage golfers here almost irrespective of the quality of
courses, but in fact its six courses, five of which are dotted
around the resorts of southern Tenerife, include some
excellent and challenging terrain. High season for golfers is
during the winter months, when the northern European
weather is at its most miserable. In consequence courses
whose green fees typically hover around €50, offer discounts of up to a third in the summer months. Most courses will rent clubs (around €18) and buggies (around €30)
as well as offering discounts to guests at certain hotels in
southern Tenerife.

GOLF COURSES

- -

Amarilla Golf & Country Golf,
San Miguel de Abona,
Autopista del Sur exit 24
℡ 922/730 319, Ⓕ 922/730
085, ⒺＥamarilla@redkbs.com.
Thoughtfully designed
eighteen-hole, par 70 course
beside the sea, where a round
costs €55. Daily
7.30am–7.30pm.

Golf del Sur, San Miguel de
Abona; Autopista del Sur exit
24 ℡ 922/738 170, Ⓕ 922/738
272,
ⓌＷwww.canaryweb.es/golfsur.
Large bunkers and wide
fairways make for difficult iron
shots on the three courses
here (each par 70), that share
twenty-seven holes. The

green fee is €60. Daily
10.30am–7pm.

Palos, Ctra. Guaza, Las
Galletas, km. 7. Exit 26 from
Autopista Sur ℡ 922/730 080,
⒡ 922/731 898,
ⓦ webtenerife.com/golf. Small
nine-hole course in the south
of the island that specializes
in instruction, though even the
experienced will be
entertained by the tricky
course that costs only €21 for
eighteen holes. Daily
8am–8pm.

Real Club El Peñon, Guamasa,
2km north of Los Rodeos
Airport ℡ 922/636 607. Stylish
eighteen-hole, par 71 course
with a €48 green fee. Mon–Fri
8am–1pm.

Las Américas, Exit 28 off
motorway Autopista Sur
℡ 922 552 005, ⒡ 922/795
250, ⓦ www.golftenerife.com.
New eighteen-hole, par 72,
public golf course between
Playa de Las Américas and
Los Cristianos, that has
turned the unattractive
wasteland between the two
towns green. The easily
walkable course contains
scattered palms and plenty of
water features. The green fee
is €63. Daily 7.40am–7pm.

Costa Adeje, Costa Adeje
℡ 922/710 000, ⒡ 922/710
484, ⒠ golfcostaadeje
@interbook.net. New
eighteen-hole, par 72 course,
with a nine-hole extension
underway, at the northern
edge of Las Américas. The
course design has been much
praised for elegantly fitting
around existing features –
particularly the large amount
of restored agricultural
terracing. The green fee is
€55. Daily 7.30am–7pm.

SPECTATOR SPORTS

Whereas traditional Canarian sports such as wrestling and
stick fighting are undergoing a renaissance on Tenerife, it is
football, and in particular support of Club Deportivo
Tenerife, that impassions most of the locals. Tickets to
either wrestling matches or football games are hard to find,
but well worth the bother if you do. If you want to catch

the island's men at their most animated, it's worth trying to secure a ticket to the home matches of local team **Club Deportivo Tenerife**, who play in Santa Cruz. With a well-respected pedigree in the Spanish league, it's often hard to get hold of tickets for CD-Tenerife's games. But if you call the box office at Estadio Heliodoro Rodríguez López (Mon–Fri 10am–1pm & 5–8pm; ☏922/291 699 or 922/240 613) a couple of weeks ahead you might be lucky; seats cost €36, stands €11.

Any sizeable place is likely to have a ring for contests of **Canarian wrestling** (*Lucha Canaria*) and information on fixtures can be gained from the Federación de Lucha Canaria, Callejón del Capitán Brotons 7, Santa Cruz (☏922/251 452) – where bouts are held on Friday and Saturday evenings. The rules of this relatively non-violent sport are simple and involve two barefoot men in a round, sandy ring attempting, by gripping the bottom of the opponent's shorts, to manoeuvre each other to the ground. Kicks and punches are not allowed. If any more than the soles of a man's feet touch the ground he loses the round. There are three rounds altogether and winning two rounds secures a point for the victor's twelve-man team. The winner can then choose to stand against a new opponent or let a team-mate take over. Bouts continue until one team has the twelve points it needs to win, and the whole contest can take around three hours. Although most wrestlers are beefy, balance, strength and grappling technique – along with generous helpings of *gofio* (see p.32) – are said to be the key.

A more minor tradition, and one primarily making appearances as a demonstration sport at fiestas, is **stick fighting** (*Juego del palo*). This contest, a derivative of Guanche stick-and-stone duels, uses large, two-metre-long staffs to both attack and defend, with the aim of trying to knock an opponent off his perch on a relatively small flat rock.

The only other traditional Canarian sport that occasionally rears its (ugly) head, is the now illegal practice of **cockfighting**, where cocks armed with spurs are encouraged to carve each other up. Incidentally, bull-fighting never caught on in the Canaries, although a speculatively built ring still stands in Santa Cruz.

Shopping and souvenirs

Given the low rate of sales tax, Tenerife is something of a shopper's paradise, with hundreds of small shops in the resorts selling luxury items, such as jewellery and perfume, to tourists. These items, and all the consumer durables locals need in their daily lives, are also available (sometimes more cheaply) in two large out-of-town shopping centres near Santa Cruz: Las Chumberas, beside the motorway near La Laguna, and Continente, between Santa Cruz and Candelaria (jctn 4 off the motorway

Autopista del Sur). **While opening hours for the shops here and in the tourist resorts are long (typically daily 8am–8pm), the rest of the island's shops keep more traditional hours – usually Monday to Saturday from 9am to 1pm and 4pm to 8pm.**

For unusual souvenirs, head for the fleamarket outside the African Market building (*Mercado De Nuestra Señora de África*) in Santa Cruz on Sunday mornings.

Traditional souvenirs of Tenerife and La Gomera include handcrafted goods such as wooden carvings, basketware, pottery, embroidery and lacework. The lace is considered particularly fine and comes from one of two main traditions – that of La Orotava, where a wooden frame is used and that of Vilaflor, where small rosettes are sewn together to form larger pieces. Various consumables are also popular souvenirs, including cigars, said to be inferior only to their Cuban cousins (and much cheaper), novelty liqueurs such as the *cobana* banana liqueur that comes in a bottle shaped like a bunch of bananas and the honey rum *mistela* from La Gomera. Some local foodstuffs might also be worth picking up, including the fine honeys collected from hives around Teide, some of the popular and varied goats' cheeses or even some *mojo*, the traditional local spicy dip (see p.33).

Drugs, trouble and harassment

Almost all the problems visitors to Tenerife encounter relate to petty crimes (pickpocketing, bag snatching, confidence tricks, burglary of accommodation or theft from cars) and serious physical confrontations are rare. Exercising caution, by leaving passport, tickets and valuables in the hotel safe, should spare you some of the worst travelling scenarios, and having photocopies of your passport and separate records of travellers' cheques and credit-card numbers is also a good precautionary measure.

If you are robbed you need to report it to the **police**, not least because insurance companies require a report to process claims. Of the three types of police – the Policia Municipal, the Guardia Civil and the Policia Nacional – you should always try to approach the Policia Municipal (blue-and-white uniforms with red trim). In some situations, particularly in rural areas, there may only be the Guardia Civil (in green uniforms) who should also be able to help you. The brown-uniformed Policia Nacional are mainly seen in cities guarding key installations and will not provide help for visitor needs.

In **emergencies**, contact the Policia Municipal on ☎092.

To prevent an unintentional entanglement with the law, it's worth being aware of a few offences you might commit unwittingly. Spanish law requires you to carry some kind of identification at all times, and the police can stop you in the streets and demand to see it – though in practice, if they do stop you, and you don't have anything with you, but are clearly a visitor, it is rare that the matter will be taken any further. Activities that may cause you to brush with official-dom include nude bathing or unauthorized camping – though a warning to cover up or move on is the most likely response to being caught committing either activity. Topless tanning is commonplace at the resorts, but may upset local sensibilities elsewhere. Despite being decriminalized in the 1980s, using cannabis is once more forbidden in Spain. Even so, the police are rarely interested in crimes of person-al use, though larger quantities (and possession of any other drugs) are a very different matter. Should you be arrested on any charge, contact your embassy or consulate for help and advice (see p.9).

Living, working and studying on Tenerife

EU nationals and citizens of Norway and Iceland are allowed to work in Spain without a work visa, but those intending to stay longer than three months will need a residency permit (*permiso de residencia*; see p.8). Citizens of most other countries need to get a work permit from the Spanish consulate in their home country. Before either the residency or work permit is issued, applicants usually have to have a work contract in place.

Most of the work available on Tenerife is casual work in resort bars or with time-share companies. Certification in skills such as diving instruction, or English teaching will attract better rates of pay, though these jobs are harder to come by. One of the few opportunities for voluntary work on the islands is offered by Proyecto Ambiental Tenerife, who have an office in London (59 St Martins Lane, Covent

Garden, WC2H 9DG; ☎020/7240 6604, ⓦwww
.interbook.personal/nt/delfinc), who organize whale and
dolphin research and conservation work during the summer
– this costs around €110 per week, half board. Qualified
divers can also take part in the organization's work in its
marine habitat survey.

Language courses are on offer in many major towns and
resorts on both Tenerife and La Gomera. Well-respected
courses are also offered by the University of Laguna (contact the *Secretaria de Los Cursos de Español para Extranjeros*; ☎
& ⓕ 922/603 345), where three week intensive (five hours
tuition per day) courses are offered for a variety of levels.
Courses include discussion groups and excursions and costs
around €300.

Travelling with specific needs

Though specific facilities or allowances for the disabled are rare in Tenerife, most major towns, resorts and, by law, all new public buildings are required to be fully accessible by wheelchair-users. The wheelchair-bound are likely to find most older town centres difficult (sometimes impossible) to negotiate, however – littered as they are with steps and narrow pavements – but should have an easier time in new resorts, particularly Los Cristianos where the pedestrianized centre has been designed with wheelchairs in mind. As a disabled traveller you are advised to make accommodation arrangements before you go. You will generally be restricted to package accommodation, the suitability and location of which you should check with your travel agent. Most travel agents will keep a number of accommodation gazetteers on hand which should be able to provide enough information to make sure your hotel or apartment won't cause unforeseen problems. In addition it's well worth browsing the well-designed Travel for All Web site, ⓦ www.cabtfe.es/sinpromi/index2-en.html, which includes an extensive searchable database listing disabled-friendly accommodation and attractions.

Transport is still the main problem for wheelchair users, since buses are not equipped to deal with these. Taxi drivers are usually helpful, though, and it's also well worth contacting the experienced local company Disabled Travellers Le Ro in Puerto de la Cruz (☏ 922/373 301) or Los Cristianos (☏ 922/750 289), who can organize island trips in a specially designed tour bus. The company also services and delivers equipment and can be of considerable general assistance. Their Los Cristianos office is in the wheelchair-friendly Mar y Sol (see p.157), whose resident dive school teaches diving to the disabled.

ORGANIZATIONS OFFERING HELP TO DISABLED TRAVELLERS

Australia Council for the Rehabilitation of the Disabled, PO Box 60, Curtin, ACT 2606 ☏ 02/6282 4333.

Belgium Mobility International, Rue de Manchester 25, Brussels B1070 ☏ 00322/201 5711, ⓕ 201/5763.

Britain RADAR, 12 City Forum, 250 City Rd, London EC1V 8AF ☏ 020/7250 3222.

Ireland Disability Action Group,

2 Annadale Ave, Belfast BT7 3JH ☏ 01232/491011; Irish Wheelchair Association, Blackheath Drive, Clontarf, Dublin 3 ☏ 01/833 8241.

New Zealand Disabled Persons Assembly, 173 Victoria St, Wellington ☏ 04/801 9100.

North America Mobility International USA, PO Box 10767, Eugene, OR 97440 ☏ 541/343-1284.

Directory

ADDRESSES are commonly abbreviated as: C/ for Calle (street); Ctra for Carretera (main road); Avda for Avenida (avenue); Edif for Edificio (a large block) and CC for Centro Commercial (a commercial centre or shopping centre or mall, often in an Edificio). Addresses within Edificios or Centro Commercials are rarely accompanied by the unit number of a premises.

COMPLAINTS Conscious of its reliance on tourism, Tenerife keeps all businesses dealing directly with visitors up to scratch by obliging them, by law, to have a complaints book (*Hoja de Reclamación*), into which complaints can be lodged. Noted in this form, complaints are treated extremely seriously by authorities, making this a last resort if those concerned will not make amends. If you feel you are being overcharged in a hotel, restaurant or bar, check the price list that needs to be present, bearing the stamp of the local issuing authority.

TIPPING The law requires the inclusion of service charges, making a 5–10 per cent tip perfectly adequate in most restaurants, bars, cafés and taxis.

ELECTRICITY Voltage on Tenerife and La Gomera is 220 A/C. Sockets take European two-pin plugs, so travellers from Britain, Australia and New Zealand will need a standard adapter plug for their electrical appliances, and travellers from North America will need this plus a voltage transformer.

GAY TENERIFE As a gay destination in the Canaries, Tenerife is completely overshadowed by neighbouring Gran Canaria. Though there is a small gay scene on the island (almost exclusively in Santa Cruz and Puerto de la Cruz), it can be hard to find. To help in the search pick up the magazine *Guía Gay Visado*, a comprehensive guide to gay and lesbian bars, clubs, discos and contacts throughout Spain, usually in some bookshops and newstands. On the Web Ⓦwww.guiagay.com also has (a few) listings that can help get you started. If you intend to spend some time on the island, it may be worth getting in touch with the Colectivo de Gays y Lesbianas de Las Palmas, P.O. Box 707, Las Palmas de Gran Canaria ℡928/433 427), who can furnish you with contacts on Tenerife. The age of consent for homosexuals in Spain is 16.

LAUNDRIES In the absence of many self-service laundries, clothes often have to be left for a full (and somewhat expensive) washing, drying and ironing service. A dry cleaner is a *tintorería*.

TIME In the same time zone as the UK and Ireland, so in line with GMT during winter and one hour ahead of GMT during the summer; between five hours (east coast) and nine hours (west coast) ahead of North America; between seven and nine hours behind Australia; and eleven hours behind New Zealand.

THE GUIDE

THE GUIDE

Santa Cruz and around

Nestling between giant steep-sided and inaccessible mountains and a large natural harbour, the dynamic city of **Santa Cruz** is where the Spanish conquest of the island began in the fifteenth century. Now the island's capital, Santa Cruz was then simply the landing site for Alfonso de Lugo who planted his holy cross here in 1494 before heading his party inland to found the island's first town – **La Laguna**, based around a lagoon and well inland, out of easy range of pirates. The first island government was located in La Laguna, but was moved to the flourishing port of Santa Cruz in 1723. La Laguna, instead, reinvented itself as a university town, and is now the major one in the Canary Islands. Today the two towns have more-or-less become one, thanks to the almost uninterrupted strip of residential and commercial developments that has grown up between them.

To the east of Santa Cruz rise the magnificent **mountains** of the Anaga peninsula. Sinuous roads climb through mist-shrouded laurel forests to reach the remote communities tucked into the deep valleys and knife-edge ridges of

ACCOMMODATION PRICE CODES

Throughout the *Guide*, accommodation has been graded according to price, based on the cost of the cheapest double room in high season – but excluding the time around Christmas and New Year, when rates can rocket. In the case of apartments that sleep more than two, the price for the smallest available unit, as described in the body text, is given; where apartments are available by the night, the price refers to the cheapest two-person apartment. Where singles – which are usually more than half the price of doubles – are available, this has also been mentioned. Travellers wanting to stay a week or more may find that nightly rate can be reduced a little.

❶ up to €12
❷ €12–€24
❸ €24–€36
❹ €36– €48

❺ €48– €60
❻ €60– €84
❼ €84– €120
❽ over €120

this ancient volcanic range. While the northern coast of the peninsula remains particularly remote, the southern side, with huge Atlantic rollers breaking against its twisted rock cliffs, is easily accessed from the city and has been turned into a playground for city dwellers, with the construction of the island's most impressive artificial beach 10km north of Santa Cruz at **San Andrés**.

A string of dormitory settlements stretches west from Santa Cruz for around 20km, petering out around the dreary modern town of **Candelaria**. Of interest solely for its church, Candelaria is host to the archipelago's most revered religious symbol – the **Virgin of Candelaria**. Inland from here the fertile terraces around **Güímar**, 6km away, were once the basis of a thriving local community. Agriculture in the area has since declined in importance and the town is now best known as the location of **pyramids**, once built by the aboriginal Guanche peoples and now painstakingly reconstructed by Norwegian archeologist Thor Heyerdahl. This major find is not only an intriguing insight into local Guanche culture but is considered of wider importance, as a stepping-stone in the migration of ancient African culture to South America.

Santa Cruz

Map 1, K2.

- -
Maps 2 & 3 cover Santa Cruz in detail.
- -

Home to the archipelago's biggest container shipping port and a number of oil refineries, **SANTA CRUZ** is no aesthete's delight, but its uniquely Canarian urban vibrance is hard to find elsewhere on the island. From the time of the landing of the first conquistadors, Santa Cruz became the island's main port and, as Tenerife became a routine stop-off for replenishing supplies before the final leg of the journey to the New World, Spanish galleons would regularly anchor here and the town was well-fortified to protect them. Santa Cruz continues to be a convenient and popular port of call for navies of the world, tankers and Atlantic trawlers. As the island's capital city and the administrative and financial centre for the four westernmost Canary Islands, it has grown into a bustling, modern Spanish town, a grid of narrow shopping streets, parks and plazas, intersected by several wide bustling avenues.

The centre is easy to explore on foot, and though there are few real sights save for a couple of churches and some

SANTA CRUZ

good museums, the pretty parks and plazas are pleasant to wander around and the absence of the resort racket makes a welcome change from the island's other major centres.

ARRIVAL AND INFORMATION

The **bus station** (Map 2, D14) is south of the centre, around ten-minutes' walk from the seafront Plaza de España; buses arrive here from almost every corner of the island (with the exception of Parque Nacional del Teide and the west coast). Those arriving by car will do best to head here, too (follow signs for the Avda Maritima), and try to find a space in the underground car park below the plaza.

The town's helpful **tourist office** (Map 2, H9. Mon–Fri 8am–6pm, Sat 9am–1pm; ☎922/239 592), on the western side of the Plaza de España, supplies good town maps for free and also has the largest stock of information on the rest of the island.

ACCOMMODATION

Unusually for Tenerife, there's a reasonably large selection of **accommodation** for the independent traveller in Santa Cruz, and finding somewhere to stay here shouldn't be a problem – except during the **Carnival** (Feb/March), at which time accommodation is generally booked up at least six months in advance.

HOTELS

Atlántico
Map 2, F8. C/Del Castillo 12.
☎ 922/246 375
🅕 922/246 378

Cramped and ageing hotel on the town's main pedestrian thoroughfare. Rooms, all with a TV, are fine for short stays. There's a pleasant roof terrace and breakfast is included. Singles available. **⑤**.

Horizonte

Map 2, F5. C/Santa Rosa de Lima 11.
Ⓣ & Ⓕ 922/271 936
Inexpensive hotel on the edge of the central pedestrian area with worn and dated 70s decor, but large en-suite rooms and some good-value singles ❸.

Mency

Map 2, D2. C/del Doctor José Naveiras 38
Ⓣ 922/276 700
Ⓕ 922/280 017
Ⓦ www.sheraton.com
This swanky, 286-room palace is located by the busy Rambla General Franco. The building's architecture is inspired by 1920s casino hotels and includes a large pool and tennis courts in its palm garden. The plush interiors reflect Classical design and are furnished with antiques. ❽.

Océano

Map 2, F8. C/Castillo 6.
Ⓣ 922/270 800
Good value hotel, above the shops of the town's main pedestrian street and a few doors down from the *Atlántico*. The functional rooms here are cramped, but rather grandly appointed with a surfeit of marble. Room rates include breakfast. ❹.

Pelinor

Map 2, G7. C/Béthencourt Alfonso 8
Ⓣ 922/246 875
Ⓕ 922/280 520
Large, airy, tiled rooms in a labyrinthine hotel complex at the heart of the pedestrian centre. Though the straightforward rooms have been renovated recently, the hotel as a whole has a slightly rundown feel – but it's clean throughout and prices include breakfast. ❻.

Plaza

Map 2, G8. Plaza Candelaria 10
Ⓣ 922/272 453
Ⓕ 922/275 160
Well-run hotel with small, plain but comfortable rooms, facing onto the town's main plaza. A popular business hotel, it keeps itself busy on weekends by offering good-value weekend rates, for minimum two-night stays. Its

SANTA CRUZ

singles offer the best value in town and taller visitors will be pleased to know that some extra-long beds are available. Prices include a breakfast buffet. **6**.

Taburiente

Map 2, D3. C/Dr José Naveiras 24A

ⓣ 922/276 000

ⓕ 922/270 562

ⓦ www.canaryweb.es/htabu

Grand, stylish, modern hotel opposite the Parque Garcia Sanabria on the northern edge of the pedestrian area. Many rooms have a good view over the park and all are en suite, with TV, fridge and direct-line telephone. Communal facilities include a roof terrace with small pool, a Jacuzzi and a sauna. The good facilities make the hotel's prices very reasonable. **6**.

PENSIONS

- -

Casablanca

Map 2, D6. C/de Viera y Clavijo 15.

ⓣ 922/278 599

Despite the friendly, English-speaking new owners and their creative decoration, beds remain well worn and the shared bathrooms less than appealing. But a small roof terrace, friendly atmosphere and location on a pleasant pedestrianized street make this a convenient, quiet and central option. Singles are available. **2**.

Mi Lema

Simón Bolívar 3.

ⓣ 922/225 879

Spartan rooms, all with shared baths, in a friendly pension 2km outside the city centre. To find it follow Peréz Armas out of town to its junction with Avda Benito at a plaza. The Pension is just off Avda Benito. **3**.

Mova

Map 2, F3. C/de San Martin 33.

ⓣ 922/283 261

Perhaps the pick of the low-budget bunch, with singles and doubles available (with or without private baths) in a slightly dilapidated part of town that's nevertheless handy for the nightlife along the Avenida Anaga. The owners speak some English. **❸**.

Padrón

C/Gral. Mola 114.
☎922/222 876
Large, basic rooms, all with shared bathrooms, in a large apartment building 2km out of town along the main arterial road Peréz Armas.

Valverde

Map 2, D6. C/de Sabino Berthelot 46.
☎922/274 063
Well-turned out, but not very friendly pension above a bar on a centrally located pedestrian street. Some rooms have private bathrooms. **❷**.

THE TOWN

Despite its age and importance, Santa Cruz itself has relatively few sights, with most of the island's most elegant historic buildings being erected in La Laguna, the capital until 1722. However, it's easy to spend a pleasant and worthwhile day wandering the parks, plazas, bustling pedestrian streets and good museums of the island's biggest city.

Plaza de España and around

The city's most distinctive landmark – a huge controversial memorial to the 39 soldiers from the island who fought and died on Franco's side in the 1936–39 Civil War – is located in the middle of the seafront **Plaza de España** (Map 2, H8), which makes a good place to start a tour of the city. Adjoining this plaza, and lined with shops and cafés, is the long, narrow **Plaza Candelaria** which turns into the town's main pedestrian drag, **Calle del Castillo**.

SANTA CRUZ

Teatro Guimerá and the Centro de Fotografía

A few streets down from Calle del Castillo, on C/Imeldo Seris is the **Teatro Guimerá** (Map 2, F9), an imposing Classical building with elaborate stuccowork. Home to performances of ballet, opera and Classical music, its box office is at the side of the building. A similar building over the road houses the **Centro de Fotografía** (Map 2, F9. Mon–Sat 11am–1pm, 6–9pm; free) a photographic museum with frequently changing, imaginative, engaging and sometimes eclectic exhibitions.

Iglesia de Nuestra Señora de la Concepcion

The seafront area south of the centre contains some of the town's major attractions, including Santa Cruz's most significant church, the **Iglesia de Nuestra Señora de la Concepcion** (Map 2, G10. Mass Mon–Sat 9am & 7.30pm, Sun & church holidays same times plus those posted outside). Construction began in 1502, but took over two centuries to complete, and it has since been gutted by fire several times, so that today most of what remains dates from the seventeenth and eighteenth centuries. Relics and articles of historic significance kept here include part of the *Santa Cruz de la conquista* (Holy Cross of the Conquest), which dominates the silver Baroque main altar and gave the city its name.

Museo de la Naturaleza y el Hombre

The city's premier museum **Museo de la Naturaleza y el Hombre** at C/Fuentes Moreales (Map 2, F11. Tues–Sun 9am–8.30pm; €5; ☎922/209 320), is directly south of the main church and contains informative and well-constructed displays on Canarian natural history and archeology, the most fascinating of which relate to the Guanches. Their pottery and tools and examples of their rock art are displayed here, but most memorable perhaps are the gruesome mummified bodies.

Maercado de Nuestra Señora de África and around

Further south still and a little inland is the bustling, covered market, the Moorish-style **Maercado De Nuestra Señora de África** (Map 2, E11). Selling almost exclusively groceries from its three hundred stalls, the market is a good place for picking up inexpensive local produce (as good a selection of local goat and sheep's cheeses is hard to find elsewhere), but also for people watching. There is little of interest further south along the seafront, though those prepared to walk five minutes along it will find the stout little seventeenth-century portside fort the **Castillo San Juan**, which not only once guarded the town's harbour, but was also the site of a bustling trade in African slaves.

Iglesia de San Fancisco and the Museo de Belle Artes

North of the town centre, another pedestrian street, running parallel to and two blocks east of Calle del Castillo is Calle Villalba Hervás. Here you'll find the **Iglesia de San Francisco** (Map 2, F7), a seventeenth-century monastery with intricate wall paintings and a traditional Canarian wood ceiling; known for its excellent acoustics, the monastery hosts regular organ concerts. Around the corner and next to the small **Plaza Princípe Asturias**, with its magnificent stand of trees, is the **Museo de Belle Artes**, C/José Murphy 12 (Map 2, F7. Mon–Fri 10am–8pm; free),

NELSON'S ATTACK ON SANTA CRUZ

In 1797 Admiral Nelson, commanding a fleet of eight men-o'war, launched a bungling, unsuccessful and ultimately embarrassing attack on Santa Cruz, that cost the lives of many of his men and, more famously, the Admiral's right arm.

The assault on Santa Cruz was carried out after four years of war against Spain, with the intention of capturing New World gold from the galleon *San José*, currently sheltering in the town's harbour. Nelson based his battle plan on the successful capture of Caprina the previous September, and wrote that the planned assault "could not fail...[It will] immortalise the undertakers, ruin Spain and has every prospect of raising our country to a higher pitch of wealth than she has ever attained".

On June 22 a party was landed east of Santa Cruz, with the intention of encircling the town before battleships were moved into bombarding position. But the island's predictably unsettled local weather conditions, particularly strong winds and swirls known by local fishermen as "the white sheet", caused the attack to be slowed down, removing the element of surprise and causing panic and a mass exodus of the town's populace and administration to La Laguna.

Nevertheless, the landing party stuck to its plans and laboured up the loose rocky slopes of Jurada, mistakenly assuming this hill to be an extension of a ridge. Tired and frustrated, the men camped on top, positioning and firing their artillery at the town and its hastily assembled militia, both of which were out of range.

Despite the failure of his landing-party's mission, Nelson decided to continue with a full frontal attack. Under heavy cannon fire from the shore's 84 guns, the British landing force separated along the seafront in some disarray, unable to communicate with each other, or retaliate thanks to damp gunpowder. Many of Nelson's men were sucked into the town's dark alleys to be picked off by snipers, but the Admiral, never one to shrink from the action, was among the second wave of landing craft. He was about to land when he was struck by grapeshot on his right arm, shattering the bone and severing a major artery. By all accounts, Nelson bore this stoically, his first action being to switch his sword to his good hand, even before the life-saving tourniquet had been strapped to his arm.

Returning to his own ship, Nelson sent a message to the ship's surgeon to ready his instruments, knowing that he must lose his arm, and that the sooner it was off the better. Nevertheless, on arrival at the ship's surgery, Nelson is said to have insisted on waiting in line for treatment, rather than pulling rank on the other wounded. Within half an hour of the amputation, the admiral was up, giving orders and practising his left-handed signature for an ultimatum demanding the town give up the galleon. The letter would never be sent, however, since by daylight a boat returned from the shore informing him that all seven hundred English on shore had holed up in the Convent of Santo Domingo and decided to surrender on condition that they would be returned to their ships accompanied by "full military honours with beating of drums, flags and arms ...". This Governor Don Antonio Gutiérrez of Santa Cruz granted, lending the attackers boats with which to return to their ships, having given treatment to their wounded.

In recognition of this honourable conduct, Nelson sent the Spaniard a gift of beer and cheese, a gesture which was returned by sending back a barrel of Malmsey wine. With only a dozen Spanish dead, over one hundred and fifty English killed, a further hundred wounded and his enterprise having failed, Nelson left the scene deeply regretful of his misjudgement and depressed that the whole affair and his own disablement might spell the end of his naval days.

an eclectic mix of weapons, coins, sculptures and paintings (including a Breughel).

Museo Militar

A ten-minute walk north of the town centre, on C/de San Isidro, is the **Museo Militar** (Map 2, G1. Tues–Sun 10am–2pm; free), which has exhibitions on the evolution of weaponry through the ages, but largely concentrates on the town's finest military hour: its repulse of the attack by Lord Nelson (see box on previous page). The cannon "El Tigre", that allegedly blew off Nelson's arm, is on display, as are flags captured from his men.

EATING

Bars and **cafés** spill onto the plazas and pedestrian streets of central Santa Cruz. While the obvious choices for a quick coffee or snack are around the Plaza Candelaria, most of the cafés here are nothing special and a bit overpriced. A couple of minutes inland you'll find more interesting and better value places favoured by locals. Likewise, though there is a fair selection of **restaurants** near the Plaza Candelaria, and particularly along the Avenida de Anaga, there's a bigger selection among the pedestrian streets of the centre and there are a number of cafés and restaurants around Plaza de la Paz, a ten-minute walk northwest of Plaza Candelaria. Finally, as you might expect in a capital city, expect to pay a little more for your food in Santa Cruz than in other towns on the island.

Each restaurant listed in the *Guide* has been categorized as either inexpensive (under €6), moderate (€6– €10) and expensive (above €10) – indicating the price of an average main course.

Cañas y Tapas

Map 2, H4. Avda Anaga 15.
Branch of the Iberian
restaurant chain with dark
wood and tile decor and
some outside seating,
opposite the city's main
harbour and beside one of its
busiest roads. Large selection
of long-standing tapas
favourites such as blood
sausage, a salami platter and
octopus are available. As
usual, eating an entire meal
based on numerous tapas
works out to be quite
expensive, but at least
selections here are
dependably good and
vegetarians will find quite a
few options. Moderate to
expensive.

Cervecería Central

Map 2, F5. Santa Rosalia 47.
Large restaurant in pleasant
plaza-side location. This is a
good option for lunch, with a
fair selection of tapas,
sandwiches, omelettes and
scrambled-egg dishes and an
acceptable gazpacho. More
substantial meals are provided
by a predictable range of local

fish and meat dishes.
Moderate.

Coto de Antonio

Map 3, D1. C/General Goded
13.
☎922/272 105
This elegant simply decorated
restaurant is a consistently
popular choice with locals
and visitors alike. The
excellent menu is based
around Basque and Canarian
cuisine, with superb and
varied daily dishes made from
local produce from the town's
market as well as regular
favourites including roast kid
from the restaurant's own
farm. Closed Sun & Aug.
Expensive.

Da Gi Gi

Map 2, H2. Avda De Anaga 43.
☎922/284 607
Italian restaurant, with two
outlets – the other is at
Rambla General Franco 27
(Map 3, D1. ☎922/274 326)
– each with stylish brick
interiors and located in the
city's most popular dining
areas. The menu features a
good selection of antipasta,

SANTA CRUZ

●

an excellent range of fresh pastas and a large selection of fantastic thin-crust pizzas. Service is quick (take out is also available) and the restaurant on the Avda De Anaga has some outdoor seating. Moderate.

El Libano
Map 3, C2. C/Santiago Cuadrado 36.
℡ 922/285 914
Simple Lebanese restaurant tucked in a side street and popular with the locals. The large menu includes old favourites such as kebabs and stuffed vine leaves, but also includes some more unusual dishes such as *beme*, an excellent traditional vegetable dish. Superb selection of vegetarian dishes. Moderate.

El Rincon de la Píedra
Map 3, E2. C/Benavides 32.
℡ 922/249 778
Stunningly cavernous and beautiful old house with restored woodwork, beamed ceilings and a friendly atmosphere. The food includes a good range of fine salads and some fish, but the restaurant is best known for its meat dishes including a superb *solomillo*. Closed Thurs. Expensive.

Mesón Castellano
Map 2, C7. C/de Lima 4.
℡ 922/271 074
Atmospheric basement restaurant serving Castilian food, fish and meat, and specializing in a range of sausage-based dishes. The rustic little bar on the ground floor above the restaurant is pleasant place for a quiet drink. Closed Sun. Expensive.

Pans & Company
Map 2, F7. C/Villalba Hervás 18.
The fast-food ambience created through the glass-and-plastic decor belies the restaurant's good healthy menus that include salads and *bocadillos*, which are particularly good value when chosen as part of a set meal. Open until 3am. Inexpensive.

Pavarotti Pizzeria
Map 2, F6. C/de la Luna 4.
Popular restaurant for various

Italian specialities, where the bulk of the seating is in a pleasant broad pedestrian alley. The predictable (but good) range of pizza and pasta on the menu is joined by more creative house specialities such as giant stuffed tomatoes and an excellent selection of marinated vegetables. Moderate.

Viet-Nam
Map 3, D2. Paseo 4.

Smart but unpretentious restaurant where diners have the option of sitting outdoors in an alley of bustling bars. The 150-dish menu offers a wide range of Vietnamese and oriental cuisine. The excellent seafood dishes are well worth trying. Moderate.

DRINKING AND NIGHTLIFE

Inevitably, Santa Cruz's **nightlife** is at its best during Carnival (see below), which can make the other fifty weeks of the year seem like one long anticlimax. But, by normal standards the capital has a good range of **bars** and **clubs** (supplemented by a number of huge outdoor venues nearby in the summer) and a respected venue for the **performing arts**.

Most of the town's trendiest **bars** and **clubs** line the **Avenida de Anaga**, which follows the coast northwards from Plaza de España, and though they don't tend to get going until midnight, most pump out chart music until around 5am – one longstanding (though rather nondescript) favourite on the strip is Nooctua at no. 37 (Map 2, H2). During the summer months the clubs along this strip are largely eclipsed by the building of temporary outdoor bars and discos, so-called **terraces**. Locations vary each year, as do the "in" places.

The town's other main nightlife area is rather more sedate and tends to cater for an older clientele who like to stroll

CARNIVAL

Santa Cruz's **Carnival** is one of Europe's most vibrant and colourful festivals. Every year proceedings aim to outstrip the efforts of the year before, so much so that in recent years up to 280,000 people – from all over the world and particularly South America – have been dancing in the streets at peak times during the celebrations.

Though originally following the religious calendar, the event has now extended deep into Lent itself. Each night the Plaza de España and surrounding streets fill with revellers from around the island, dancing to vibrant salsa beats from bands performing on various stages, or to various pop and rock tunes pumping out of the hundreds of kiosks lining the street. The party is at its height from 11pm until dawn and is particularly well-attended at weekends. Fancy dress is almost compulsory for all who attend, and many will dress in the annual theme.

The highlight of the week is the **Grand Procession** on Shrove Tuesday – a cavalcade of floats, bands, dancers and entertainers, who march and dance their way along the dock-side road. Also popular is the ironically comical **Burial of the Sardine** on Ash Wednesday, when the effigy of a ridiculously large sardine is burnt before an entourage of wailing widows. Many participants get into the spirit of the event by dressing in mourning clothes. Traditionally, the sardine's cremation, followed by fireworks and a huge open-air ball should signify the last day of the carnival, and the beginning of Lent, but this carnival now comes to its climactic end the following weekend – at which point smaller towns around the island often start their own carnivals.

For the latest on the current year's carnival preparations and plans check Ⓦ www.carnaval-tenerife.org.

down Rambla General Franco, the main arterial road inland and to the north of the centre, which is lined with kiosks, cafés and some unusual modern sculptures.

The **Plaza de la Paz** is a vague focus for another area of bars including the Cervecería Metro, Rambla de Pubido 89 (Map 3, D3), a pleasantly furnished popular place where a varied crowd meets in the dingy pub-style bar. Opposite the entrance to this bar is a small alley, the Paseo, into which half a dozen small bars spill. El Desvan, at no. 17 (Map 3, D2), is one of the more stylish along here. Relatively undisturbed by nearby main roads, the bars in the alley hum for most of the night – with a good mix of age groups represented.

There's little in the way of live music in Santa Cruz with only occasional **pop concerts** taking place on Plaza de Toros (for ticket and concert information enquire at the tourist office). However, the capital's main performing arts venue, the Teatro Guimerá, C/de Imeldo Seris (Map 2, F9. ☎922/29 08 38), is rather busier with its programme of **Classical music** and **theatre performances**. The annual Classical-music festival, the *Festival de Música de Canarias*, is the highpoint of the annual calendar here, and includes numerous performances by the well-respected symphony orchestra of Tenerife (☎922/239 801, ⓦ www.cabtfe .es/ost/) – which puts on its own festival here in March.

LISTINGS

Banks and exchanges Virtually every Spanish bank has a branch in the town centre, several of them on Plaza Candelaria, including the Banco Credito at no. 1 and Banco Banesto at no. 9.

Car rental Cicar, at the quay Muelle de Ribera (☎922/292 425); Rent-a-Car Ada, C/Emilio Calzadilla 10 (☎922/274 953).

SANTA CRUZ

Cycling The sports megastore Decatholon (☎ 922/627 900) in the shopping centre Las Chumberas (by the motorway, opposite La Laguna) rents out mountain bikes for €11 a day.

Hospital Hospital de Nuestra Señora de la Candelaria (☎ 922/275 563), by the motorway to La Laguna. For an ambulance, call ☎ 922/281 800.

Internet café El Navegante, Callejón del Combate 12 (daily 11am–5pm; €5 per hour).

Laundry Lavandería Autoservico, C/de San Antonio 59 (Mon–Fri 9am–1pm & 5–7pm, Sat 9am–1pm).

Pharmacy Saavedra Pérex Avda Anaga 37 (☎ 922/275 563).

Police The Policía Municipal office is on Avda Tres de Mayo 79 (☎ 922/606 092).

Post office The main office is on the Plaza de España and offers a fax service.

Swimming The Parque Maritimo (☎ 922/203 244), a César Manrique-designed pool, is a ten-minute walk along the coast from the bus station at the southern end of town.

Taxi ☎ 922/210 059.

Travel agents Halcón Viajes, Plaza del General Weyler 9 (☎ 922/249 371); Iberia, Avda Francisco la Roche 34 (☎ 922/227 051).

La Laguna

Map 1, J2.

Map 4 covers central La Laguna in detail.

Now a lively and historic university town, **LA LAGUNA** was Tenerife's first major settlement and, for over two hundred years, its capital. Though the government may have moved, and its bland suburbs now melt with Santa Cruz, its well-preserved centre remains a showpiece of Canarian architecture and the city remains the cultural, religious and learning centre of Tenerife.

A good deal higher than Santa Cruz and so with a considerably cooler, cloudier and rainier climate than at the coast, the town took its name from its proximity to a former lagoon which was drained as late as 1837, after having already shrunk as a result of logging in the area. Today, La Laguna is seen at its best during festivals, particularly Corpus Christi, when many of its central streets are bedecked with complicated patterns of flowers.

ARRIVAL AND INFORMATION

La Laguna's **bus station** is an easy ten-minute walk north of the centre. From here, frequent buses cut through central La Laguna to connect it with Santa Cruz day and night. If arriving in town by car, you are advised to park as soon as you can as it's difficult to find a space within the centre.

There's a small **tourist information** kiosk (Map 4, G4. Mon–Sat 9am–7pm) on Plaza del Adelantado, the town's main square, which can provide a list of available accommodation in the area, useful town maps and a couple of glossy brochures on local architecture (in Spanish).

LA LAGUNA

ACCOMMODATION

The selection of **accommodation** in La Laguna is limited to a couple of pleasant but fairly expensive options. The very central *Hotel-Apartamentos Nivaria*, at Plaza del Adelantado 11 (Map 4, F4. ☎922/264 298, ℉922/259 634; ⑤), is a restored eighteenth-century house with large rooms that are simply decorated with a mix of old and new furnishings. The small complex also contains a bar and even a squash court. The *Hotel Aguere*, C/del Obispo Rey Redondo 57 (Map 4, A2. ☎922/259 490, ℉922/631 633; ⑤) is in a stylish old building, where uncluttered rooms surround a pretty central courtyard. Singles are available here and prices include breakfast.

THE TOWN

La Laguna does little to court the tourist industry, and despite being crammed full with examples of the vernacular architecture, its most impressive buildings can be viewed within a couple of hours. Though the old town is in a geographic sense its centre, it's the university district, just to its south, that is the busiest area of town. This grid of streets buzzes with students and is awash with all the usual student hangouts – bars, cafés and bookshops. Though founded in town in 1701, the present university campus, just beside the motorway, was built in the 1950s and is nothing special.

Plaza del Adelantado

Map 4, F4.

Plaza del Adelantado is at the heart of the historic centre. Centrepiece of the square is a statue of the friar Anchieta who was born in La Laguna before emigrating to South America, where he is said to have converted over two million natives to Christianity. Bordering the plaza are a busy indoor grocery market and a convent, the **Convento Santa Catalina** dating from 1611. The wooden grill on the upper floors of the convent covers a pavilion overlooking the plaza and was constructed to enable nuns to view the goings on on the square without being observed themselves. On February 15, around 17,000 people head to this convent to pay their respects to one of its most generous and pious nuns, a Sister María de Jesús, who died well over 200 years ago.

Museo de la Historia de Tenerife

Map 4, E2. C/de San Agustín. Tues–Sun 10am–8pm; €4;
☏ 922/825 943

On one of the main old streets in La Laguna is the atmospheric and beautifully restored sixteenth-century Casa Lecaro. This, one of a line of beautiful houses, is the former home of the wealthy merchant Lecaro family and now houses the **Museo de la Historia de Tenerife**. On display in this museum are numerous documents, maps and artefacts relating to the town's history and that of the Lecaro family, Genoese merchants, moneylenders and speculators, who having made their fortune running mercantile operations on spice routes through Asia, became one of Tenerife's most powerful families.

Iglesia de la Concepción

Plaza de la Concepción. Daily 10.30am–12.30pm.
As the island's first major town and its religious centre it is inevitable that La Laguna has several grand and impressive churches. The oldest of these, in fact the island's first, is the **Iglesia de la Concepción**, which has evolved over the years to contain a number of different styles of which

LA LAGUNA

Gothic is most in evidence. The green-glazed baptism pool, an original fitting in the church, was once the scene of many Guanche baptisms. The church's impressive ceiling collapsed in 1972, but the replacement is, if anything even more splendid.

Santa Iglesia Cathedral

Map 4, D3. Plaza de la Catedral. Mon–Sat 10.30am–1.30pm & 5.30pm–7pm.

The town's largest church and technically the religious centre of Tenerife, is the **Santa Iglesia Cathedral**, which was consecrated in 1913. Though its exterior is rather drab, the interior is a more impressive mixture of Baroque and Gothic. The latter can be seen particularly clearly in the pointed arches of the presbytery and in the decorated windows of the east end. The church treasury contains the figures that head the Christmas, Easter and Corpus Christi processions and behind the ornate altar is the tomb of Alonso de Lugo, conqueror of the islands, who died 1525.

Museo de la Ciencia y el Cosmos

In the southern suburbs of La Laguna, and on the (indirect) bus line (#14) to Santa Cruz is the **Museo de la Ciencia y el Cosmos** (Tues–Sun 10am–10pm; €4), a good interactive science museum in a futuristic-looking red building. An educational, if eclectic, range of displays on subjects ranging from biology, through physics, to astronomical – and, strangely, astrological – exploration, is designed to keep inquisitive children occupied for a couple of hours. A more unusual and distinctively local section includes a computer that can translate you name into Guanche script. Most displays have some information in English.

LA LAGUNA

LOS RODEOS AIRPORT DISASTERS

Before Tenerife became well-known as a holiday destination, it was world famous as the site of the worst-ever air-traffic disaster. Los Rodeos airport was built in 1930 beside La Laguna, 600m above sea level in the misty centre of the island, a location which had always been questionable. During its opening ceremony, poor local weather conditions left a local dignitary stranded on the island for two days. Then, in 1972 a charter plane crashed on take-off in poor visibility killing 155 people on board – a tragedy which finally prompted the construction of another airport in Reina Sofia, the sunny south of the island. Unfortunately, this was not completed in time to spare Los Rodeos its worst accident yet. On March 26, 1977, two jumbo jets – both headed for Gran Canaria but diverted to Tenerife due to a bomb scare there – collided. Confusion on take-off, combined with the presence of dense fog on the runway, led to one plane crossing the path of the other as it took off at over 200km per hour. All 583 people on board the two planes died. They are commemorated by a memorial in Los Rodeos airport – which still functions as an airport, though handling almost only domestic flights, and thankfully with a clean accident record since 1977.

EATING, DRINKING AND NIGHTLIFE

Students provide the bulk of the custom for the town's **bars** and **bistros**, so that most of these have gathered south of the historic centre near the university campus. The largest concentration of eateries is along Calle Heraclio Sánchez, while the bulk of the bars line Calle del Doctor Antonio González. The **live-music** scene in town is surprisingly small, but occasionally posters will announce gigs along this strip. **Jazz** enthusiasts should visit *El Buho*, C/Catedral 3, a

LA LAGUNA

good live music venue just north of the main collection of bars.

Each restaurant listed in the *Guide* has been categorized as either inexpensive (under €6), moderate (€6– €10) and expensive (above €10) – indicating the price of an average main course.

Bar Lucerna

Map 4, D5. C/Heraclio Sánchez 10.

Unpretentious, strip-lit bar with a predictable range of bar food and a good range of fish and meat dishes. Good value menu of the day, great potato and lentil soup and a fine range of fruit juices. Inexpensive.

El Gran Café

Map 4, C8. C/Heraclio Sánchez 50.

Hip café targeting students with snacks and tapas on the menu. In the evenings it becomes an unpretentious and sociable place to sit and drink and smoke. Inexpensive.

El Tonique

Map 4, D6. Edif. Galazia, C/Heraclio Sánchez 23.

Wine cellar-style decor, and 150 varieties of wine accompany a large selection of imaginative and unusually large tapas. A good place for an evening drink, but only open until 1.30am. Closed Sun. Moderate.

Maquila

Map 4, A2. Callejón Maquila. ☎ 922/257 020

In business for over a hundred years, in which it has had plenty of time to build its reputation as the best restaurant in town. The decor is suitably rustic and simple, as are many of the restaurant's recipes for rabbit and goat in spicy sauces and its oven-baked lamb dishes. The stuffed squid is the house speciality. Closed Tues & Aug. Expensive.

Tasca La Tropical

Map 4, C7. C/Heraclio Sánchez & C/Catedral.

Offers a good selection of snacks and small meals including a huge range of excellent scrambled-egg-based dishes in unusual combinations for example with asparagus. Moderate.

Rico mango

Map 4, C6. Avda de la Trinidad 47.

The only vegetarian restaurant on the island, this offers lots of great South American veggie favourites. Decor is somewhat Bohemian – customers visit Mars or Venus toilets. Open 1–4pm & 7.30–11.30pm. Closed Sun. Moderate.

San Andrés and around

Map 5, H7

About 6km northeast of Santa Cruz, the leafy hillside village of **SAN ANDRÉS** is known for its large artificial beach, **Playa de las Teresitas**, built to provide Santa Cruz with a great bathing area beside the towering Anaga mountains. A large man-made breakwater eliminates waves and currents around the palm-studded beach, and local facilities, including showers, changing-rooms and bars, make the beach a practical, easy-going and pleasant place for a day of sunbathing. Frequent buses (#910 & #245) serve the beach from Santa Cruz.

Though the bars by the beach serve good snacks, for more substantial meals it's worth heading into town to one of a couple of good seafood **restaurants**. The simple but elegant *La Gran Paella,* C/Pedro Schwartz 15 (closed Tues), behind the ruined Castillo de San Andrés, a stocky round tower that once protected the village, not only makes a great paella, but also does a large number of sauces to accompany its seafood dishes. Other local fish and seafood specialists line the seafront and include *Bar Monterrey*, C/Dique 25, a low budget place offering basic but good fresh fish dishes as well as numerous set meals.

Bus #245 continues east to the end of the road at Igueste, 6km away on top of the cliffs bordering a beautiful stretch of coastline. Along the way is the steep access road down to the next cove from Las Teresitas, **Playa de Las Gaviotas** – a much quieter beach frequented by nudists, though it is the seagulls that the grey-black sands are named after. A bar serves snacks down by the beach.

Las Montañas de Anaga

Map 5 covers the Anaga region.

The back door of Santa Cruz opens out onto the **Anaga,** one of the most spectacular mountainous regions of the island. Geologically the oldest part of the island, the range has been eroded into deep valleys, leaving wildly rugged and forested knife-edge ridges with peaks and slopes smothered in ancient laurel forests. Once dominating the Mediterranean basin, the laurel has in the last 20 million years retreated from advancing ice ages to small pockets in the Canary Islands, most notably in the Parque Nacional de Garajonay in La Gomera (p.260) and along the misty central ridge in the Anaga. From here tremendous views plunge seaward to rocky, unspoilt coastlines, against which large Atlantic rollers crash. Small communities have survived in isolated hamlets in this remote region. Once largely sustained by arduous farm work on tiny terraces cut into steep-sided slopes, agriculture's importance has diminished and though many have left the area in search of other work, today a small but steady flow of visitors into the area has helped to stabilize the local economy.

One **main road** runs along the length of the Anaga, climbing up onto the ridge from La Laguna to the **visitors' centre** and one of the most popular viewpoints at **Cruz del Carmen**. East along the main road it is crossed by another twisting main road that joins the north and south coasts and links the remote **Taganana**, the region's largest town, with San Andrés (see p.87). Further east the main road through the range follows along its back bone and through dense misty forests to reach the peaceful village of **Chamorga** – the best gateway to the region's network of excellent **hiking** trails. But neither here nor anywhere else in the Anaga will you find any **accommodation** (unless you wish to join those who camp illegally on Playa de Benijo near Taganana). So the area is best explored on long day trips, taking advantage of the small bars in all the main villages that serve simple, inexpensive Canarian food such as stews and goat meat.

Information and getting around

The area's **visitors' centre** is at Cruz del Carmen (Map 5, B5. Tues–Sun 9am–3pm; ☎922/633 576). It can supply you with a basic hiking map that's rather wanting in detail (many paths are even missing) – but generally fine to negotiate the area's main well-marked trails. Though **buses** ply the routes between the small villages of the Anaga, they are infrequent and using them requires some careful planning, as does bringing your car – since only a few of the hikes work well as loops.

Cruz del Carmen and around

CRUZ DEL CARMEN (Map 5, B5), only 9km from La Laguna is a good gateway to the region and easily accessed by those relying on the bus service. Though there's not much here, save a viewpoint, a visitors' centre, a bus stop (#75, #76 or #77 run from La Laguna) and a restaurant, there is a good **hike** (2–3hr) that begins from here – with excellent views from the outset – and leads north past the village of **Las Carboneras** (Map 5, B3) 2km away, to the hamlet of Chinamada, a kilometre beyond.

CHINAMADA (Map 5, A3) is known for its houses built around natural caves in the rock, but there's little to see here. More spectacular are the views from the **Mirador Aguaide** just beyond the village (accessed via a track off the town's plaza). From here there are dizzying views down the cliffs to the ocean and across to Punta del Hidalgo. A track branching off the path to the viewpoint heads down to Punta del Hidalgo and if you are using the bus service, you might consider heading down to the town on a steep three-hour hike taking a bus back from there (#105) to Santa Cruz. If this sounds tempting consider doing the trek the other way around – starting from Punta del Hidalgo and hiking to Cruz del Carmen (approx. 5hr) – since this will be a more rewarding climb and will give you a wider choice of bus services back to your base. For those travelling by car, it's better to retrace your steps, though it's worth deviating slightly by taking the quiet road from Chinamada to Las Carboneras before either heading back to Cruz del Carmen the way you came, or extending the hike to **Taborno** (Map 5, C3), the village on the opposite side of the valley, from where you can walk around the imposing

volcanic rock monolith the **Roque d**
C2). This adds around another two to
hike.

Taganana

By far the largest settlement in the Anaga, th
TAGANANA (Map 5, F3), 13km north of ...a Cruz
was once the local centre of sugar cane production and then
later wine production. Precariously sprawling over several
ridges and steep hillsides, it was long remote from the rest
of Tenerife and was only connected to the road network in
1968. Nowadays it's easy to reach, with regular buses from
Santa Cruz (#246 via San Andrés) negotiating a good,
though steep and narrow twisting road to the town.

Taganana is worth a quick stroll around for its narrow
streets lined with simple old Canarian houses, before carrying on along the coast to the villages of **Almaciga** (Map 5,
H2) – terminus of the bus from Santa Cruz – and **Benijo**
(Map 5, I2) by way of the pebble beaches **Playa del San
Roque** (Map 5, G2) and **Playa de Benijo** (Map 5, H2),
both of which are popular with local surfers and have a few
little bars and restaurants. High winds along this coast can
make for awe-inspiring breakers, but even in calm conditions visitors should be wary of the dangerous currents and
rocky surf and follow the advice of locals before bathing.
From Benijo it is possible to hike east along a dirt road that
hugs cliffs high above the sea to the village of **El Draguillo**
(Map 5, J2), so called for its surviving dragon tree, 2km
away.

From El Draguillo paths head to **Chamorga** (Map 5, K2)
and Roque de Bermijo (see p.92). If you are after a longer
hike (10km; 4–5 hour) it is well worth getting off the bus (or
parking the car) at El Bailadero, near the **Mirador Cabezo
del Tejo** (Map 5, J2) – not far from the intersection of the

LAS MONTAÑAS DE ANAGA

91

west route through Anaga and the road from San ... – and walking down to El Draguillo and on to ...maciga (a further 3km away) to catch the bus back to El Bailadero or on to Santa Cruz from there. Note that buses don't stop directly at the viewpoint. To reach it follow a path from opposite the bus stop and parking area at El Bailadero and head east along the road for just over a kilometre before turning onto a track signposted El Pijara. This track is one of the best in the region and takes you through premium laurel forest along the spine of the Anaga range, but without requiring any real climbing. Following the path as it joins then leaves the road you eventually come to the Mirador Cabezo del Tejo, which affords stunning views across the rugged coastline around Playa de Benijo. A little further along from the viewpoint the path comes to a crossroads where you turn left to head down to El Draguillo, right to Chamorga (less than 1km away), or straight on to Roque Bermijo (4km).

Chamorga

At the far eastern end of the twisting and often misty main road thorough the Anaga, lies **CHAMORGA** (Map 5, K2) a small tidy collection of houses spread across a valley that's studded with palms and dotted with neat and productive terraces. The village feels incredibly remote, yet is easily accessible on a day trip from Santa Cruz (bus #247), and is well worth it since some of the best walks in the region start from here. One good, straightforward **hike** (7km; approx. 3hr) follows a loop down from Chamorga to a small cluster of houses near **Roque Bermijo** (Map 5, M2), a sharp crag in the sea. From here you climb back to Chamorga by way of a ridge walk that starts near the **Faro de Anaga** (Map 5, L1), a lighthouse that overlooks the craggy shore. From along the ridge there are good views over the rugged northern coastline.

For a **longer loop** (14km; approx. 5hr) hike west out of Chamorga, following the path down to El Draguillo and then east along the remote and little-used coastal path to Faro de Anaga. Leaving Chamorga, look for the sign to Cabezo del Tejo, and walk up the lush valley, terraced with fruit trees. Head straight on, ignoring signs for Cumbrilla and to the Mirador Cabezo del Tejo (though you might want to detour to the latter – a ten minute round trip from the main path – for its great views across the whole north side of the range). Instead continue down to El Draguillo, then east along a stunning coastal path, above steep-sided cliffs – in places 300m above the sea and with imposing views. At the small hamlet of Las Palmas (Map 5, J2), ignore the path that forks uphill and instead head downhill across a small barranco, then back up through stunning scenery to the lighthouse. From here you have the choice of a well-graded ridge walk back to Chamorga, or to head a short way down to Roque Bermeijo and take a rocky path back along the valley floor – which adds more variety to the walk, but at the expense of some of its best views.

South along the coast

The 20km of coast south of Santa Cruz, includes a number of unattractive small dormitory towns as well as the two larger, but equally dull, towns of **Candelaria** and **Güímar**. It's only the presence of Tenerife's most significant contemporary spiritual site, the **Basilica de Nuestra Señora de Candelaria** and the most important find relating to pre-Spanish spirituality the **Pirámides de Güímar** that make these towns a worthwhile trip.

BASILICA DE NUESTRA SEÑORA DE CANDELARIA,

Map 1, I4. Mon–Fri 7.30am–1pm & 3pm–6.30pm, Sat & Sun 8am–7pm. Masses Mon–Fri 8am & 6pm, Sun 8am, 9.30am, 11am, 12.30pm, 5.30pm & 6.30pm.

Devoted to the patron saint of the archipelago, and built to house a famous statue of the Virgin Mary, the **Basilica de Nuestra Señora de Candelaria** is the most important religious site in the Canaries. The main day of celebrations is August 15 (coinciding with the Feast of the Assumption and *Beñasmen*, a Guanche harvest festival), when pilgrims from all over the island converge on the town, the most devout making at least the last part of their journey on their hands and knees. Sheep and goats are paraded behind the Virgin in a procession which ultimately leaves the statue surrounded with garlands of flowers and greenery, while the devotees spend the night singing and dancing.

The **foundation of the church** was inspired by the arrival of an image of the Virgin Mary (thought to have been the wooden bust off the prow of a wrecked ship) which washed up on the beach here in the 1390s. It was initially kept in a cave and worshipped by the local Guanches, before passing into Spanish hands after the conquest. For many years the statue was in the care of monks, who built a sanctuary on the site of the present church in 1526. This was replaced by a church and convent in the nineteenth century, which in turn was destroyed by a tidal wave that washed the beloved Virgin back out to sea in 1826. So today, it is a replacement statue of the Virgin that forms the centrepiece of the splendid late-nineteenth-century colonial-style basilica. The statue stands atop a platform draped in gold and silk cloth, adorned with gold and jewels, a baby Jesus in her arms. Throughout the year her feet are surrounded by flowers left by those wishing her blessing, who touch the ribbon that flows from her clothes before making their wish.

The **church plaza** is guarded by ten larger-than-life statues of Guanches, their backs to a small sandy beach and the Atlantic. These are the work of local sculptor José Abad, who depicts the Mency of Güímar, one of the chiefs who sided with the conquistadors, with doves of peace, while Bencomo, the Mency of Taoro, who for a while successfully rallied against the Spanish, is given the look of the noble savage.

PIRÁMIDES DE GÜÍMAR

Map 1, H5. Daily 9am–5pm; €14; ☎922/514 510, Ⓦ www.fredolsen.es/piramides

The so-called **Pirámides de Güímar** are located in a valley near the once rich agricultural centre of Güímar, surrounded with breathtaking canyons and large banana plantations. Now signposted as "pirámides" from the centre of Güímar, the structures were long dismissed as simply heaps of stones cleared by farmers. Fearing research into the piles of angular and precisely assembled rocks would reveal something about the island's heritage that might encourage Canarian separatism, the Franco government prevented research into their origins and their significance continued to be dismissed for some time afterwards.

It wasn't until Norwegian holiday-makers brought the structures to the attention of archaeologist **Thor Heyerdahl** (best known for his Kon Tiki voyages across the Pacific), who immediately interrupted his research on Incas in South America to fly to Tenerife, that international attention was directed to this site. On closer inspection it emerged that the three pyramidal structures of carefully squared stones had been laid out with considerable geometric exactitude, so as to point to the sun during the winter and summer solstices, with the stairs up the side of each flat-topped pyramid being aligned to face the rising sun.

SOUTH ALONG THE COAST

Now owned and run by a fellow Norwegian, **Fred Olsen** (the Canarian shipping magnate), the three pyramids, known collectively as **Chacona**, have been carefully rebuilt to what is thought to be their original form and opened up to visitors. Though you can't actually climb onto the structures, a well-positioned platform gives you a good view over them. In the adjacent museum, parallels are drawn between these pyramids, the culture of their architects (including a comparison of petroglyphs and pottery) and those found in North Africa and South America. Though the museum doesn't go so far as to say that the Canaries are a missing link between ancient Egyptian and South American societies, the vast amount of circumstantial evidence it has assembled certainly suggests this is the case. And the success of Heyerdahl's journeys across the Atlantic in reed boats, a significant part of his life's work, helps to back up the feasibility of this thesis.

THE OLD ROAD TO SOUTHERN TENERIFE

Two routes head to southern Tenerife from Güimar. The **old main road** still twists its way south high above the coast, but since the completion of the motorway, traffic along this decaying stretch has declined, as has the local economy which is based solely on farming. The drive along the winding road, heading in and out of steep-sided gorges, is a slow and hard one, but luckily there's not much traffic, fine views over the coast and at least one small local bar at which to eat or drink in most of the villages.

Just 2km outside Güimar and beside the **Mirador Don Martin**, a large well-appointed, but now ruined hotel clearly illustrates the decline in business along the road but continues to provide a spectacular panorama over the small farms of the Güimar valley and further up the coast beyond Santa Cruz. Further southwest along the road are some of the island's earliest Spanish settlements, such as those at **ICOR**, 20km south of Güímar, which has some of the oldest buildings on the island dating from the late sixteenth century. Originally built without using mortar, some of their crumbling walls have since been patched with cement. Some of the many caves along the road were also used as dwellings, not only by Guanches, but also by Spanish settlers – a number of families were still registered as cave dwellers as recently as the 1930 population census.

The main town along the route is **ARICO** (Map 1, G7), 5km beyond Icor, actually a number of scattered villages. Located among a pretty cluster of whitewashed houses in Arico Nuevo is the *Hotel Viña Vieja* (☎922/161 131, ⓕ922/161 205; ❺). It offers comfortable, rustically decorated rooms in a large nineteenth-century house. Facilities include satellite TV and a large outdoor garden and patio. The hotel also organizes hiking trips and other excursions. In nearby Arico Viejo, the restaurant *Casa Manolo II*, Avda Del Cabildo 9 (closed Thurs & Oct) has been specializing in fresh fish for over twenty years. The prices are moderate and local wines are served from the barrel.

Puerto de la Cruz and the Orotava Valley

Green and fertile northern Tenerife contains some of the island's richest farmland and so has been one of the most densely populated areas of the island since pre-Spanish times. The region's terraces have played host to most of Tenerife's cash crop monocultures, including sugar cane, vineyards and today mostly bananas – though wine is still produced here and the local wine industry, centred on the **Orotava valley**, has recently undergone something of a renaissance. In the past, the fortunes of the locality have, however, fluctuated with the vines, which have been susceptible to mildew and the ravages of the vine weevil *viteus vitifolii*. As a result, the cultivation of bananas has been encouraged, and the economy of the valley has been increasingly dominated by its tourist infrastructure. **Puerto de la Cruz** is at the heart of this industry - the formerly modest port has become the island's major holiday resort

ACCOMMODATION PRICE CODES

Throughout the *Guide*, accommodation has been graded according to price, based on the cost of the cheapest double room in high season – but excluding the time around Christmas and New Year, when rates can rocket. In the case of apartments that sleep more than two, the price for the smallest available unit, as described in the body text, is given; where apartments are available by the night, the price refers to the cheapest two-person apartment. Where singles – which are usually more than half the price of doubles – are available, this has also been mentioned. Travellers wanting to stay a week or more may find that nightly rate can be reduced a little.

❶ up to €12   **❺** €48– €60
❷ €12–€24   **❻** €60– €84
❸ €24–€36   **❼** €84– €120
❹ €36– €48   **❽** over €120

outside the south coast. Adjoining it is the wealthy colonial town of **La Orotava**. And, despite its moody weather, treacherous seas and the steep slope of the land, other parts of the north coast have also been developed for tourism. Ugly, misbegotten, small-scale resort areas thrown up in the mid 1960s, as typified by Punta Del Hidalgo and Bajamar, are best avoided, though the occasional traditional fishing village has survived.

Puerto de la Cruz

Map 1, F3.

Map 6 covers Puerto de la Cruz in detail.

With over a hundred years pedigree in the field, **PUERTO DE LA CRUZ** does resort tourism well. The bustling, former harbour town, which still acts as a focal point for the business communities in the Orotava valley, was historically much favoured by British traders who erected the imposing **Grand Hotel Taoro** here in 1889. The hotel itself helped to define Puerto de la Cruz as a tourist destination. In the 1890s it became a fashionable spa town and since then it has been a preferred haunt for wintering European royalty and dignitaries such as Winston Churchill and Bertrand Russell. Despite the influx of various high-rise complexes and the associated tackiness of mass tourism, Puerto has managed to retain something of the style and flair of a cosmopolitan spa as well as keep the feel of a small, friendly and busy Spanish town. It has maintained an individuality and character that the southern resorts lack. Particularly popular with a more mature holidaying clientele, much in evidence promenading and pottering happily there, Puerto boasts the highest rate of return visits of any resort in the world.

ARRIVAL AND INFORMATION

Buses arrive at the station on C/del Pozo (Map 6, D6) on the western side of the town centre. The **tourist office** is a ten minute walk away beyond the Plaza del Charco on the Plaza de Europa by the seafront (Map 6, H3. Mon-Fri 9am-8pm, Sat & Sun 9am-1pm; ☎922/386 000)

ACCOMMODATION

There's no shortage of accommodation in Puerto de la Cruz, with not only the usual selection of large resort lodgings but also a good selection of small **hotels** and **guest-houses** right in the centre of town. One of the best areas to stay is the old fishing quarter of Ranilla. Despite the town's popularity it's not too hard to find accommodation here, except during peak times (Christmas, Easter and the summer months) when it's worth booking ahead. Listed below are some of the best places in town; the tourist office can supply a comprehensive list of other options. For help finding an **apartment**, contact the Agency Apartmentos-Puerto de la Cruz, CC Olympia 7, Plaza del Charco. (☎922/373 759 or 922/381 124).

HOTELS

Alfomar

Map 6, D4. C/de la Peñita 6
☎ & ℱ 922/380 682
A small hotel housed in a 1970s building and containing what's now notalgically chic decor. En-suite double rooms, most with balcony overlooking a quiet pedestrian street at the centre of town. ❸.

Botánico

Urb. El Botánico
☎922/381 400
ℱ922/381 504
ⓌWww.hotelbotanico.com/home.htm
A large five-star hotel, within immaculately maintained and imaginatively laid-out gardens to the east of town. The hotel's many facilities include three restaurants, a couple of swimming pools, a sauna and a health and exercise centre, plus tennis courts and an eighteen-hole putting green. ❽.

Chimisay

Map 6, G4. C/Béthencourt 14.
☎922/383 552
ℱ922/382 840
ⒺChimisay@mx2.red.estb.es
Despite an uninviting exterior and faded interiors the large, clean rooms here are well kept and overlook quiet pedestrian streets. Its four storeys contain 67 en-suite double rooms, and there's a small pool on the roof. ❺.

Maga

Map 6, G4. C/Iriarte 11.
☎922/383 853

This simple hotel is in an old building in the centre of town near Plaza del Charco. Despite the worn furnishings, the place is good value with room rates including breakfast. ❹.

Marquesa

Map 6, G3. C/de Quintana 11.
☎ 922/383 151
🅕 922/386 950

A long-standing hotel in an early-eighteenth-century Canarian building overlooking a plaza in the town's pedestrian zone. Alongside the building's Colonial flair and elegance – particularly its ornate stained pine woodwork balconies – are good modern facilities, including a reliably good restaurant and a small pool. Breakfast is included in the room rate. Singles available. ❺.

Miramar

Map 6, I7. Parque de Taoro.
☎ 922/384 811
🅕 922/371 067
🅔 hotel.miramar@mx3
.redestb.es

A six-storey building, a good hike up from centre of town,

this large, old atmospheric hotel has rooms with a homely atmosphere and rustic furnishings and is particularly popular with Spanish visitors. A large pool is available in the pleasant garden setting (with views across town), as are a number of tennis courts, minigolf and table tennis. ❻.

Monopol

Map 6, H3. C/de Quintana 15.
☎ 922/384 611
🅕 922/370 310
🅦 www.interbook.net/empresas
/monopol

This elegant building dates from 1742, although it didn't become a hotel until later. Lots of wooden balconies overlook the courtyard, where wicker furniture is provided for guests to sit and relax. A lush atrium, pool, roof terrace and Jacuzzi are also available. The rooms are exquisitely presented, though some of the less expensive ones are somewhat cramped. Guests should not miss the stunning 1970s leather-effect modular furniture in the bar. Prices include breakfast. ❻

Régulo

Map 6, F4. C/San Felipe 6.
℡ 922/388 800
Ⓕ 922/370 420

Small, newly renovated house in the old central quarter, and opposite the top quality restaurant of the same name. Facilities include a sun terrace. The rooms facing the courtyard are significantly quieter than those facing the road. Half-board deals, with dinner at the *Régulo* restaurant, are around twice the price of the room-only deal. ❸.

San Borondón

Map 6, C5. C/Agustín Espinosa 2. ℡ 922/383 313
Ⓕ 922/371 365
Ⓦ www.ashotel.es/sanborondon/

Cheerful, Colonial-style group of buildings with over a hundred rooms. Centrally located, but outside the busiest town areas, with a good-sized pool, pleasant grounds, tennis courts, fitness rooms, and restaurant, this place is just 200m from the beach. All prices include breakfast and dinner. ❻.

Tejuma

Map 6, F6. C/Péres Zamora 51.
℡ 922/383 613

Basic rooms, but all with telephone, balconies and en-suite facilities. The gloomy brown decor may be off-putting for some, but this budget hotel is superbly located in a quiet area just five-minutes' walk from the centre of town. ❸.

Trovador

Map 6, E4. Puerto Viejo 38.
℡ 922/384 512
Ⓕ 922/384 549
Ⓦ www.canaryweb.es/trovador
/index.html

Central and pleasant enough, most rooms here are en suite and have balconies, TV and minibar, and there's a small pool on the roof. The elegant and decent breakfast buffet is included in the room rate. ❻.

Turquesa Playa

Urb. Turquesa Playa.
℡ 922/371 308
Ⓕ 922/372 923

New and generously built place with 350 rooms, from the outside, this can look unprepossessing, if not dreary.

PUERTO DE LA CRUZ

The lobby is extremely glitzy, however, and the facilities here are good – there's a pool, gym and sauna – and there's basic kitchen facilities and easy wheelchair access. Some rooms have a balcony. A five-minute walk from the Playa Jardin. **⑤**.

PENSIONS

La Platanera
Map 6, G6. C/de Blanco 29.
Ⓣ922/384 157
Both single and double rooms are available in this modern house a five minute walk out of town. All are en suite, and some have balconies and overlook a charming little garden - that's unfortunately located beside a busy road. **❸**.

Loly
Map 6, F6. C/de La Sala 4.
ⓉT91922/383 693
A friendly, simple and clean pension just outside the old town with double rooms, all with shared bath. **❷**.

Los Geranios
Map 6, E3. C/del Lomo 14.

ⓉTel922/382 810
Fantastically clean and well-kept hotel-quality rooms (all en suite) in a friendly, family-run pension. A basic continental breakfast is also offered for a small extra charge. No singles rooms available though. **❷**.

Rosamary
Map 6, E4. C/de San Felipe 14.
ⓉTel922/383 253
A small, friendly and immaculately kept place, where all rooms are en suite. While some rooms have a balcony, these overlook a busy road and so are noisier than the rooms that don't. TV lounge and sun terrace. No singles available. **❷**.

APARTMENTS

Florasol
Map 6, G9. Camino del coche 7.
ⓉTel922/389 848
ⒻFax922/389 574
Ⓦwww.aparthotelflorasol.com
On the edge of the Taoro park, this small, new complex offers excellently equipped, tastefully decorated and very

generously sized apartments. Many of these have views over Teide on clear days. Communal facilities include a pool, tennis courts and a restaurant. Four person apartments have two separate bedrooms and prices include breakfast ❺.

Florida Plaza
Map 6, E4. C/Puerto Viejo 30.
☎ 922/371 140
🖷 922/387 051
🌐 www.floridatenerife.com
Modern, fairly characterless hotel, centrally located on a plaza in the pedestrianized Ranilla district. The well-equipped apartments all have kitchens and a TV. The

simple rooms sleep three, though one ends up on the sofa. There's a small pool here. ❺.

Park Plaza
Map 6, F4. C/José Arroyo 2.
☎ 922/384 112
🖷 922/371 338
A modern block of well-equipped apartments, each with a kitchen, TV and a balcony. Though it feels well-worn and the brown bath fittings are probably to few people's taste, the central location and small roof top pool and sun deck help make up for this. All apartments sleep two. ❹.

THE TOWN

The centre of Puerto de la Cruz is focused around the small **Plaza del Charco**, in the heart of a pedestrian district and beside a now little-used small harbour. From here the pedestrian area spreads west into **Ranilla**, a quaint old fishing quarter and east along the seafront and through the town's shopping district, to a charmless jumble of high-rise hotels, bars, discos and international restaurants at the eastern end of town. While the centre of town is always a pleasant place for strolling aimlessly, there are actually few real sights here – Puerto's main attractions are its **beaches**, **lido** and the nearby **Loro Parque zoo**.

PUERTO DE LA CRUZ

Plaza del Charco

Map 6, F4.

The busy shady **Plaza del Charco** is the focal point of the Puerto and filled with cafés and (mostly elderly) tourists pottering around or sitting on benches overlooking the fountain at its centre. The plaza itself, which took its name from the shrimp pools that once formed here at high tide (its full title is Plaza de Charco de Los Camerones), has always been the focal point for local activity since the adjacent harbour took off in the seventeenth century. Though trade is now absent from the port, a handful of small fishing boats still put in here beside the town's oldest building, the **Casa de la Aduana** (Map 6, G3), the former customs house, built in 1620. Most of Puerto's other historic buildings also lie within the vicinity of the square.

Iglesia de Nuestra Señora de la Peña Francia

Map 6, H4. Mass daily 8.30am, 6.30pm & 7pm.

Puerto's main church is the seventeenth-century **Iglesia de Nuestra Señora de la Peña Francia**, just west of the Plaza del Charco. The imposing building is only open to the public for mass, when its worth sneaking in to have a look at the simple interior, the fine *Mudéjar* ceiling, the Baroque retable and a sculpture of the Virgin by Luján Pérez.

Casa Iriarte

Map 6, G4. Mon–Sat 10am–7pm.

This eighteenth-century house was once home to various over-achievers from the Iriate family including various politicians, diplomats and, most famously, the playwright

Thamás Iriarte who was born here in 1755. Iriarte's plays satirized the sloth of the nobility, while championing the industry of the working classes.

Today, the courtyard of the old house is given over to the peddling of **handicrafts**, with an abundance of embroidery and lace for sale. A room on the first floor at the front of the house is devoted to a somewhat scrappy little collection of photographs and calls itself the **town museum** (free). The rest of the first floor is accessed from the back of the building and is devoted to a **naval museum** (€1.50). This is centred on a good range of painstakingly constructed, dusty models of boats from the sixteenth century onwards. Other nautical odds and ends include a copy of the last letter Nelson wrote with his right arm and the first he scrawled with his left (see p.73). But without doubt the most (unintentionally) entertaining display of all here is a diorama depicting the island's conquest – three truly dreadful life-sized models of a conquistador, a priest and a Guanche with an afro hairdo prostrating himself.

The Ranilla district

Just to the west of the centre of town is the former fishermen's quarter, the **Ranilla district**, an area of squat, old houses and narrow roads. The **Archeological museum**, C/de Lomo 9a (Map 6, E4. Tues–Sat 10am–1pm & 5pm–9pm, Sun 10am–1pm; €1) is on a quaint pedestrian street at the heart of this district, but contains only a modest and not really worthwhile collection of Guanche pottery.

On the western edge of the district old homes give way to large modern hotels and apartment blocks. Just in front of these, and now almost out of place, stands a stout early seventeenth-century fort, the **Castillo de San Felipe** (Map 6, A5. Mon–Sat 11am–1pm & Mon–Fri 6pm–9pm; free), which opens to allow access to visiting exhibitions.

PUERTO DE LA CRUZ

Beside the fort is the town's premier beach, the popular sandy **Playa Jardín**, where the sea is sometimes calm enough for bathing, but otherwise is left to experienced surfers to catch waves.

Loro Parque

Daily 8.30am–6.45pm; €18, under 12s €9; ☎ 922/374 081.

A ten-minute walk west on a promenade alongside the landscaped gardens that separate Playa Jardín from the road leads to a cluster of houses on a headland known as the **Punta Brava**. Beside this small town lies Tenerife's best publicized tourist attraction, the **Loro Parque**. Opened in 1978, the zoo originally contained only 150 parrots, a few of which performed in a show. The show is still put on several times a day, but everything else in the park has changed dramatically – the collection of parrots having grown to 1400 and several far more high-profile attractions have been added. These include other animal performances (you should study the timetable on entering if you plan to catch them), some impressive aquariums (including a shark tunnel), and large gorilla and chimp enclosures.

The latest and most impressive addition to the zoo has been the remarkable, if rather out of place, **Planet Penguin**, the world's largest so-called penguinarium, powered by the equivalent of two thousand fridges and running a filter system that process over one million litres of water per hour. The park promotes itself as a kind and sensitive zoo, having nursed and cared for various maltreated animals (particularly parrots and chimps used by unscrupulous photographers). Some of the animals have even been happy enough here to successfully breed – but of course the essential moral problems associated with the incarceration of birds and animals in zoos remain unresolved. In any case the zoo remains an aggressively commercial venture.

Parque Taoro

Map 6, H7.

High above Puerto on its southern side with commanding views of all sits the grand old **Hotel Taoro**, the town's major landmark. As the islands first large purpose-built hotel, the building is also a major landmark in the history of the development of Tenerife's tourism. Built by an English company as a sanatorium in 1889, but since rebuilt, having been dramatically gutted by fire in 1929, the building no longer provides any accommodation, but houses a **Casino** (daily 7pm–3am; €3) and a restaurant. There are great views over the roofs of Puerto from in front of the casino. **Parque Taoro**, the vast neat grounds surrounding the casino, contains some newer hotels, including the Tigaiga, a venue for **folklore shows** (Sun 11am; €2) that sound dreadfully kitsch, but are actually quite fun. These include traditional dancing and singing as well as a display of Canarian wrestling (see p.50).

Botanical Gardens

Daily 9am–6pm; €0.80.

The impressive, varied, subtropical **Botanical Gardens** are home to around three thousand species from around the world. The variety of species that thrive in the gardens is impressive – Californian palms and Brazilian shrubs grow alongside one another – but all told the garden is not really very big and doesn't take long to wander around.

The gardens were originally created by **Carlos III** in 1788, who had an ambition to display species from all his colonies in his palace gardens in Spain. He hoped Tenerife would be a good place to acclimatize the plants, and to that extent he was right. But unfortunately, though most species thrived on Tenerife, few could withstand the cool Spanish

PUERTO DE LA CRUZ

winters, meaning overwhelming failure for his tropical-garden project. No longer necessary as a place for acclimatization, the gardens soon fell into disrepair, and it wasn't until almost a century later that they were nursed back to health by the renowned Swiss botanist **Hermann Josef Wildpret** – who also catalogued and gave his name to a number of Canarian flora.

Lago de Martiánez

Map 6, L1. €2.50, kids half-price. Mats and shade extra.

Although there are several good beaches in and around Puerto, the strong currents and large waves along the coast mean that it's rarely possible to bathe safely. The vast and beautiful open air salt-water lido, **Lago de Martiánez** was built to compensate for this and has done so successfully, attracting over a million annual visitors. The complex contains a number of predictable facilities: pools, sunbathing areas, bars, cafés and changing facilities, but is unusual in its design. The work of Canarian surrealist artist **César Manrique** (1920–92), the complex houses many soft curves and quirky attentive touches – the upside-down trees add a surrealist touch that Manrique could obviously not resist.

Playa Bollullo

- -

Puerto is a popular base for hikers. Several companies here offer escorted trips of the island: Gregorio (☎ 922/383 500 or 639/332 761, ⓕ 922/384 055) is an experienced guide who works out of the Hotel Tigaiga. British operator, KWA (☎ 922/372 770 ex.343; call before 8am) does similar trips from Nov to April.

- -

CASA DEL VINO LA BARANDA

Those with private transport and interest in local wines should make the trip to Tenerife's wine museum, the **Casa Del Vino La Baranda** (Tues–Sat 11am–8pm, Sun & public holidays 11am–6pm; free; ☎922/572 535; ⓦ*campo-canarias.com*), in the town of El Sauzal 16km east of Puerto. The museum is housed in a beautifully restored seventeenth-century hacienda in a major agricultural region, known particularly for its fine grapes and excellent wines. Informative displays give details of the surrounding wine region and there's the opportunity to sample the produce in the adjoining tasting room. There's also a good, **restaurant** on site, the *Tasca* (☎922/563 388; closed Mon), offering Canarian food and, of course, wine at moderate prices. In the summer the museum's central courtyard becomes a tasteful venue for Classical music concert's every other Tuesday (8pm; €6).

The large, pleasant, sandy beach Playa Bollullo is one of the areas best **beaches** – though its frequently enormous waves mean that it would be optimistic to expect to be able to swim once there. It's a good four-kilometre (approx. 1hr) coastal cliff-top **hike** from Puerto, starting with a steep climb uphill from behind the shopping Centre Plaza along Viera y Clavijo, then continuing up Calle las Cabras, and following the steps leading onto Camino San Amaro. Excellent views over Puerto soon open up, and **Mirador de la Paz** is a good place to pause to enjoy them. From the viewpoint head east onto the Camino de la Costa, a cliff-top path just below the main road (Carretera del Este), which follows the coast line to Playa Bollullo. A flight of stairs leads down the cliff to the beach, although a path continues east, alongside a stone wall connecting several more, smaller beaches (the first about a fifteen-minute scramble away), where both nudism and wild camping are tolerated.

PUERTO DE LA CRUZ

EATING

Puerto de la Cruz is well-supplied with **cafés** and **restaurants**, with over a hundred in the centre of town alone. In comparison with the island's southern resorts, the food here is generally good quality and value, but beware of the early closing times of many of the restaurants – it's unusually hard to find a restaurant here that will serve food after 10pm.

RUTE DE LA CARNE

Along the old main road to Orotava, above the motorway, are a number of old unpretentious working communities of the agricultural heartland that more or less fuse with one another – the three most sizeable towns are La Matanza, nearby La Victoria (both sites of major battles between conquistadors and the native Guanches) and Santa Ursula, which straddles the edge of the Orotava valley. Although the old farm buildings of these towns are a pleasant enough backdrop, there would be little to encourage visitors here if it weren't for the fact that this area has somehow earned the reputation for great, substantial, traditional and inexpensive food in the basic restaurants that line the main road that links them – known locally as the **Rute de la Carne**. Many of the restaurants along the road are similar, and its perhaps most interesting just to take pot-luck at one of them, but if you need a recommendation, head for the consistently good, if a little expensive, *Casa Juan Ahumadero*, C/de Acentejo 77 (closed Sun & Mon), signposted from the petrol station in La Matanza. Both the smoked fish and home-made sausages are good and, unusually for this kind of restaurant, vegetarians will find some options, too. On the road out of Santa Ursula, *El Larga* is another popular choice, particularly for fish and seafood, which comes straight from the restaurant's tanks and is offered at moderate prices. Arrive after 9.30pm, however, if you don't want to be eating alone.

Capricho on the Plaza del Charco is a great little bakery with
a splendid array of fresh pastries, cakes and bread.

Azucar

Map 6, G5. C/Iriarte 1.
☎ 922/387 014
Cuban food – mostly rice-based dishes but including black bean stews, fried green bananas, croquettes and tapas-like snacks – are served in a restored house in the centre of the old town. The restaurant has a stylish ambience and artistic soft-earth tones and lively Latin American music. Service can be painfully slow. Closed Mon 8.30pm–2am. Moderate.

Daisy Burguer

Map 6, F5. C/Doctor Ingram 18.
Cheerful and bustling burger bar, extremely popular with the locals. Omelettes and a few tapas are also on offer. Open all day and well into the small hours. Inexpensive.

El Caldosa

Playa Chica, Punta Brava.
☎ 922/389 018
Good little seafood restaurant off the end of Playa Jardín in Punta Brava, a small town 2km from the centre of Puerto and location of the Loro Parque (see p.108). Superb fish and seafood served in cheerful stylish surroundings with large windows that swing open, so that the waves crashing in on the tiny beach can be heard. Moderate.

El Limón

Map 6, H4. C/de Esquivel and C/de B.Miranda.
Vegetarian place serving great veggie burgers, soups, salads, sandwiches and one main dish for dinner, plus lots of fresh shakes and juices. Closed Sun lunch. Moderate.

El Pinguino

Map 6, G4. Plaza del Charco.
Good café in one of the best spots in town to people-watch. Has a great line in a large variety of inexpensive, superb, home-made Italian ice-cream. Sit down here and gorge on

extravagant sundaes, or pick up a cone to eat on the hoof.

La Carta

Map 6, D4. C/San Felipe 53. ☎922/381 592

This place has a number of standard Spanish and Canarian dishes but also offers seasonal dishes such as asparagus and brown rice in June. Smart and well-presented, the setting still doesn't really justify the cost, except in the case of the good-value daily menu. Moderate to expensive.

La Papa

Map 6, E4. C/San Felipe 33.

Cosy restaurant with a range of Canarian food and, unusually, a couple of veggie options, and good Puchero or Cabra (goat) dishes. Moderate.

La Rosa Di Bari

Map 6, E4. C/del Lomo 23. ☎ & ⓕ 922/368 523

Possibly the best Italian restaurant on the island, this place has oodles of panache and great food, including excellent and generous portions of fresh gnocchi and

pizza and good fish dishes. Expensive.

Peruano

Map 6, C6. C/El Pozo 18.

Decorated and named to make its Peruvian credentials quite clear, the cuisine here follows suit. Many of the dishes are the usual local meat and seafood dishes with a Peruvian spin. Dried lamb sirloin is the house speciality. Closed Wed & May. Inexpensive.

Pizzera Pomodora

Map 6, I3. Puta Viento.

Not a gourmet choice, though the Italian food is tasty and the views over the coast are beautiful – the restaurant is set into the cliff, well within earshot of the sea as it crashes into the cliffs of the rugged coast. Moderate.

Régulo

Map 6, F4. C/Pérez Zamora 16. ☎922/384 506

One of the classiest restaurants in town, located in a restored town house, with much of the seating in a stylish courtyard. There's a good spread of

Canarian cuisine on offer, and the place is particularly known for its seafood. The local fresh fish, such as hake and parrot fish are also particularly good. There are no vegetarian options. Closed Sun & July. Expensive.

DRINKING AND NIGHTLIFE

There's no shortage of **bars** and **clubs** in Puerto, and from June to September the town is heaving all night with Spanish holiday-makers. In the winter months nightlife tends to be more limited, though there are dependable favourites along the Calle La Hoya, such as the nondescript bar and disco *Penny Farthing* at no. 32 (Map 6, J4) or the grotto-themed bar *La Gruta* at no. 24 (Map 6, I4), where there's occasionally live music. The bulk of the clubs and discos are clustered along the Avenida del Generalisimo. There's plenty of variety (including, unusually for Tenerife, a few gay clubs), but in this fast-changing scene its hard to predict what will be "in" next. Most clubs stay open until around 5am most nights – and often won't get going until well after midnight – so there's plenty of time to explore.

LISTINGS

Banks and exchanges There are over twenty different banks in town and even more exchange booths. The most convenient are to be found around the Plaza del Charco.

Car rental Niza Cars, Hotel Turquesa Playa (☎922/388 456, ⓦwww.nizacars.com); DCC, C/Puerto Viejo 42, Edif. Brisas del Mar (☎922/381 123).

Cycling Mountain Bike Active, C/Mazaroco, Edif. Daniela 26 (☎922/376 081, ⓦwww.espanabike.com) rent out good quality mountain bikes (€12 a day) and arrange tours for cyclists of all abilities.

Hospital Clinica Tamaragua, Agustin de Bethencourt 3O, (℡ 922/380 512, ℱ 922/380 850), is a private hospital with 24-hour emergency service and English-speaking staff. For an ambulance call ℡ 922/383 812.

Internet Centro Soth's, CC La Cœpla (€4 for 30min).

Laundry Lavenderia Minosa, Edif. Daniela C/Mazaroco (Mon–Fri & Sun 9am–1pm & 4-7.30pm, Sat 9am–1pm).

Pharmacy Farmacia Pérez y Pérez, San Felipe 9; Farmacia Padilla, Avda del Generalisimo, 21.

Police Policia Municipal, Avda de José de Campo Llaren, just west of the centre (℡ 922/381 224).

Post office Opposite the bus station on C/el Pozo.

Scuba Diving Atlantik Diving centre, Hotel Maritim (℡ & ℱ 922/362 801, ⓦ www.arrakis.es/-atlantik) offers both CMAS and PADI courses; also organizes night dives, and dives to a DC3 plane wreck and cave.

Taxis ℡ 922/384 910

Travel agents The Travel Shop, Ctra Botanica (℡ 922/371 422, ℱ 922/370 356, ⓦ www.travelshoptenerife.com).

La Orotava

Map 8, C4.

Map 7 covers La Orotava in detail, while map 8 covers the the Orotava valley in general.

Only 6km from Puerto de la Cruz, La Orotava is an easy day trip from the resort. Not only the town's name, but also the bulk of its original wealth has come from the prosperous, **lush valley** surrounding it – the town quickly grew as cash crops were developed in the valley in the sixteenth century.

THE TOWN

LA OROTAVA's well-preserved old town centre, with its network of steep, cobbled streets is particularly known for the presence of twelve striking Canarian-style mansions, the **Doce Casas** – the former residences of the area's leading families. Only some of these are open to the public, mostly as souvenir shops, so their exploration and that of the rest of the old town, which includes a large ornate garden, the **Jardín Victoria**, and a reasonable handicraft museum, the **Museo de Artesania Iberoamericana**, can easily be done in around half a day. One particularly good time to visit the town is before or during the celebrations of Corpus Christi, when the streets are decorated with a multitude of flower petals, baked leaves and volcanic sand. This tradition began in 1847 and the displays mostly involve biblical motifs.

Jardín Victoria

Map 7, D5. Plaza de la Constitución. Daily 8am–9pm; €2.50.
Just beside the old town's busiest square, the tree-lined Plaza de la Constitución, is the **Jardín Victoria**, the nineteenth century-style gardens of the Ponte family. The immaculately kept and tightly regimented gardens may not be to everyone's taste, but they are laid out to take advantage of views over the coast below. Just west of them are La Orotava's own tiny **Botanical Gardens** (same opening

LA OROTAVA

times), though they are not really worth a detour, particularly if you've already seen those in Puerto de la Cruz (see p.109) other than to see an impressively proportioned dragon tree (see p.127).

The gardens here were the work of **Sabin Berthelot**, a French diplomat, whose main interest was in the acclimatization of tropical plants and fauna. Berthelot arrived in 1820, aged 26, and by the middle of that century he had compiled his authoritative and still respected *Histoire naturelle des Iles Canaries*.

Museo de Artesania Iberoamericana

Map 7, C3. C/de Tomds Zerolo 34. Mon–Fri 9.30am–6pm, Sat 9.30–2pm; €2.

Housed in a former convent, the Convento de Santo Domingo, the **Museo de Artesania Iberoamericana**, devotes itself to exhibiting handicrafts from Spain and Latin America. Apart from textile and ceramics displays there's an array of musical instruments, mostly from Peru and Nicaragua. The museum also houses a scale model of the reed boats used by Thor Heyerdahl to prove the feasibility of the ocean link to South America (see p.95). Whilst the handicrafts and folk art in the museum are beautifully exhibited, there is unfortunately little explanation of the displays provided – so that the opportunity to look around the beautiful old convent buildings becomes as interesting as the collections themselves.

Iglesia de la Concepción

Map 7, B4.

The original church on the present site of the **Iglesia de la Concepción** was destroyed in the earthquakes of 1704 and 1705. Today's church was built shortly after this and, thanks

LA OROTAVA

to the relatively wealthy local community at the time, was replaced with this grand structure. Its facade is considered a particularly notable piece of Baroque architecture, making it a Spanish national monument.

Doce Casas

Mon–Sat 9am–6pm; free.

From the Iglesia de la Concepción, Calle del Colegio climbs south to become Calle de San Francisco, which is known for its impressive seventeenth- and eighteenth-century mansions, including the grandest of the town's **Doce Casas** (Twelve Houses), the Casa de Los Balcones –also called the Casa Mendez-Fonseca – and the Casa de Los Turistas – also called the Casa de Los Molína.

As the name would suggest, the **Casa de Los Balcones** (Map 7, B6) is best known for is splendid, ornately worked Canarian pine balconies – facing both the street and into the house's pretty courtyard. The lower level of the house now contains a lace and linen centre. The upper level (access to which costs €1.50) contains opulent dark-wood clad rooms (all Canarian pine), furnished in much the same way the Fonseca family would have had them in the eighteenth century. A couple of rooms here have also been furnished to reconstruct the living quarters of simpler folk at the same time.

Across the road from the Casa de Los Balcones is the **Casa de Los Turistas** (Map 7, A6), an equally impressive building, but completely devoted to pedalling Canarian handicrafts (it's packed with embroidery, lace, cigars and local wine), with occasional displays of pottery and weaving in the courtyard. The courtyard also has an extensive example of the local floor collages with which the town is decorated during Corpus Christi, as well as some excellent wide-open views of Teide, the western Orotava valley and the coast.

LA OROTAVA

Another house well worth a quick visit (and also selling handicrafts) to appreciate its woodwork is the sixteenth-century house **Casa Terrehermosa** (Map 7, B3), located opposite the Museo de Artesania Iberoamericana at C/Tomás Zerolo 27.

El Farrobo

Further south along the Calle de San Francisco from the Casa de Los Balcones and Casa de Los Turistas is the town's old mill quarter, **El Farrobo**, where the local speciality, *gofio* (see p.32) has for centuries been produced. Nowadays, seven of the original gofio mills still survive along Calle de San Francisco. The one at no. 3 (Map 7, B7. Mon–Fri 8am–1pm &2pm–7pm; free) still operates, albeit with an electric motor now. Photos inside depict bygone days when the quarter still clattered with the sound of the mills.

Opposite the mill the nineteenth-century **Hospital Sant'sima Trinidad** (Map 7, A7), still used as a hospice, is worth a quick look for the views over the valley from its entrance and for its peculiar front door, which contains a revolving drum, designed to be used as a receptacle for abandoned babies.

PRACTICALITIES

From La Orotava's **bus station** (Map 7, G2) it's a ten-minute walk west to the old town, where you'll find the **tourist office** (Map 7, C4. Mon–Fri 10am–6pm, Sat 10am–2pm) on C/de la Carrera del Escultor Estévenez 2.

Only two places in town offer **accommodation**: *Pension Silene* C/de Tomás Zerolo 9 (☏922/330 199; ❸), whose overpriced rooms have en-suite showers and small balconies with good views over the town; and the smart, but pricey

Hotel Victoria C/de Hennano Apolinar 8 (☎922/331 683, ⓕ922/320 519, Ⓦwww.victoria.teneriffa.com; ❼), in a refurbished 400-year old Canarian mansion, which has thirteen double rooms, all with satellite TV, fax and modem connections.

The **restaurant** at *Hotel Victoria* (closed Mon & Sun) is also the best of the handful of places to eat in the old town centre – dishes such as the fine sole in a prawn sauce with asparagus are served in the courtyard. Other options include *Sabor Canario*, C/Carrera 17 (closed Sun), part of the Museo El Pueblo Guanche. Try their roast cheeses with *mojo* or *ropa vieja*. *Casa Egon*, C/Leon 5 (closed Mon), is one of the best of the more moderately priced restaurants in town. A bistro-style restaurant, it specializes in omelettes and tapas.

The upper Orotava Valley

Beyond the densely settled and farmed slopes of upper Orotava valley the island's largest pine forest takes over, nourished by the mists that shroud these heights. The area is crisscrossed by many paths, most of them wide forest tracks that can be linked to form good hiking routes. A useful starting point for hikes in the area is **La Caldera** (Map 8, E7) a picnic spot, in an old volcanic crater 2km north of the village of Aguamansa (Map 8, E6); there's plenty of parking here and the regular buses (#345) from Puerto de la Cruz also stop here. A kiosk beside the crater also does light meals, including fresh trout – from a farm (open for viewing) a few hundred metres south down the road to Agaumansa. A rudimentary **information centre** serving the local woodland areas, beside the farm (daily 8am–3pm; ☎ 922/330 701) can give advice on local hikes.

The best **hikes** from La Caldera head east towards **Los Organos** (Map 8, F7), a row of massive basalt pillars moulded by crystallization to resemble organ-pipes. The best place to view these is along the easy level track to the small forest shelter El Topo (Map 8, F6). The **trail** (2hr loop) begins from the northeast side of the car park at La Caldera and continues on the well-graded dirt road past the large pine trees draped in silvery-green lichen, taking in the views stretching 1200m below to Puerto de la Cruz. Follow signs to Aguamansa (or for a longer route head on to the tracks that link the forest shelters El Topo and Perez Ventoso, before heading to Aguamansa) where you arrive at a minor sealed road, linked to the main road where the bus to Puerto de La Cruz stops.

A more strenuous, and more rewarding **longer hike**, takes you south on a sixteen-kilometre (5hr) loop around Los Organos along a narrow track above the cliffs, before descending to the wide forest track that links La Caldera with the base of Los Organos. From the south side of La Caldera, climb up a broad track marked "Zona de Encampa", following this to a bench and overlook, turning up a track behind this which turns into a steep climb before leading to the shelter at Chimoche (Map 8, E8). On approaching the shelter head east along a trail that soon hits a dry stream-bed where it turns slightly downhill before becoming a narrow track, which in turn soon climbs alongside a steep gorge. From here the trail ducks in and out of a number of dry gorges, with few real climbs, and up into a cliff face, until it beings to descend. Good views fan out from this trail over the whole Orotava valley, but none better than that offered from a promontory two thirds of the way along this section (once the site of a viewing-platform,

THE UPPER OROTAVA VALLEY

now marked by its crumbling former foundations). Beyond this are some short narrow sections where ropes have been attached for support and not long after is a turn-off to the left, where a trail heads past a rocky outcrop before zigzagging steeply downwards. Though easy to recognize this essential turn-off is easy to miss if you're not looking out for it. The narrow path soon joins a wider forest trail. Keep left here, then turn right at the T-junction further down. On reaching the densely lush and atmospheric forest, ignore signs to Aguamansa, instead going back to La Caldera on a well graded flat forestry trail, past some buildings and a shelter to return to the start point.

THE UPPER OROTAVA VALLEY

The west

The west of Tenerife is largely defined by the colossal and ancient **Teno mountains** which encompass most of the island's northwest tip. The sheer sides of this range mean that the region's coastal towns have to squeeze into narrow flat areas, or spread up steep roads. The coastal road on the northern side of the mountains links several of the island's oldest towns, including **Icod de Los Viños**, home of the largest specimen of the endemic dragon tree, and the quaint formerly bustling harbour town of **Garachico**. The impressive bleak peaks of the Teno rise from here and in their midst lies the remote village of **Masca** in a stunning precipitous valley of the same name. The trail to the sea from here is one of the most impressive on the island and ends at a beach surrounded by staggeringly huge cliffs, the Acantilados de Los Gigantes or Cliffs of the Giants, after which the modest neighbouring resort of **Los Gigantes** has been named. Connected to Los Gigantes are two other coastal resorts, **Puerto de Santiago** and **Playa de la Arena**, the last major towns between here and Playa de Las Américas. The coast south of them is dominated by farming and fishing, though occasional small resort developments have begun to take hold.

Map 9 covers the west coast of Tenerife and the Teno region

ACCOMMODATION PRICE CODES

Throughout the *Guide*, accommodation has been graded according to price, based on the cost of the cheapest double room in high season – but excluding the time around Christmas and New Year, when rates can rocket. In the case of apartments that sleep more than two, the price for the smallest available unit, as described in the body text, is given; where apartments are available by the night, the price refers to the cheapest two-person apartment. Where singles – which are usually more than half the price of doubles – are available, this has also been mentioned. Travellers wanting to stay a week or more may find that nightly rate can be reduced a little.

❶ up to €12
❷ €12–€24
❸ €24–€36
❹ €36– €48

❺ €48– €60
❻ €60– €84
❼ €84– €120
❽ over €120

The north coast

West of the Orotava valley, the slope of the north coast becomes progressively steeper, the coastal strip – on which numerous small towns and villages are built – narrower. The major towns along here are the workaday **Icod de Los Viños** and the small, historic **Garachico**. The coastline is generally rocky and mostly unsuitable for bathing, although a scattering of sea-water pools along the coast make up for this. West along the coast and beyond sprawling banana plantations is the island's most westerly point, **Punta de Teno**, marked by a lone lighthouse on a pretty rocky outcrop.

ICOD DE LOS VIÑOS

Map 1, D4.

The main attraction in **ICOD DE LOS VIÑOS** is the giant yucca-like **dragon tree**, El Drago; and though the town is one of the oldest inhabited sites on the island, only a small portion of it is particularly historic. Luckily for visitors, this area of sixteenth-century houses with ornate balconies is right beside the tree, making exploration of the most interesting parts of town an easy one-stop trip.

El Drago, the world's largest and oldest specimen of the endemic dragon tree, stands above the main road at the western end of town. Though its dimensions make the tree commanding enough – seventeen metres high and with a six metre trunk circumference – its true impressiveness arises from its age. In the late eighteenth century the German scientist Humboldt proclaimed it to be the oldest living thing on earth, and estimations of its age have ranged from about 3000 years to around 500 years – the last the best current estimation of its age. Even at a sprightly 500 years old, it pre-dates all the buildings that surround it.

The tree stands in a garden, to which admission is charged (€3), but many visitors satisfy themselves with looking at it for free from an elevated shady square nearby, next to the late sixteenth-century **Iglesia de San Marcos**. The church is worth a look, too, for its Baroque interior, fine Canarian pine ceiling and the two-metre high filigree silver cross on the altar.

For a closer look at a dragon tree, albeit not the oldest on the island, head a short way up Calle de San Antonio past stylish sixteenth- and seventeenth-century buildings to the **Drago Chico**. This old town district also contains the **Mariposa del Drago** (daily 9.30am–6pm; €4; ☏922/815 167), a tropical garden swarming with butterflies, and the *Restaurante Carmen*, Avda de Las Canarias 1, a reasonable-

THE DRAGON TREE

With its twisted trunk and many-branched crown, the dragon tree has the appearance of a giant frayed rope. Once common around the Mediterranean, ice-ages pushed its habitat further south around twenty million years ago, eventually restricting the tree's habitat to the Canary Islands, where the climate has remained remarkably stable.

The tree's unusual characteristics – the gnarled wood, geometric buds and the sheer longevity of each specimen have earned it plenty of attention and respect over the years. Guanche elders and kings held court beneath the canopy of these trees, and the people believed the tree could foretell the future – a fine blossom pointing to a fine harvest. But the dragon tree's most striking feature – the bleeding of red rubbery sap, or dragon's blood, when cut – has not only given the tree its name, but has also been used in a wide variety of applications. The Guanches used it in various healing salves, to keep their teeth healthy and even in their mummification process. More recently it has been used as dye in toothpaste, marble, Italian violins and Venetian ladies' hair.

The popularity of the sap has meant many dragon trees were tapped to death, and now only a sprinkling of large specimens survive in the Anaga and Teno regions of Tenerife. Though clearly aged, these specimens are notoriously hard to date, since they don't form annual rings like most other trees. A dragon tree's roots encircle and conceal the original stem which gradually rots away inside, leaving estimations of its age to be based on the tree's habit of throwing out a new branch every ten to twelve years.

quality Canarian restaurant with fairly moderate prices whose menu includes a good local stew, the *Puchero Canario* (€5).

Playa de San Marcos

Just below Icod a small, steep-sided bay contains the black-sand **PLAYA DE SAN MARCOS**. Though surrounded by the holiday homes of Canarians, fishing boats bob in its small harbour and outside weekends and the holiday season the bay retains a traditional feel. The beach generally offers quiet and relatively uncrowded bathing opportunities and is also lined with a few good, inexpensive fresh-fish restaurants, such as the *Tasca El Pescador* and the *Marítimo*, next door to each other on the harbour front. For holiday **accommodation**, privately owned apartments, to which local bartenders can direct you, are rented out for around €30 per night.

GARACHICO

Map 1, C4 & Map 9, N2.

Clustered on a small flat shelf base of immense cliffs beside a deep harbour, **GARACHICO** was, along with La Laguna and La Orotava, one of the first crop of important towns on the island. The town's narrow cobbled streets, rough fisherman's cottages and grand town houses were once part of Tenerife's most important sixteenth-century port, until a series of natural disasters plagued the town and ultimately ruined its harbour. But at least for visitors the results of this drama – lava rock-pools in the town's bay and charming old streets frozen in time – are engaging and picturesque.

Originally both town and harbour grew up on the grant of Genoese banker Cristóbal de Ponte who developed the land that he'd received as payback from Alonso de Lugo for financing the island's conquest. Thanks to a deep natural harbour, the town blossomed as a stop-off for numerous ships to the Americas, and a point of export for sugar cane and wine from the north. But in 1645 natural forces interrupted the good times, when a volcanically induced landslide spread over the town, sinking forty boats and killing a hundred people. Undeterred, the town quickly rebuilt its houses and port, only to see much of it destroyed again in 1706 when two slow-moving prongs of lava crept into town. Though no-one died in this eruption, the harbour was mostly filled in and so rendered useless to large-scale commercial traffic – a death knell for the commercial concerns, which moved on to Puerto de la Cruz to the east. In 1905 an earthquake reminded locals of the continued threat posed by nature, while more recent studies of satellite images have revealed worrying and as yet unexplained subsidence of up to 20cm around town.

Arrival and information

Buses connect Garachico with other towns along the north coast and Santa Cruz, dropping passengers off beside the main coastal road at the centre of town. The **tourist office** is at C/de Esteban Ponte 9 (Mon–Fri 10am–3pm; ☎922/830 185), a road which runs parallel to the main coastal road.

Accommodation

With only one hotel and one pension (which runs a couple of apartments) in town, **accommodation** options are limited. But luckily there's a further selection of places to stay on a banana plantation 2km east of here, near the village of **El Guincho**. All three accommodation options at El Guincho have access to a beautiful little rocky bay, **El Charco**, whose idyllic aquamarine waters make an enticing bathing spot.

In town

Pension El Jardín, C/Estaban de Ponte 8 (☎ & ⓕ 922/830 245, ⓔargonaut@arrakis.es; rooms ❷, apartments ❹), just behind the main waterfront road, is the least expensive place to stay. This impressive and creaky old town house contains five double rooms (one with its own shower) and a pleasant little bar in its courtyard. The owners also run a diving shop from the building and a couple of apartments around town for short-term lets. The *Hotel San Roque*, C/Esteban Ponte 32 (☎922/133435; ⓕ922/133406; ⓌWwww.hotelsanroque.com; ❽) is in an equally atmospheric, but more fully refurbished and much grander town house. The former home of the Ponte family, the house is now an extraordinarily elegant, well-thought-out and attentively run hotel. The entire building has been decorated and furnished with artistic flair, bringing out the best from the dark wood of its ceilings, internal balconies and floors. While no two of the beautiful rooms are the same, all are equipped with TV, video, CDs, minibar and direct-line phone. The hotel also has a gourmet restaurant, rooftop-terrace, pool, sauna and tennis court, and can lend bikes and fishing equipment to guests. There are some singles available and all room rates include breakfast.

At El Guincho

Inconspicuously signposted from the road at **El Guincho** and tucked away in the middle of a massive banana plantation, are three stylish places owned by the aristocratic Puente family. The sixteenth century colonial-style *Hotel El Patio* (☎ 922/133 280, ⓕ 922/830 089; ⓌWwww.hotelpatio.com; ❼) has airy rooms set around a grand and impressively lush courtyard. Facilities include a swimming pool and rates include breakfast. *Finca Malpais Trece* (☎ & ⓕ 922/133 068; ❺), further down the road, is a large old farmhouse with incredible views over plantations and the coast from its large courtyard and sun-terrace. This property has a more limited selection of facilities, including a few communal living rooms and a dining room where meals can be ordered in advance. Self-catering apartments are also available on the estate at *Apartamentos Las Terrazas* (☏ & ℱ 922/133 120 or 619 133 120; ❹), where eleven new, simply and stylishly furnished, roomy apartments with private balconies have commanding views out over the coast and ocean. Weekly rates are available.

The Town

Garachico's few landmarks aren't exciting sights, though the walk around its small centre is well worth it for a closer look at old fishermen's houses as well as ostentatious town houses with ornate and typically Canarian balconies.

One of the town's oldest and most striking buildings is the stocky little harbour-side fort **Castillo de San Miguel**. Built in the sixteenth century to protect Garachico from pirates, the fort was one of the few buildings to survive the 1706 eruption and is now home to a vaguely diverting rock and fossil collection (daily 10am–6pm; €0.60). More engaging are the views from the castle ramparts across the village and out to the Roque de Garachico, a lone rock monolith in the bay.

One of Garachico's unique attractions is a series of **rock pools** behind the Castillo de San Miguel. The lava here is part of that which closed off the harbour and ruined the town in 1706, but locals have made the best of it by creating paved walkways between the natural bathing pools. Formed as lava cooled on contact with the sea, these are fed and cleaned by the tidal action – making bathing possible only at low tide during calm seas.

Parallel to the main coastal road is the inland Calle Esteban Ponte. This narrow road separates out rows of elegant and mostly wooden town houses and runs to **Plaza de Juan Gonzalez de la Torre**, which includes a small park whose centrepiece is the **Puerta de Tiera**, a one-time gate to the town's harbour. There's also an old wooden winepress on display in the park.

To the west of the plaza and park are several narrow streets lined with traditional fishermen's cottages, while to the east is the town's main square, **Plaza de la Libertand**. The centrepiece of this square is a statue of Simon Bolivar, the nineteenth-century South American freedom fighter. His tenuous connection to Garachico was his grandmother, who emigrated from here after the 1706 disaster.

On the western side of the plaza stands the grand **Iglesia Santa Ana**, the town's main church, destroyed and rebuilt after the tragedies of 1706, with a fine wood ceiling. On the opposite side of the square, the **Convento de San Francisco** (Mon–Fri 9am–7pm, Sat 9am–6pm, Sun 9am–2pm; €0.60) houses the town's small and ramshackle museum. Its collections include a number of shells, stuffed birds, and an exhibit of locks and keys through the ages. More interesting is the scant information on Garachico's history, particularly its role as a major port. Most rewarding of all, however, is the wander around the extraordinarily pretty old wood balconies and atriums of these former convent buildings.

Finally, fans of the elegant and accomplished woodwork on balconies around Garachico might like to visit a small museum at the western end of the seafront, the **Museo Capinteria Antigua** at Avda República de Venezuela 17 (daily 9am–7pm; €1.50). Old artisans' tools have been beautifully displayed here alongside photos of their craft around town.

Eating and drinking

Many of the town's **restaurants** are located along its seafront strip and specialize in seafood. The most strikingly positioned of these is *El Caleton,* between the Castillo de San Miguel and the waves that crash into the town's volcanic rock pools. The restaurant offers a wide selection of reasonably priced fish and meat dishes, including light snacks such as sandwiches and soups, though the food is generally nothing special. A better bet for good seafood is the slightly more expensive and grander *Casa Gaspar*, Avda República de Venezuela 20 (closed Sun), beside the town's harbour. A good selection of fresh fish and seafood – what's on offer depends on the luck of the local catch – can be picked from an iced display and is priced by weight. Further back towards the town centre, at no. 9 on the same street is *Bar Bacco*, which serves excellent pizzas, though it's only open Friday, Saturday and Sunday after 7pm and so popular that you're likely to have to wait for a table.

For good, inexpensive food it's also worth investigating the **bars** and **bistros** that are scattered about the town's seafront and centre, around the Plaza de la Libertand. *Casa Ramón*, Esteban de Ponte 4, is a particularly good choice, not so much for the limited menu of excellent seafood dishes, or the distinctive, spicy home-made *mojo*, but more for the atmosphere of the old, dingy wood-clad restaurant and the manner of its elderly proprietor, who makes you feel as though you've dropped by your Canarian grandmother for lunch.

The road west

The road west along the coast travels through the heart of Tenerife's banana industry and links small uneventful towns. The pretty little **LOS SILOS** (Map 9, J3) is one of the major towns along the way. It's from here that you can gain access to a dirt road that runs along the rocky coast – a pleasant place to hike and watch local fishermen cast off the rocks in one of the island's fishing hotspots. A large sea-water pool complex (daily 11am–11pm; free) beside the sea in nearby **LA CÁLETA** (Map 9, K2) includes a good and inexpensive fish restaurant.

Further down the coast, **BUENAVISTA DEL NORTE** (Map 9, F2) is another unspectacular town, but again has good fish restaurants. *El Pescador* C/Los Molinos 27 (9am–midnight; closed Tues), serves a great range of inexpensive seafood, including particularly good king prawns in three different sauces; while *La Cabaña*, C/El Puerto 26 (closed Wed), offers particularly good fish stews.

A remote road often beset by rock and mudfalls runs 10km west of Buenavista to Tenerife's most westerly point, the **Punta de Teno** (Map 9, A5), a jagged volcanic-rock headland jutting into the ocean. Marked by an old light-house, the headland attracts local fishermen and the clear waters of its sheltered bay is an inviting bathing spot. But it's the views from the rocky promontory itself that most come for, particularly at sunset when the last rays disappear behind La Gomera and La Palma. Equally impressive views also extend inland from here, up the dusty green, immense Teno mountains and the huge coastal cliffs.

The Teno region

Like the Anaga at the eastern end of Tenerife the **Teno region** is an area of steep gorges carved out of ancient vol-canic rock. At around 17 million years old, the Teno is also one of the oldest parts of Tenerife and over time its rock has been eroded into deep and inaccessible ravines that cut down to a rugged coastline and its few accessible beaches. Unlike the Anaga, where laurel forests dominate the scenery, the landscape is much bleaker here and the area is largely treeless and exposed since most of its timber was cleared to fire sugar mills in the sixteenth century. Now it is protected and only traditional land uses are permitted.

The inland edge of the range is pretty much defined by the road between Icod de los Viños and Los Gigantes via Santiago del Teide. To the east of this road are the comparatively recent lava landforms stemming from the Teide region, to the west, the smaller of the Teno's bold craggy peaks, including **Montaña Jala**. The other main road in the area passes through the centre of the Teno, leaving Buenavista del Norte to climb up into the range and then descend to Santiago del Teide via the picturesque, improbably steep-sided **Masca valley**. This contains the region's most popular hike, down its narrow gorge to the sea, although views of the region's mountains common to other great hikes in the Teno are absent here.

- -

You can watch **rough-hewn traditional pots** being made at Centro Alfarero (Tues–Sat 10am–1pm & 4–7pm, Sun 10am–2pm; ☎ 922/863 127) in the village of Arguayo near Santiago del Teide (Map 9, J8). The pots are made without the help of a wheel, using thousand-year-old Guanches techniques. A tiny shop sells a few examples of this pottery.

- -

THE NORTHERN TENO

The road from Buenavista del Norte snakes its way south into the heart of the Teno region, via a handful of small rural settlements scattered in the area's largest valley. Among these is **EL PALMAR** (Map 9, G4), home to the **park**

information centre (Mon–Fri 8am–3pm), which hands out free, but fairly simple, hiking maps. The restaurant here, along with those further up in Teno Alto, serves good, basic upland Canarian fare – mostly grilled meat and chicken, along with fresh goat's cheese and local wines that are well worth sampling.

The best views over the valley are from **Mirador La Tabaiba** (Map 9, F6) at its southern edge, beside a hairpin in the road which then dips out of sight on its way to Masca. The views north towards Buenavista or west over uninhabited gorges and massive cliffs are spectacular, and the viewpoint marks the start of an excellent, relatively flat, ridge walk. From here its 11km back to Buenavista, a hike of about four hours, which passes grazing goats in gullies and along stunning ridges, and past meadows filled with wildflowers in spring, to the village of Teno Alto. From here you follow a minor road, before finally descending a steep slope down to the road between Buenavista and Punta de Teno. The best way to reach the start of the hike is by public bus (Mon–Fri 9.30am) from Buenavista.

MASCA

Map 9, H7.

Second only in popularity on the island to the Parque Nacional del Teide, the village of **MASCA**, in an impressively isolated and picturesque gorge, is generally considered Tenerife's prettiest village. And outside the hours of 11am and 5pm, when streams of crowds and tour buses beset the village, it's hard to argue with this opinion – the village's pretty old stone houses looking out across palm-trees and improbably steep ravine walls towards the Atlantic Ocean. So, if you're happy to arrive in the village early, and are fit and energetic enough for the **hike** down the incredible, narrow gorge to the sea, then visiting the valley is likely to be among your most memorable experiences on Tenerife.

Considering it was only connected by road to the outside world in 1991, and is a good three-hour hike from the coast, it's hard to imagine quite what inspired the village of Masca in the first place. However, fertile valley soils spawned a relatively large six-hundred strong community here at one point. Now the population hovers around one hundred, with many of the old stone houses of the village lying vacant and most of the villagers remaining here only to service tourist needs.

For the hardy, the six-hour return **hike** down the impressive steep-sided Barranco de Masca, from the village to the sea, is a must. The path down the gorge is straightforward to follow – it starts just left of the ridge that runs through the centre of the town – and, despite requiring the use of hands for support in a couple of places and often being steep and full of loose rock, is easy enough for relatively experienced hikers. Along the walk, the sides of the ravine climb as high as 600m above the sea, and at its narrowest the gorge is only 20m wide. These narrow sections are the most memorable since they're filled with bizarre, swirling rock formations and curious endemic vegetation. After around two hours of hiking down the gorge, the noise of waves breaks into the still, humid air which soon gives way to a sea breeze. The path terminates at a pretty little beach – a great place to relax, but the sea currents here are usually too strong to allow for safe swimming.

Practicalities

The easiest way to get to Masca is by car. But if you want to save money, or don't fancy the drive up the steep sinuous roads, then you can either use the infrequent public **buses** (Mon–Fri 2 daily from Santiago del Teide; Mon–Fri 4 daily from Buenavista del Norte), or take a guided **hiking trip**

THE TENO REGION

to the valley. Companies offering this trip operate out of most of the main coastal resorts and usually offer a shuttle bus to the village and a **boat** to pick you up from the beach after your hike through the Masca canyon. From the western resorts these trips cost around €35 per person, from the southern resorts costs rise to around €45. If you want to organize your own transport to Masca, but would like to take a boat from the beach to Los Gigantes, contact Excursions Maritimas (☎922/861 1918) who charge €9 for this service, which leaves the beach at 3.30pm.

Almost all visitors come to Masca on day trips as there's very little **accommodation** in town – only the German-run *El Guanche* (☎922/861 405; ❺) in the village's old schoolhouse offers basic rooms (with outside toilet) and half-board. Several **restaurants** and **bars** have opened up around town, most opening between noon and 6pm. The most beautifully positioned, and consequently one of the busiest, of these is *Chez Arlette* (closed Sat), just below the main road near the church. The restaurant terrace has particularly great views over the valley and serves excellent, refreshing, home-made lemonade as well as good Canarian food, such as crispy corn cakes and tangy grilled lamb.

MONTAÑA JALA

Map 9, I7.

The hike up **Montaña Jala** at the western perimeter of the Teno range is one of the easier hikes in the area, but climbs through an interesting mix of vegetation – including some prime laurel forest – and is well rewarded by some of the best possible views over the Teno.

A practical place to start the hike is the roadside **Restaurant Fleytas** (Map 9, J6), from where the eight-kilometre loop up Montaña Jala takes around three hours. Buses between Icod de Los Viños and Las Américas stop outside this restaurant and its owners allow private vehicles to be left in their car park.

The **trail** begins over the road from the restaurant, immediately descending into a wide valley with a few small ponds. The path passes these and follows a zigzag route up towards a ridge to the right, where it splits into three. The right branch heads northeast along the ridge, the left climbs up a wide dusty track in the opposite direction. You can follow the latter up the mountain, but a much more enticing option is the narrow track straight ahead through thick vegetation. The dense canopy along this laurel forest path blocks most of the light, making the trail moist, overgrown and in places difficult to follow. Look out for a fairly well-trodden track branching off this path on its uphill side and follow it to a wider track, where you turn right, following it a short way, before climbing again on a small track. This short path soon follows a smooth, dry stream bed gouged into the soft earth here before it leads out to a forestry road that circles the base of Montaña Jala. To climb to the summit turn left here, or to walk around the hill first turn right. The ascent of Jala takes about half an hour from this spot, up a little-used road to phenomenal views from the summit. The other route is fairly flat and leads through a pine and laurel forest, before meeting the same road. The hiking loop ends by descending down this road, turning left off it just shy of the main road, then descending on a narrow track that leads back to the ponds and then to the restaurant.

The West Coast

Due to the proximity of the stunning and colossal **Acantilados de Los Gigantes** (Cliffs of the Giants), the presence of a couple of small beaches and predictably good local weather along the west coast, three fairly large resorts – **Los Gigantes**, **Puerto de Santiago** and **Playa de la Arena** – have sprung up on the steep slopes of the southern edge of the Teno range. Further south the rocky coast is lined with a handful of modest commuter towns and fishing villages, as well as a couple of fledgling resorts such as **Callao Salvaje** and **Playa Paraiso**.

THE WESTERN RESORTS

The western resorts of **Los Gigantes**, **Puerto de Santiago** and **Playa de la Arena** fuse with one another along the steep rocky coastline and are based almost entirely around providing holiday accommodation and services to visitors. Together, the three offer a more modest and low-key modern-resort alternative to Playa de Las Américas, 30km to the south, and attract those looking for good weather and a quiet resort; nightlife is almost entirely absent here.

Arrival and information

Buses connect the three resorts with each other and the island-wide network via routes down the coast to Las Américas and inland to Santiago del Teide. The local **tourist office**, at Edificio Seguro de Sol 36–37 (Mon–Fri 9.30am–3.30pm, Sat 9.30am–12.30pm; ☎922/860 348), overlooks the beach in Playa de la Arena.

Accommodation

Apartments Neptuno
Playa de la Arena
☎ 922/861 606
⚞ 922/860 584

Large, well-equipped but functional apartments in a modest complex containing a small pool and sun deck next to the black Playa de la Arena. The friendly local owners offers one- and two-bed apartment for weekly rental, sleeping two to four people. A number of shops and restaurants are close to the complex. ❹.

Aparthotel Poblado Marinero

Puerto de Los Gigantes
Ⓣ 922/860 966
Ⓕ 922/860 943
Ⓔ pobladomarinero
@cajacanarias.net

Attractive Canarian-village-style complex surrounding a pebble-dash courtyard beside Los Gigantes port. Apartments include kitchen, bathroom and lounge and can sleep up to six. The balconies of the best apartments face the Los Gigantes cliffs. The complex has its own rock-pool swimming area. ❹.

Hotel Barceló Santiago

Puerto Santiago
Ⓣ 922/860 912
Ⓕ 922/861 808
Ⓦ www.barcelo.com

Multistorey, cliff-top hotel centred around a massive sun deck, pool and with an activity programme that includes volleyball, quizzes and bingo. Facilities include a fitness centre, tennis and squash courts. Most rooms have a balcony and overlook the sea with views of La Gomera. The hotel is opposite a small shopping centre, CC Santiago, that contains a few restaurants and the usual array of tourist services. ❺.

Hotel Playa La Arena

Playa de la Arena
Ⓣ 922/795 778
Ⓕ 922/791 686
Ⓦ www.step.es/spring

Large, new multistorey edifice containing over four hundred air-conditioned rooms with satellite TV – most with balcony and sea views. Hotel facilities include three bars, a restaurant (with a good breakfast buffet), two large pools (featuring waterfalls and a waterslide), tennis courts and a minigolf course. ❼.

THE WEST COAST

The Resorts

Though largely characterized by densely spaced low-rise apartment complexes, **LOS GIGANTES** (Map 1, B6) has the advantage of a spectacular setting beside the huge cliffs from which it gets its name. A single, one-way main road descends into town and loops around its central collection of shops, which hide a tiny pedestrian plaza in their centre. Below the commercial area is a neat little marina crowded with boats and yachts and lined with cafés and restaurants. North of here is a small, clean and rarely crowded black-sand beach beside the sheer rock walls of the massive **Acantilados de Los Gigantes**. It is these cliffs that form the only real local attraction here, and a spectacular one at that. Marking the boundary of the volcanic Teno range, the cliffs were formed by lava squeezed under high pressure through multiple parallel cracks. Most visitors join a boat tour to their base, which also offer an opportunity to see the dolphins in the Gomeran Channel and stop for a swim. Expect to pay from around €18 per person for these trips, which are hawked by a number of operators based beside the town's marina. A couple of diving firms are also located in the marina, including Aquascuba (℡ & ℻ 922/867 217, ⓦwww.aquascubacanarias.com) – a good outfit that offers beginner courses and dives for certified divers.

South of Los Gigantes, and effectively joined to it, are **PUERTO SANTIAGO** and **PLAYA DE LA ARENA**. Both are a rather modern, sprawling mixture of homes, hotels and apartments and not really worth going out of your way to explore – particularly since most restaurants, bars and cafés are along the main seafront road anyway. The local highlight is the small and busy black-sand beach from which Playa de la Arena gets its name.

The opportunity to bathe along the coast beside the three resorts is often compromised by the huge waves and dangerous undercurrents in the sea so, to compensate, two private complexes offer pools and sun terraces on cliffs above the sea, just south of the marina in Los Gigantes. The larger of the two, El Laguillo (daily 10.30am–6.30pm; €4, kids €2) has a more imaginatively laid-out bathing area using lakes, waterfalls and islands, than does the rather dull, older, but greener (including a bowling green) Oasis (daily 10am–6pm; €3, kids €1.50) nearby.

Eating and Drinking

Each restaurant listed in the *Guide* has been categorized as either inexpensive (under €6), moderate (€6– €10) and expensive (above €10) – indicating the price of an average main course.

Each of the three resorts has a small and predictable assemblage of touristy **restaurants** and sports **bars**. While the bulk of restaurants serve mediocre meals (inevitably including English breakfasts), you can find a few more interesting places if you look hard. Los Gigantes has the biggest selection, with several restaurants and cafés beside its marina, and a couple more in the centre of town. Most of the restaurants in Puerto Santiago are clustered in CC Santiago beside the Hotel Barcelo Santiago, while the small number of restaurants in Playa de la Arena are along the beachfront road where the wide selection includes Chinese, Italian, Mexican and Austrian cuisine.

Beeches

CC Santiago II
℡ 922/862 403
Small, thoughtfully run restaurant with plenty of fresh gourmet options, including quite a few veggie choices. Dishes are prepared with considerable attention to detail and include a broccoli,

leek and brie angelhair pasta and Mediterranean fish-pie topped with saffron – one of several seafood options that vary according to what's fresh. Reserving one of the handful of tables is advisable. Closed Fri. Moderate to expensive.

Gran Cañon

Ctra Gral Tamaimo 105, La Caldera

☎ 922/860 323

Laid-back place, a short drive or a steep twenty-minute walk from the upper limits of Los Gigantes, that provides great views over the valley and La Gomera. Run by unconventional German ex-pats, the restaurant offers organic produce (also on sale separately) accompanied by favourite Canarian dishes such as grilled chicken, rabbit and goat. Closed Mon. Moderate.

Miranda

C/ Flor de Pascua 25, Los Gigantes

☎ 922/860 207

Good and unusually imaginative Canarian restaurant in the centre of Los Gigantes, where local specialities are blended with international cuisine producing a variety of interesting dishes. The excellent boneless sole in prawn and mushroom sauce is the house speciality. Vegetarians will find a couple of (odd) choices here too, including a curry and a sweet and sour stir-fry. Moderate to expensive.

Pancho

Playa de la Arena.

Pleasant Canarian restaurant in a great location – its terrace directly beside the beach and beneath a shady, heavy tree canopy. Lots of great fish dishes are offered here, including good Canarian-style bass and a great two-person paella. Open for both lunch and dinner, but closed Mon & June. Moderate to expensive.

THE ROAD SOUTH

The main road south from the western resorts connects a number of coastal communities before turning into a motorway near Playa Las Américas. Inland, this region is thick with (mainly banana) plantations, while along the coast the small towns exist mostly to service the resorts to the north or south of them, though a small community of fishermen still survives along the rocky coastline of secluded coves, bays and beaches.

The main town south of the western resorts and the nearest to them is the unpretentious little **ALCALA**, surrounded by banana plantations. Town life is centred on a little plaza, near its small sheltered harbour and beach. Just north of the harbour is the town's only **accommodation** option *Pensión Alcalá*, C/Marrucos 2 (☎922/865 457, ©922/865 976; ❷), a Bohemian place run by an eccentric Gomeran who provides autobiographical leaflets about his life as a South American revolutionary. The influences of this continent are well in evidence in his rich abstract paintings that line the guesthouse walls and in the food served in his small **restaurant** (closed Sun). Meals here are set – and rather expensive – affairs, involving a series of small tapas dishes, but if you are staying at the pension, the owner will happily cook other dishes for you. Otherwise, for good fish, fresh from the restaurant's tanks, try *El Pescador de Alcalá*, a big restaurant with moderate prices overlooking the harbour and open for lunch and dinner.

Further south along the main road, the next major settlement is the functional little commuter town of **SAN JUAN**. Though a bland little place consisting mainly of ugly two-storey buildings, it's worth a detour to the short promenade beside its harbour where there are a few inexpensive bars and restaurants serving fresh fish.

Further south, the proximity of Playa de Las Américas is announced by two small resorts, Callao Salvaje and Playa Paraiso, occupying separate headlands and each beside a small sheltered beach. **CALLAO SALVAJE**, for some reason a Danish enclave, has the usual combination of tourist bars and restaurants and a pleasant little apartment block, the *Aparthotel Kiwi-Club*, (T 922/741 510, F 922/741 004; ❹), whose facilities include large gardens and a pool. The nearby **PLAYA PARAISO** is a slightly larger and considerably uglier resort, mainly due to the presence of a couple of twenty-storey apartment blocks and a considerable amount of building work by the coast. The apartments of one of these well-worn 70s blocks, the *Paraíso Floral* (T 922/740 722; ❹), sleep four and have access to down-at-heel facilities that include restaurants, a pool and a mini-golf course. The nearby *Oasis Paraíso* (T 922/741 049; W www.h10.es; ❸) offers a similar deal. The highlight of the resort is its pleasant little sheltered bay with good snorkelling, and a good local diving outfit, the Barakuda Club (T 922/74 18 81; W www.divers-net.de/teneriffa), which organizes dives and courses for beginners.

The last little, surprisingly serene, settlement, a couple of kilometres from the northern fringes of Las Américas, is **EL PUERTITO**. Though the small hamlet itself is clustered around a beach, it's best known for a beautiful and unspoilt beach half an hour's walk south along clifftops, where hippies camp and naturists bathe. To find the trail to this beach head south out of town, down alleys that extend from the beach up onto a headland. A rough path begins here and crosses this headland and two more before heading down to the beach.

Playa de Las Américas and Los Cristianos

Once a sparsely populated rocky shoreline, the arid coast that stretches from **PLAYA DE LAS AMÉRICAS** and **LOS CRISTIANOS** in a contiguous string of developments is now the centre of commercial tourism on Tenerife. By averaging 320 days of sunshine a year, this area has become a **package-tour heaven** for sun seekers, with vast swathes of land occupied by huge, impersonal hotels and consistently crowded beaches that are home to two thirds of the island's visitors and countless expatriate hangers-on.

With the exception of the old harbour town of Los Cristianos, most of this conurbation has been built from

---
Maps 11, 12 & 13 cover Las Américas and Los Cristianos in detail.

ACCOMMODATION PRICE CODES

Throughout the *Guide*, accommodation has been graded according to price, based on the cost of the cheapest double room in high season – but excluding the time around Christmas and New Year, when rates can rocket. In the case of apartments that sleep more than two, the price for the smallest available unit, as described in the body text, is given; where apartments are available by the night, the price refers to the cheapest two-person apartment. Where singles – which are usually more than half the price of doubles – are available, this has also been mentioned. Travellers wanting to stay a week or more may find that nightly rate can be reduced a little.

❶ up to €12
❷ €12–€24
❸ €24–€36
❹ €36– €48

❺ €48– €60
❻ €60– €84
❼ €84– €120
❽ over €120

scratch in the last thirty years. It must have taken a considerable leap of imagination to see economic potential in the barren, baking-hot land, particularly when even the most basic aspects of the local environment had to be adapted for tourism. Not only did engineers have to pipe in water and build desalination plants, but they even shipped in sand from the Sahara to make beaches, constructing huge concrete breakwaters to prevent them from being washed away. The vast scale and complexity of the engineering that went into making these resorts is phenomenal, and given the speed at which it has been created, it is a tribute – of sorts – to human achievement.

Most visitors spend a good part of their time on one of the area's half-dozen **beaches**, which are crowded with regimented lines of sunshades and loungers. The breakwaters that shelter these beaches produce a gently lapping sea which is perfect for swimming. A range of **water sports** and equipment is also on offer – from pedal boats, jet skis and motorboats to parascending or being towed on an inflated banana. The more adventurous might also like to try learning to scuba dive, with one of a number of local dive operations. And should resort life become too much to bear, you'll find that even the tackiest resorts have their quiet and exclusive spots, and the well-developed tourist infrastructure makes it easy to escape to the region's quieter parts, making this a good base from which to explore the rest of the island.

In addition, there are a couple of attractions within easy reach of the resorts – **Parques Exóticas** is an imaginatively laid out animal park and **Jardines del Atlantico:Bananera** is, as you might expect, a Banana farm with exhibitions on the locally grown fruit.

ARRIVAL AND INFORMATION

Most visitors will arrive in Las Américas on a **free shuttle-bus** provided by their tour operator, taking them from the airport directly to the door of their hotel. Independent travellers can make use of the frequent **public bus service** from the airport, which comes through Los Cristianos and Los Moritos before heading for the **bus station** (Map 12, F1), between Central Las Américas, San Eugenio and the motorway.

Las Américas has two **tourist offices**, one for each of the two administrative regions it straddles. The centre and north. is covered by the Adeje-region office at Avda de Rafael Puig 1 (Map 12, C2. Mon–Fri 9am–1pm; ☎ 922/750 633), just north of CC Veronicas in central Las Américas, while the south is covered by the Arona-region office near the Parque Santiago II building (Map 12, C6. Mon–Fri 9am–1pm & 4–7pm, Sat 9am–1pm; ☎ 922/797 668, ⓦ www.arona.org), a fifteen-minute walk south down the same road. The tourist office in Los Cristianos (Map 13, J4. Mon–Fri 9am–3.30pm, Sat 9am–1pm) is downhill from the bus station in the town's cultural centre.

GETTING AROUND

Getting around Las Américas is fairly straightforward since all regional **buses** – as well as local services – make frequent stops here. **Motorists** will, however, find the road system unreasonably chaotic for such a recently built place, and parking spaces are usually hard to find. Using one of the ubiquitous **taxis** (hail them around town, or pick them up at the numerous ranks along the seafront road Avda de Rafael Puig) is often the best bet if you're short on time – though the pleasant seafront promenade, which runs almost without interruption along the resort, makes a pleasant route for **walkers**.

ACCOMMODATION

With over a hundred hotel and apartment complexes in Las Américas, you'd think you'd be spoilt for choice. But, since almost all the accommodation is designed to serve the booking systems of the **package-holiday industry**, it doesn't make life terribly easy for the independent traveller. If you want to stay in this resort it's easiest and usually cheapest to work within the accepted system. Turning up on spec is ill-advised, but if you do, try the **apartments** and **hotels** listed below, all of which have some rooms set aside for independent travellers. You're better still approaching one of the listed **accommodation agencies** who can help find vacant apartments in large complexes, many of which they manage on behalf of absentee owners. Agencies can generally offer a week's apartment rental (usually the minimum booking period) from around €300.

As well as a large number of block-booked hotel and apartment complexes, there are also quite a few **pensions** in Los Cristianos. However, these are almost always full at any time of year, so don't rely on finding a bed, particularly late in the day. To maximize your chance of finding a room turn up around noon, just after available rooms have been vacated – given the great demand for rooms, advance reservations are rarely accepted.

AGENCIES

Anyka Sur
Map 13, C3. Edif. Azahara, Los Cristianos.
☎ 922/791 377 or ☎ 649 837 836
ⓕ 922/751 957
Ⓦ www.anykasur.com

Apolo Services
Map 13, XL3. CC Apolo, Los Cristianos
☎ 922/790 251
ⓕ 922/797 026
ⓔ apoloprop@arrakis.es

Custom Holidays
Map 12, E5. Aparthotel California 6, Las Américas.
☎ 922/796 000
ⓕ 922/796 211
Ⓦ www.custom-holidays.com

Marcus Management
Map 13, C2. Apartamentos Portosin, Avda Penetracion, Los Cristianos.
☎ 922/751 064
ⓕ 922/753 725
Ⓦ www.tenerife-apts.com

Tenerife Holiday Rent
Map 12, E6. Edif. Tenerife Garden, Las Américas.
☎ 922/790 211
ⓕ 922/795 818
Ⓦ www.tenerife-holiday-rental.com

HOTELS

Andreas
Map 13, E5. C/Antigua General Franco, Los Cristianos.
☎ 922/790 024
ⓕ 922/794 270
Ⓦ www.hotelsreveron.com

ACCOMMODATION

151

Straightforward hotel, close to the centre of town, but without any on-site facilities. Many of the ample rooms have balconies, some of which face a busy road, and all rooms have a private bathroom. ❺.

Colón Guanahani
Map 11, B2. C/Bruselas, Playa de Fañabé, Las Américas.
ⓣ 922/712 314
ⓕ 922/712 121
Massive, stylish four-star hotel containing over one and a half thousand plush, spacious, air-conditioned rooms with generous balconies, plus facilities that include a sauna and heated salt-water pool. Guests are also offered a weekly themed gala buffet, reduced green fees at local golf courses and substantial reductions for stays of five nights or more. ❼.

Esmerelda Playa
Map 11, C4. Torviscas, Las Américas
ⓣ 922/714 710
ⓕ 922/715 875
ⓔ tenesur@jet.es
Characterless four-star hotel

with over three hundred rooms. Great ocean views from the sun terrace and pools on the hotel's large roof compensate for the tacky vinyl furniture, as does its location close to the beach and near plenty of shops and restaurants. Facilities include tennis and squash courts, a sauna and a mini-golf course. Guests also receive discounts at the local golf courses. ❻.

Gran Hotel Arona
Map 13, L9. Avda Maritima, Los Cristianos.
ⓣ 922/750 678
ⓕ 922/750 243
Large classy hotel beside the promenade, a ten minute walk east of town. All rooms have balconies with sea views as well as a satellite TV and a minibar. The hotel has an extensive sun terrace and large pools on site. ❽.

Gran Hotel Melia Bahía del Duque
Fañabé, Los Américas
ⓣ 922/713 000
ⓕ 922/712 616
ⓦ www.canaryweb.es/hduque
Luxurious modern

development, constructed in the style of nineteenth-century Canarian town houses. The complex's extensive facilities include eight restaurants, nine bars, an Internet café, a library, an observatory, five swimming pools, squash and tennis courts and a jogging path. One particularly well-appointed building within the complex, the *Casas Ducales*, has its own butler service. If money is no object, ask for the royal suite which costs around €1200 per night. Be warned, however, that for all the luxury within the grounds, the area outside the complex is largely devoid of facilities and is pockmarked by numerous building sites. ❽.

Jardín Tropical
Map 11, C8. San Eugenio, Las Américas
☎ 922/746 000
🖷 922/746 060
Ⓦ www.tropical-hoteles.com
Moorish hotel beside the sea with a sense of style that's lacking in the surrounding architecture. Its central courtyards are filled with lush subtropical gardens and facilities include a large fitness centre and five good restaurants, open to non guests, who can also use the pools and rent a sun bed for €3 per day in the adjoining, cliff-top Las Rocas Beach Club overlooking the sea. The hotel has negotiated discounts at golf courses for guests, who in low season can also get a good deal on rooms, which are offered at half the high-season price. ❽.

The Mare Nostrum Resort
Map 12, E8. Avda Las Américas, Los Moritos, Las Américas
☎ 922/757 500
🖷 922/757 510
Ⓦ www.marenostrumresort.com
Large resort complex, backing onto the sea and dominating the landscape of southern Los Moritos. There are five separate five-star hotels on the site – *Mediterranean Palace, Sir Anthony, Julio Cesar, Marco Antonio* and *Cleopatra Palace* – plus twelve restaurants and the ostentatious Casino

ACCOMMODATION

Royal. Facilities include four pools, tennis and squash courts, and several first-class fitness studios with spa facilities. The hotels also offer packages for golfers, the most deluxe including seven nights bed and breakfast, a six-day spa programme, a rental car and green fees for €1355. **❽**.

Oasis Moreque
Map 13, K7. Avda Penetración, Los Cristianos.
☎ 922/790 366
🖷 922/792 260
🖳 www.h10.es

Late-1960s building beside the promenade, with good facilities, including a pool and tennis courts, and fairly swish rooms. The hotel usually runs to capacity with guests on packages – vacancies tend to arise from cancellations – and as a consequence independent reservations are only accepted a couple of days in advance. Prices are generally reasonable and include a good breakfast. The single rooms are particularly good value at only half the price of standard doubles. **❼**.

Park Club Europe
Map 12, C7. Avda Rafael Puig, Los Moritos, Las Américas
☎ 922/757 060
🖷 922/793 352
🖳 pce@europe-hotels.org

Comfortable hotel beside the Mare Nostrum Resort, in easy walking distance of Playa de Las Vistas, many local restaurants and Los Cristianos. The hotel includes good sport facilities, among them a fitness centre with sauna, tennis and squash courts, as well as a scuba-diving outfit and the hiking- and mountain-biking tour operator, Diga Sports (see p.177). The reasonably sized rooms boast understated decor and large balconies. Room rates halve in low season. **❺**.

Reverón Plaza
Map 13, H5. Plaza Del Carmen, Los Cristianos
☎ 922/757 120
🖷 922/757 052
🖳 www.hotelesreveron.com

Swanky modern hotel in the heart of the centre. Amenities include a good-sized pool and sun-lounge area on the roof, plus exercise, sauna and steam rooms, a Jacuzzi and a squash court. There are great views, particularly from the hotel's exclusive restaurant, the *Mirador Plaza*. The spacious rooms are tastefully decorated and all have balconies. Good singles rates. ❼.

PENSIONS

Casa de Blanca
Map 13, G5. C/Ramón Pino 28V, Los Cristianos
☎ 922/751 975
Basic pension in a quiet side street with rudimentary rooms and shared bathrooms. No singles, but one good-value triple. ❷.

Corisa
Map 13, I5. C/Amalia Alayón 18, Los Cristianos
☎ 922/790 792
Clean and simple rooms sharing bathrooms on the upper floors of the dreary modern block that houses the restaurant of the same name. Many of the rooms are taken as long-term lets. ❸.

La Paloma
Map 13, F6. C/Paloma 7, Los Cristianos.
☎ 922/790 198
Pleasant, basic rooms, most sharing bathrooms, in the pedestrianized centre of town. Several singles available. ❸.

La Playa
Map 13, F6. C/de la Paloma 9, Los Cristianos
☎ 922/792 264
The most consistently full pension in town, with good long-stay room rates attracting migrant workers from around the island. All rooms with shared baths Some singles available. ❷.

Lela
Map 13, F6. C/Juan XXIII 34, Los Cristianos
☎ 922/797 150
Friendly owners run this nondescript pension spread over several floors above shops in the town's pedestrianized centre. All rooms with shared baths. ❷.

Teresa
Map 13, F5. C/Ramón Pino 44,

ACCOMMODATION

Los Cristianos
☎ 922/791 230
Newly renovated, friendly boarding house just outside the pedestrianized part of the centre. All rooms have shared baths. A few singles available. ❷.

Venezuela

Map 13, F5. Avda de Suecia 24B, Los Cristianos
☎922/797 931
The newest pension in town, centrally located, but near the busy and noisy through road. Clean, spartan rooms with shared bathrooms offer the best and cheapest deals in town for lone travellers. ❷.

APARTMENTS

Aparthotel Jardin Caleta

La Caleta
☎ 922/710 992
🅕922/711 040
The only accommodation in La Caleta – a small fishing village on the northern fringes of the ever-expanding Las Américas that still offers a pleasant respite from the noise and bustle down the coast. This nondescript apartment block contains over two-hundred neat little apartments sleeping up to three people, that surround a pool and terrace area, where a programme of social activities takes place. ❺.

Aparthotel Villamar

Map 11, C8. C/Eugenio Domínguez, San Eugenio, Las Américas
☎ & 🅕 922/750 004.
Bland architectural pile in a busy part of town, close to numerous shops and restaurants and handy for the beach – just as well, as the terrace that surrounds the pool is very cramped. On the up side, kitchens are well-equipped and prices are reduced by a third out of season. ❻.

Lagos de Fañabé

Map 11, B3. C/Londres, Fañabé, Las Américas
☎922/712 563
🅕922/712 129
Good value one- and two-bedroom apartments (sleeping up to four) in two-

storey buildings clustered in a small village between Fañabé's commercial area and the sea. Shared facilities include a pleasant garden and somewhat cramped sun decks and pools with chutes and slides to keep kids busy. ❺.

Mar y Sol
Map 13, N7. C/del General Franco, Los Cristianos.
ⓣ 922/750 540
ⓕ 922/790 573
ⓦ www.marysol.nu
Unspectacular but well-managed apartment block, thoughtfully developed so all facilities fully accommodate wheelchair users, for which the resident dive school also caters. Both studios and apartments are offered and the complex's facilities include three pools. Spa programmes and massages are also available. ❼.

Puerto Cólon Club
Map 11, B7. Puerto Cólon, Las Américas.
ⓣ 922/793 526

ⓕ 922/794 550
Simple, pretty harbour-side apartments owned by a private club that will rent accommodation to non-members at the last minute if they're not fully booked. Prices halve in low season. ❼.

Tenerife Sur
Map 13, M5. Avda Las Galletas, Los Cristianos.
ⓣ 922/791 474
ⓕ 922/792 774
Popular apartment complex built around a common busy pool and children's play area. Of the several different styles of apartment, most are relatively small, but stylish and well-equipped and come with a balcony. All units sleep up to four people (two on a sofabed in the living room) but are far more comfortable for two. On-site facilities include a squash court and a sauna. Rates are halved between mid-April and June. ❼.

ACCOMMODATION

PLAYA DE LA LAS AMÉRICAS

The reputation of Playa de las Américas as a concrete jungle of tackiness and hedonism is second to none in the Canaries. This three-kilometre long sprawl of hotel and apartment complexes, housing some 100,000 beds, divides up into a number of districts with subtly different characters.

Central Las Américas was thrown up in the 1970s to cash in on the booming tourist trade. What emerged was a number of particularly ugly complexes – but they were cheap and holidays here sold well, at least at first. By the mid-1980s the resort's popularity began to dwindle, partly from competition elsewhere and partly because many of the resort's facilities were becoming tatty and unappealing. Despite renovation attempts since, the bland concrete commercial centres at the heart of the resort remain – though they now house the throbbing nightlife for which the resort is notorious and as such form the main attraction for many young visitors to the island.

To improve the resort's image and finances there has been some effort to attract more affluent tourists, with four- and five-star hotels apearing in the more salubrious districts on the edges of Playa de las Américas. Just north of central Las Américas, **San Eugenio** and its British-dominated northern neighbour **Torviscas** have successfully become family destinations, while the new yachting marina **Puerto Colon** between the two is slowly emerging as a trendy stop-off for the yachting set. At the northern fringes of Las Américas is the soulless but relatively stylish and rapidly expanding resort of **Fañabé** – though visitors should be aware that its beach is still under construction as are many of its swanky hotels, which huddle around empty shopping centres. The **Gran Hotel Melia Bahía del Duque**, the most luxurious accommodation on the island, is at the northern end of this district.

Attempting to project a similar, exclusive image as Fañabé, **Los Moritos**, to the south of central Las Américas and bordering Los Cristianos (leaving it no space to sprawl) is near some of the least crowded beaches – the extravagant architecture of the five-star **Mare Nostrum Resort** setting the local tone.

Central Las Américas

One of the prettiest stretches of Las Américas' promenade is that by the narrow and rocky **Playa de Troya** (Map 12, C3), one of the few natural stretches of coastline on this part of the island. Though few visitors spend time here, it's popular with local surfers and bodyboarders who come to dodge rocks when the surf's good.

At the northern end of Playa de Troya are two commercial centres, **CC Vernoicas** (Map 12, C3) and **CC Starco** (Map 12, D3) – the centre of Las Américas and its least attractive part. By day there's not much going on in the bars and fast-food outlets here, but by night this area is packed with clubbers and touts (see p.174) To the north of this area are two very popular, but unattractive beaches – **Playa Las Cuevitas** (Map 12, C1) and **Playa del Bobo** (Map 11, C9) – where, in addition to the usual water sports, the Escuela del Vela Las Américas (☎922/792 050) teaches windsurfing and sailing; courses for beginners start from around €150.

San Eugenio

Busy **San Eugenio** flanks central Las Américas' northern side. Despite having a large commercial centre, the CC San Eugenio (Map 11, D7), and a harbour, Puerto Colón (see below), the resort is short of a good beach – the small **Playa La Pinta** (Map 11, B6) is a miserably crowded little cove surrounded by restaurants and by the harbour which obscures views out to sea. These shortcomings are partly compensated for by the presence of the **Octopus Aquapark** (Map 11, F6. Daily 10am–6pm; €13, under-14s €8, sun beds and lockers €1.50 each; ☎922/715 266; free buses from marked stops along the seafront road in Las Américas and near the bus station in Los Cristianos), a waterpark 1km inland and a good substitute for a beach. Sporting the usual array of pools, slides, islands, bridges and waterfalls the aquapark also puts on two daily **dolphin shows**. The complex is smaller than the ubiquitous advertising might suggest, so in high season it's best visited on Tuesdays or Fridays, the main flight days, when many holiday-makers are busy travelling – and avoided at weekends, when large numbers of local school kids often take over. The park's couple of cafés and bars are overpriced, so packing a lunch is a good idea. Try to remember regular doses of sunscreen when playing on the slides – many forget and fry.

San Eugenio's the small attractive marina, **Puerto Colon** (Map 11, A6) is a relatively recent addition to the area and one that has spruced up its image. The port's busy commercial centre is crowded with businesses and agencies organizing a range of **boat trips** from here and the harbour at Los Cristianos on a range of boats, including old wooden vessels and luxury yachts, glass-bottomed catamarans and so-called "booze cruises". Most trips head out to look for dolphins (see box on p.164) in the channel between Tenerife and La Gomera, or head north along the coast to the imposing cliffs of Los Gigantes, usually stopping for a swim and a snorkel along the way with sometimes a meal included. Typically, a two-hour trip will cost around €12 per person, a five-hour trip around €30. Some boats offer deep-sea fishing trips, starting from around €48 per person for a five-hour trip.

Torviscas and Fanabé

North of San Eugenio, the seafront promenade passes into Torviscas and past a large bazaar-like commercial centre overlooking **Playa de Torviscas** (Map 11, B4). This beach is crowded and nothing special, although Torviscas Watersports rents out kayaks and pedal boats for €9 an hour, as well as offering all the usual motorized thrills – jet skis, water-skis, parascending and inflated bananas.

A more promising beach is **Playa de Fañabé** (Map 11, A3), flanking the classier resort area of the same name. Most of the beach is still under construction, though some sections have already been populated by sun loungers and tropical-style thatched shades. Fañabé itself is emerging as the smartest resort in Las Américas, but is still rather dull, partly because many hotels here are yet to be completed.

Building work is particularly rampant on the northern fringes of **Costa Adeje** a resort based around a large golf course that seeks to differentiate itself from the sprawl of Las Américas in an effort to create a more upmarket area attracting high-spending golfers. The impressive **Gran Hotel Melia Bahía del Duque** is to be found here and by virtue of its lavish decor and extravagant architecture has developed into something of a tourist attraction. The hotel makes the most of the island's heritage – its buildings are all copies of nineteenth-century houses on the island and employees are required to wear traditional costume, which gives the place the rather odd feel of a living museum. Visitors are welcome to wander around the complex from 6.30pm onwards and though regulations stipulate a smart dress code, you should have no trouble getting in as long as you're not wearing shorts.

Casino Royal

Map 12, D8.

About as far east as you can go without being in Los
Cristianos is the Mare Nostrum Resort, and its **Casino
Royal** is the pride of Las Américas. An oversized pastiche
of Mexico's Chichén pyramids, and clearly trying to imitate
its larger cousins in Las Vegas, the casino is entered via a
Greek-style portal, past a cohort of Roman archers that
guard it from above.

LOS CRISTIANOS

Though it's difficult to tell where Los Cristianos finishes
and Las Américas begins, the centre of Los Cristianos,
nestling beside the steep bleak Montaña Chayofita and
the town's main beach and harbour is easy to identify.
The atmosphere here, while undeniably touristy, is much
less conspicuously synthetic and less tawdry than that of
its sprawling neighbour. This is mainly because it has
grown much more organically – from **fishing village** to
port and then, since the 1960s, to an agreeable and relatively **sedate resort** attracting families and a large con-
tingent of retired folk. Today, it is still home to many
Canarians. The town's pedestrianized centre is filled with
restaurants, shops and services targeting the many strolling
holiday-makers. Its relatively low-rise buildings overlook
the harbour and the substantial **Playa de Los
Cristianos**, while high-rise apartment blocks dominate
the outskirts of the town, particularly on its eastern side
towards the footslopes of the barren **Montaña Guaza**.
The town spreads a good way west of the harbour area,
too, melting with Las Américas along a rather theoretical
western boundary in the middle of the wide **Playa de
Las Vistas**.

Around the harbour

The town centre borders the pleasant busy **Playa de Los Cristianos** (Map 13, G7–H7) whose orderly rows of sun loungers look onto the bay containing the town's **harbour**. Once many fishing boats bobbed in these waters, but today they're overshadowed by pleasure boats and the many ferries carrying a million annual passengers to the neighbouring islands of La Palma, El Hierro and La Gomera (see p.225). The large array of vessels and companies offering **boat trips** from here are represented in a row of harbour-side booths, in front of which their touts cruise for custom. Similar to the trips run out of Las Américas, most trips incorporate whale and dolphin watching (see box overleaf).

Montañas Guaza and Chayofita

Map 10, F7 & Map 13 E3.

A pleasant **promenade**, popular for strolls at any time of day, passes the harbour and the Playa de Los Cristianos on its route along the town's entire seafront. It begins to the west of town, by the new and relatively uncrowded Playa de las Vistas, from where it joins the promenade running around Las Américas and hugs the coastline as it heads east past high-rise hotel blocks and touristy restaurants finishing just short of the bleak and shadeless 428-metre **Montaña Guaza** (Map 10, F7). You can climb Montaña Guaza from this point, in a route that crosses arid terrain via a steep rocky path before reaching terraced farm land higher up (2–3hr round trip). The views from the summit stretch far beyond Los Cristianos and Las Américas along the western coast and over the sea to La Gomera.

For a shorter hike, but with similar views, try the route up **Montaña Chayofita** (Map 13, E3). At 116m above the

WHALE AND DOLPHIN WATCHING

As many as twenty-six species of **whale** and **dolphin** have been spotted in the channel between Tenerife and La Gomera, but as development has grown along the coast and boat traffic has consequently increased, it appears that pods are under increased stress and have changed their behaviour patterns as a result.

While once both whales and dolphins came close to shore, they've now retreated into the deeper, less busy waters of the channel where today around forty vessels, carrying 700,000 annual whale-watchers, seek them out. Though the effects this has on the creatures has always been pondered, headlines were made and questions raised when the ferry to La Gomera collided with and killed some of them. Subsequent incidents have led to a number of studies, among them those of the Canarian Whale Institute, that have indicated that the marine life was showing clear symptoms of stress when being pursued by **tour boats**. Consequently, restrictions have been placed on boat safaris, which are now allowed no closer than 60m to the animals, or 200m if more than three boats are present. However, despite both boat and helicopter patrols, the system is hard to police and captains, keen to please passengers, tend to sneak nearer – in any case almost half the vessels don't have a whale-watching licence.

While there is talk of declaring the channel between Tenerife and La Gomera a **marine reserve**, it seems likely that this would ban fishing rather than the more lucrative leisure activities here. The possibility of incorporating radar and sonar detection equipment to ferries has also been discussed, but so far little concrete action has been taken and boat-tour operators still flatly deny their effect on the animals.

sea and near the centre of Los Cristianos, this is a good place to watch the sun set. The dirt road up begins on the hill's northern side (best found from the town centre by heading clockwise around its base) and eventually meets a path that loops around its big dusty crater.

PARQUES EXÓTICAS

Map 10, F6. Daily 10am–6pm; €10, under-13s €6 ☎ 922/795424.

Subdivided into Amazonia and the Cactus and Animal Park, this lovingly crafted zoo and park shows off its wares well. If you enjoy watching wildlife, or are a budding wildlife photographer, you will be here some time. **Amazonia** is a huge tent full of rainforest plants and animals, and though its flora is not as lush as you might expect, it does contain an interesting selection of exotic birds. It's best to take your time here, since you may well be rewarded with the sight of hummingbirds feeding. The rest of the park is given over to the **Cactus and Animal Park**. The leaflet you receive at the entrance jollies you around the cacti area, explaining the evolution of the cactus as well as, perhaps inevitably, pointing out their phallic suggestiveness. Unless you're a dedicated fan you'll probably not linger here, but head for the animal enclosures. These are exceptionally well designed, and allow entry to enclosures such as a bat cave, a butterfly garden and a small reptile house, getting you as near to the animals as they – and you – are comfortable with.

JARDINES DEL ATLANTICO: BANANERA

Map 10, G6. Daily tours 10am, 11.30am, 1pm, 3.30pm & 4.15pm; €6, under -13s €3, under-4s free ☎ 922/720 403, Ⓦ www.azulnet.com/bananer

The region's most refreshingly low-key attraction is

Bananera an adapted family **farm** near Buzanada around which tours are conducted to give a good introduction to Tenerife's agriculture. There's nothing particularly exciting about the farm, so your enjoyment of your visit will depend for a large part on the input of your guide. Each **tour** lasts around an hour and starts and finishes with a free shot of liqueur.

As you'd expect from the attraction's name, the **banana** features heavily on the tour, as do explanations of the problems associated with its cultivation. Banana trees are thirsty plants, each consuming about one hundred litres of water each month. Given the island's dearth of naturally available fresh water, Tenerife's system of underground aquifers, which together span 1600km and are explained using scale models of the island in cross-section, is an essential but dwindling reserve. Desalination plants will secure most of the water in the future, though this will price water beyond the realms of economical agriculture, a problem that is at the heart of the banana industry's future on the island, and one that is discussed along with other problems, such as the EU's ban on its export (it's too small) and its unappetising black spots (hence its nickname, El Tigre).

Tours finish with a look at a number of endemic species of non-cultivated plants grown in the farm's gardens, which also produce some of the ingredients used in the good-value set meals offered in the **restaurant**, open daily from noon to 4pm.

PARQUE ECOLÓGICO LAS AGUILAS DEL TEIDE

Map 10, E5. Daily 10am–6pm; E*14, under 13s €6; Free shuttle bus from Las Américas and Los Cristianos ☎ 922/753 001.

Though considered one of Tenerife's premier tourist attractions, this highly commercial bird park, perched on hills overlooking Las Américas, is not all that entertaining and doesn't seem like particularly good value for money. Contrasting strikingly with the aridity of the land outside the complex, the park is filled with lush vegetation. In amongst this greenery are a number of bird and animal enclosures, a metal bobsleigh run (E★1.50 per run) and an assault course made from ropes and cargo nets. The main attractions are, however, the **bird shows**. Exotic birds perform at 11am and 2pm when, among other displays, you'll be able to catch the parrot "Scoobiedoo" ride a scooter, and two Kookaburras, "Bruce" and "Sheila", wrestle a rubber snake. The show's pretty kitsch and its music doesn't help. Still, the displays of intelligence in the show, question the term "bird-brain", and consequently suggests the frustration of the hundreds of caged birds in the park. The greater attraction, as the park's name implies, is the eagle show (*Aguilas* are eagles). Here various birds of prey swoop low over the crowd to earn morsels from their trainer's hands – you're best sitting on the lower rows for maximum effect. Flying times are at noon and 4pm, but avoid visiting on windy days when neither this nor the exotic bird show works as well as it should and often needs to be curtailed. There are a number of over-priced restaurants and cafés in the complex.

EATING

For picnic food, and snacks, try the bakery *Boutique Amady,* Edif. Lord Nelson 5, which has a huge well-presented selection of quality breads, cakes and pastries.

Scattered in among the vast number of mediocre places to eat in **Las Américas** are a few good restaurants serving a fair range of international cuisines between them. Most restaurants are open longer hours than elsewhere on the

EATING

island, often not closing in the afternoon – particularly those places by the promenade. After midnight, when most of the restaurants have closed, it's still possible to get food from international fast-food outlets in the centre, and from local vendors selling kebabs and such like. Despite its seaside location, good fish- and seafood-restaurants are surprisingly rare in Las Américas, making the short trip to the popular restaurants of the small fishing village **La Caleta** (regular buses from the bus station in Las Américas) just to north of the resort worthwhile. Three restaurants are particularly popular here – *Piscis* is the most expensive and stylish, while the *La Caleta* is more moderately priced and makes the most of its seafront setting. The *Celso*, the most functional of the three, is especially good value, particularly popular with locals, and offers a range of preparation techniques beyond just grilling.

A large number of cafés and restaurants vie for custom along the seafront and in the centre of **Los Cristianos**. Few are anything special, making it worth either heading out to local favourites on the less atmospheric fringes of town or to the simple inexpensive tapas bars on the western edge of the pedestrian district. The harbour area, also just west of the centre, is notable for its small collection of good seafood restaurants. Fast-food needs are served by American chains on the beachfront, though tastier, better value local delicacies can be had from many of the town's supermarkets, which offer picnic food such as a whole freshly grilled garlic chicken for around €4.

Each restaurant listed in the *Guide* has been categorized as either inexpensive (under €6), moderate (€6– €10) and expensive (above €10) – indicating the price of an average main course.

LAS AMÉRICAS

Cantina Lupita

Map 11, B3. CC Fañabé.
Cheerful, brightly coloured
Mexican restaurant on the
promenade where it
overlooks Fañabé's new
beaches. Dishes include
burritos, chimichangas,
chargrilled vegetables, Tacos
and salads. Though the food
is a bit bland by Mexican
standards, it can be spiced up
on request. Moderate.

Cervecería Central

Map 12, F7. El Camisón, local
17–18, Los Moritos.
A branch of the classy and
popular Santa Cruz
restaurant, serving a good
range of food from coffees
and cakes, to filled rolls,
omelettes and a good variety
of tapas. Full meals, mostly
Spanish or Canarian fish and
meat dishes are also available
in the evenings. Moderate.

El Duque

Map 11, A1. Gran Hotel Bahía
del Duque, Fañabé.
☎ 922/713 000
One of the most expensive
restaurants on the island, this
place serves a changing and
carefully chosen range of
international dishes in
Neoclassical surroundings.
The menu includes the
simple but superb house
speciality, seafood lasagne,
and an extensive selection of
wines. Dress is smart casual.
Closed Sun & June.
Expensive.

El Gomero

Map 12, F2. Edif. Las Terrazas.
Straightforward Canarian
restaurant with speedy service
at vinyl-covered tables. The
menu offers a decent range of
fish dishes, including a
selection of paellas, plus good
steaks and reasonable, filling
set meals. Closed Sun.
Inexpensive.

Harley's American Diner

Map 11, C6. Torviscas.
☎ 922/713 040
Its presence announced by a
fleet of American vehicles
outside, *Harley's* is a theme-
bar and restaurant offering a
wide range of cocktails and
meals. The eclectic menu at

EATING

the bar includes large portions of American favourites such as nachos and fajitas as well as cannelloni, sweet-and-sour chicken and a number of vegetarian options. The restaurant gets busy in the evenings, so it's worth booking ahead – or being prepared to drink patiently in the back of a Cadillac while you wait for a table. Moderate to expensive.

The King And I

Map 11, E8. Local 12B Garden City San Eugenio
℡ 922/750 350

Great Thai food served in a plain little restaurant on the eastern side of San Eugenio. Though a little more expensive than surrounding restaurants, the quality of the massive range of available dishes – including good green curries, chilli squid, ginger mushrooms and a great papaya salad – ultimately makes the place good-value. Moderate to expensive.

Las Rocas Beach Club

Map 11, C8. *Hotel Jardín Tropical*, San Eugenio.

Small cliff-top beach club, where exclusive dining is offered to visitors as well as hotel guests on a terrace overlooking the sea. The restaurant specializes in rice and seafood dishes – particularly recommended are the paellas, including one vegetarian version. Expensive.

Little Italy

Map 11, B3. CC Fañabé.

A new branch of the popular local chain of Italian restaurants, serving dependably good pizza and pasta in pleasant, if unmemorable surroundings. Moderate.

Mamma Rosa

Map 12, D5. Apartments Colón II, Los Moritos
℡ 922/797 823

Smart little Italian restaurant serving delicious pasta and pizza as well as the excellent juicy sirloin steak á la Mamma Rosa – the house speciality. Meals are sometimes served to the accompaniment of live accordion music. Expensive.

EATING

Passaparola

Map 12, G7. El Camisón Local 50, Los Moritos.
℡922/798 214

Simple, small Italian-run restaurant, ten minutes' walk from Playa de las Vistas in a strip of restaurants popular with locals as well as tourists. Serves good pizza and pasta and excellent antipasta. Moderate.

Slow Boat I

Map 11, B7. CC Puerto Colon
℡922/796 423

Part of a popular and successful local chain serving quality Chinese (mostly Cantonese) meals at reasonable prices. A bottle of wine is often included in the price of the meal. Take out is available. Moderate.

LOS CRISTIANOS

Casa del Mar

Map 13, E6. Esplanada del Muelle
℡922/793 275

Large, consistently popular, first-floor fish restaurant in a great location with a terrace that overlooks the bay and harbour. There's always a good selection of fresh fish here, and though the food costs a bit above the local average, the size and quality of portions ultimately makes the place good value. Closed Mon. Moderate.

Corisa

Map 13, I5. C/de Antigua General Franco 18

Basic central restaurant with bright lights and vinyl table cloths. It serves good simple fish, seafood and meat dishes – the ménu del dia, which includes wine, is particularly good value. Inexpensive to moderate.

El Caserío

Map 13, E6. Plaza Las Fuentes

Simple Canarian restaurant, combining elements of the tourist aesthetic (dim lighting and wooden furniture) with traditional, no-frills food. The large menu includes dishes such as stews, rabbit, octopus and a good selection of fish. Open evenings only. Inexpensive.

EATING

El Gomerón
Map 13, K3. Edif. Royal
Cheap eatery, with stylish chrome tables on a shady road-side patio near the bus station. The restaurant is popular with locals for its straightforward Canarian food, including a decent range of fish and seafood and some good steaks. Inexpensive.

Little Italy
Map 13, G6. C/Pablo Abril 1
This branch of the dependable local Italian-restaurant chain has views over the beach and harbour and the option of street-side dining. The chain's formula – reasonably priced pizza and pasta served at dimly lit check-cloth covered tables – has been popular and successful enough for it to open over a dozen generic outlets around central Los Cristianos as well as one in Las Américas (see p.170). Moderate.

Pitaland
Map 13, H5. Edif. Reverón

Good local fast-food restaurant, opening as late as anywhere in town. Options here include stuffed pitas, as well as pizzas, burgers and sandwiches. Inexpensive.

Pizza Cut
Map 13, G5. CC Don Antonio
Good quality Italian fast food in a quiet, shady but sterile shopping-centre courtyard. Closed Sat & Sun. Inexpensive.

Rincón del Mero
Map 13, E6. Esplanada del Muelle
℡ 922/793 553
Functional restaurant squeezed in beside the underpass to Playa de Las Vistas. Only good fresh fish and seafood grace the menu – including dishes such as parrot fish, tuna, sole, hake, scampi, cockles and octopus. Moderate.

Slow Boat V
Map 13, I6. Edif. Bucanero
℡ 922/796 163
Branch of the reliable local Chinese-restaurant chain –

this one with views over the bay. Try the excellent varied (mostly Cantonese) banquets from around €12. Take out is also available. Moderate.

Trattoria La Foccacia
Map 13, F5. Ramon Pino 32
Strip-lit restaurant with small terrace serving some of the best value Italian food in town, including a large selection of competitively priced pizzas. The pasta in particular comes in many creative incarnations, with numerous shapes and sauces offered. Daily 2pm–11pm. Inexpensive to moderate.

NIGHTLIFE AND ENTERTAINMENT

Nightlife in Las Américas is vast in quantity but limited in variety, based as it is around clubs and fun-pubs churning out live music of dubious quality, often by celebrity lookalikes. Though numerous bars and restaurants are to be found throughout the resort, three commercial centres are particularly renowned for their high concentration of bars and clubs. The first, **CC Veronicas** is the most notorious and centrepiece of the alcohol-fuelled, nocturnal world from which this resort gets a large part of its reputation. Slightly more salubrious is **CC Starco**, across the road, which contains fewer clubs, but more bars, and tends to get busy earlier (from around 10pm) – only when bars here close (at around 3am), do patrons migrate to the clubs in Veronicas. In both of these areas you'll be accosted every few paces by a tout trying to drag you into a club or bar; for more on these, see the box on p.174. The third area, **The Patch** is in northern Los Moritos, and tends to cater to an older clientele. Filled with more than its fair share of naff restaurants and unattractive bars full of plastic patio furniture, venues here tend to dabble in vaguely music hall-style cabaret, or host musicians impersonating the likes of Elvis Presley, Elton John, Tina Turner or Billy Idol.

NIGHTLIFE AND ENTERTAINMENT

TOUTS

While being **touted** to go into the various bars and clubs in the resorts can quickly become irritating, you can use the system to your own advantage, since most clubs give discounts on your first drinks (usually well above normal island prices), if you arrive accompanied by a tout. And to make the most of the system, it therefore pays to swap bars frequently. (No cover charge is levied at any of the bars or clubs in town.) However, before going in anywhere, you'd be well advised to check it's not empty first. The proliferation of bars and clubs mean that though all usually fill with patrons eventually, particularly in the summer months, many also have long idle spells in the early evening, – particularly in the off season – when they are devoid of atmosphere.

By virtue of its popularity with an older set of holiday-makers, **nightlife in Los Cristianos** is much more sedate than that in Las Américas, with just one notable bar in the centre and a couple worth checking out on the fringes of the resort.

LAS AMÉRICAS

Aside from what's listed below, there's the flamboyant shows of the **Pirámide de Arona** at the Mare Nostrum Resort (☎922/796 360), which puts on various acts, including regular and reasonable flamenco, occasional ballet and the odd theatre performance. Tickets bought through agents and hotels are usually cheaper than those at the venue. There's also the **Casino Royal** in the same complex for classy gambling in smart dress only – note that you'll need to take your passport along as ID here. A curious but popular and well-promoted evening attraction (and served by shuttle buses from the resorts – pickup arranged with ticket purchase) is a large beige, breeze block castle, **Castillo San Miguel**, on the road to Buzanada, off the San Miguel – Autopista del Sur road (Jctn 62), that hosts mock jousting and much other medieval-style merriment (Mon, Wed, Thurs & Sat 8pm; from €24). After a kitsch banquet *The Drifters* take the stage playing 60s hits to round things off. Tickets are available through various hotels or can be bought on the door at 7.30pm.

Bobby's

Map 12, C3. CC Las Veronicas
Thanks to exposure in a Sky TV docusoap, this dark first-floor club is the most famous in Veronicas. It shares a landing with another, similar club *Busby's*. Both get busy from about 2am and concentrate on pumping out thumping dance music onto their meat–market dance floors.

Bonkers

Map 12, C3. CC Las Veronicas
Small busy basement club playing contemporary pop and many standard party favourites. The club's DJs try to showcase themselves, interspersing music with somewhat feeble, but somehow captivating, attempts at entertaining cabaret. *Bonkers* tends to get busier earlier than many other clubs, chiefly due to arrangements it has with tour operators who bring their flocks of fun seekers here on nights out.

Dubliner Pub

Map 12, C5. *Hotel Las Palmeras*, Los Moritos.
Dependable source of good craic in a fun atmosphere near The Patch. The pubs popularity is based on word-of-mouth rather than busy touts, with an enthusiastic live band playing a mix of vaguely contemporary hits to a large, mixed-age crowd. Busiest between 10pm and 4am.

Leopard Lounge

Map 12, C3. CC Las Veronicas
Stylish, though often empty club on the southern side of

Veronicas. Unusually for the area, it is patronized by a high proportion of non-British holiday-makers.

Lineker's Bar

Map 12, D3. CC Starco
Fun party atmosphere orchestrated nightly by DJs in a bar owned by former England footballer Gary Lineker and run by his brother. This is one of the few places to get going early (around 10pm) and the bar is also open during the day (from noon) to peddle souvenir merchandise and show live sporting events.

Moonlight Fun Pub

Map 11, B4. Pueblo Torviscas
Consistently popular fun-pub drawing a mixed-age crowd to its excellent location overlooking the ocean from a seafront promenade. Cheesy nightly shows feature Billy Idol and Tina Turner lookalikes.

Noctooa

Map 12, C3. Beside CC Las Veronicas
Vast club almost exclusively

patronized by locals. The place is packed and fun on weekends and devoid of the tawdry, down-at-heel atmosphere present in nearby Veronicas.

Soul Train

Map 12, D3. CC Starco
Large dark basement club serving up R&B and hip-hop, this is one of the few venues in Las Américas not playing Techno or dance music. Usually gets going from around 3am.

Tunnel

Map 12, C3. CC Las Veronicas
When most clubs are closing, this dingy basement club begins to fill, mostly with cliques of off-duty touts from the other clubs, who tend to be a bit stand-offish towards outsiders. Trance, hard house and garage thumps here until dawn.

LOS CRISTIANOS

La Bohéme

Map 13, G5. C/Juan XXIII 16
A stylish cocktail bar mostly

CHRISTIAN WILLIAMS

Carnival parade, Santa Cruz

CHRISTIAN WILLIAMS

Orotava Valley, near Los Organos

CHRISTIAN WILLIAMS

Playa de las Terisitas, near Santa Cruz

Los Cristianos

Ten-Bel Resort, Costa del Silencio

CHRISTIAN WILLIAMS

CHRISTIAN WILLIAMS

CHRISTIAN WILLIAMS

Pico del Teide

CHRISTIAN WILLIAMS

The table-top mountain La Fortaleza, La Gomera

popular with young Canarians.

Café Mestiz

Map 13, I6. Paseo Maritimo. A pleasant laid-back terrace bar with a vaguely South American theme, whose drinks menu includes some good cocktails.

Chicago's

Map 13, I6. Paseo Maritimo. An American theme bar with a large terrace that overlooks the sea, serves a good range of American–style bar food..

Establo

Map 13, G6. C/Pablo Abril 5 By virtue of being the only disco in the centre of the resort, the mediocre Establo has a stranglehold on the tiny Los Cristianos club scene. Closed mid-Nov to mid-Dec.

LISTINGS

Banks and Exchanges The travel agent, Viajes Islazul C/Juan XXIII 8, Los Cristianos (☎922/750 026, Ⓔgarvin@santandersupernet.com), usually has better rates than any of the town's many banks. American Express is represented by Viajes Insular, Residencial El Camisón, Los Cristianos (☎922/790 154).

Bike rental Bicisport (☎922/751 829), Edif. el Arenal, beside the post office, Los Cristianos; Cycling Diga Sports, Park Club Europe, Los Moritos (☎922/793 009; Ⓕ922/176 837). Diga Sports also arranges biking tours and rents out inline skates by the hour and day.

Car rental OrCar at CC Puerto Colon (☎922/714 280), Las Flores in San Eugenio (☎922/795 470), Tenerife Royal Garden (☎922/753 771), and CC Fañabé (☎922/712 068).

Fishing Crested Wave (☎922/797 469) and Nauti Sport (☎922/791 459; Ⓦwww.dotsytoo.com) organize deep-sea fishing trips from their harbour-side kiosks.

Gym Bouganville Hotel (℡922/790 200), includes sauna and massage facilities. Daily and weekly membership available.

Hospital Hospital Las Américas, on the border with Los Cristianos. For an ambulance, call ℡922/780 759,

Internet access in CC San Eugenio (€5 per hour). Word Computer Systems, C/Juan XXIII 37, Los Cristianos (€5 per hour).

Language courses Centro de Estudíos, Mercury 8 (℡922/767 059; ℮cemercury@terra.es).

Laundry In Edif. Simon, just north of the bus station (daily 9am–9pm); in the basement of the *Hotel Villamar*, central Las Américas; at the Lavandería Royale, Edif. Parque Royale.

Pharmacy There's a 24-hour pharmacy beside CC Starco. There are several pharmacies scattered around the northern side of the pedestrian area in Los Cristianos, including the Pharmacía, C/General Franco 23.

Police For the location of the nearest municipal police station call ℡922/797 850. In Los Cristianos, the Municipal Police Station is on C/Valle Mendez beside the cultural centre and tourist office at the east end of town (℡922/757 133).

Scuba diving Gruber Diving, inside the Park Club Europe building (℡922/752 708); Wreck and Reef, in Vista Sur, beside Playa de Las Vistas (℡922/796 791; ℮jedl@arrakis.es); Barakuda Club in Playa Paraiso (℡922/780 725; ⓦwww.divers-net.de/teneriffa); Club de Buceo Rincón de Arona, Muelle, Los Cristianos (℡922/79

35 50; Ⓔrincondearona@lettera.net); Aqua Sport in the Mar y Sol apartment block (Ⓣ922/797 797).

Taxi From one of the ranks along the main seafront road in Las Américas, or by calling Ⓣ922/791 407. Beside the Plaza del Carmen in Los Cristianos, or call Ⓣ922/790 352.

Tennis Tenisur, next to the Octopus Aquapark (Ⓣ922/796 167), rents out courts and organizes lessons and tournaments.

Travel agents Butterfly Booking Agency, CC Puerto (Ⓣ922/712 095), for local excursion; Flight Center, CC Americas Shopping, adjacent to Parque Santiago II, Los Moritos (Ⓣ922/793 819; Ⓦwww.tenerife-uk.com/flight-center), for charter flights to the UK, Left-luggage service, showers and changing rooms. Viajes Islazul C/Juan XXIII 8 (Ⓣ922/750 026; Ⓔgarvin@santandersupernet.com) for cheap international flights.

The southern coast

Since Tenerife's international airport is on the **southern coast**, this hot and dusty region forms most visitors' first impression of the island. Though now overshadowed by the vast resorts of nearby Las Américas and Los Cristianos, the tourist resorts here were going strong a decade earlier, and the rate of new development in them today still matches that of its larger neighbours. The massive hotel complex **Ten-Bel**, beside the small workaday town of **Las Galletas**, was one of the island's first truly huge holiday complexes and, despite the presence of only a slim shingle beach, the large bland resort area known as the **Costa del Silencio**, has grown up beside it. Further east is the **Golf del Sur**, a new resort centred around two large golf courses. Further east still is the most stylish and picturesque town along this stretch of coast, **El Médano**, whose vast, windswept beaches are the only significant natural ones on the island.

Map 10 covers southern Tenerife.

While the southern coastal region is largely flat and barren, the monotony is broken by a number of hills: **Rasca** in the west and **Roja** and **Pelada** in the east are all designated as nature reserves to protect the area's delicate ecosystems,

ACCOMMODATION PRICE CODES

Throughout the *Guide*, accommodation has been graded according to price, based on the cost of the cheapest double room in high season – but excluding the time around Christmas and New Year, when rates can rocket. In the case of apartments that sleep more than two, the price for the smallest available unit, as described in the body text, is given; where apartments are available by the night, the price refers to the cheapest two-person apartment. Where singles – which are usually more than half the price of doubles – are available, this has also been mentioned. Travellers wanting to stay a week or more may find that nightly rate can be reduced a little.

❶ up to €12	❺ €48– €60
❷ €12–€24	❻ €60– €84
❸ €24–€36	❼ €84– €120
❹ €36– €48	❽ over €120

and each offers pretty coastal **hikes** and excellent **mountain-bike** opportunities. The coastal waters also attract the active, with numerous **diving** concerns operating in the relatively clear waters beside Las Galletas and El Médano usually thronging with large numbers of **windsurfers** attracted to the world-class conditions here.

LAS GALLETAS AND THE COSTA DEL SILENCIO

Map 10, G8–H9.

Though largely given over to the tourist industry, **LAS GALLETAS** still has the feel of a small coastal town with a handful of shops, bars and restaurants scattered along the seafront and inland along its main pedestrian street. Beside Las Galletas the large **COSTA DEL SILENCIO** resort now forms a couple of miles of almost uninterrupted development containing numerous expat businesses – mostly restaurants and bars. In the absence of any real beach, growth here is spurred on by the success of the complex-oriented holiday, as begun at **Ten-Bel** in the 1960s, and an apparently boundless demand for holiday and retirement apartments in southern Tenerife.

Certainly, it's not the peace along this stretch that encourages tourism, its name – meaning "Coast of Silence" – something of a misnomer since the opening of the nearby international airport in 1978. Yet it's only at peak flying times that you notice the planes – for the most part it is the continual din of pneumatic drills and cement mixers on the numerous building sites that is most likely to disturb the peace. For this reason alone, it is worth avoiding the eastern end of town on most weekdays. Just beyond the noise of these building sites, however, is the small protected area around **Montaña Amarilla**, which provides a respite from development as does the undeveloped rocky outcrop containing some spectacular cacti just beyond. While to the west of Las Galletas, **Rasca Nature Reserve** offers a similar arid landscape and is a good location for hikes west to **Montaña Guaza**, centre of another nature reserve.

Arrival and information

Public buses link Las Galletas with Los Cristianos and the airport. Services stop along the main road skirting the town's inland side and beside the Ten-Bel holiday complex. There's a **tourist-office** booth (Mon–Fri 9am–1pm & 4–7pm, Sat 9am –1pm; ☎922/730 133) in the pedestrian avenue, La Rambla behind the seafront promenade.

Accommodation

Other than the massive holiday village **Ten-Bel**, there are only a few small simple **pensions** in Las Galletas, and although there are a large number of self-catering **apartments** in the neighbouring Costa del Silencio, most are reserved for package-holiday deals and are of no use to the independent traveller. However, an **accommodation agency**, the Trading Post, La Rambla 8 (☎922/730 058), near the tourist-office booth, can usually fix you up with an apartment in the area. One of the island's few campsites is also nearby. *Camping Nauta* (☎922/785 118) is 2km inland of Las Galletas just off the road to Guaza north of Pension La Estrella at Cañada Blanca; its basic facilities include a swimming pool and a rudimentary sports area. The tent sites (€3 per person) are dusty and uninviting, but most of the site is given over to basic cabins sleeping up to four (€12)

Pension Cano

C/Galván Bello 9, Las Galletas
☎922/731 138
Slightly cramped rooms, all with shared baths, this is the cheaper of two pensions in Las Galletas (the other is *Pension Los Vinitos*). ❷.

Pension La Estrella

Avda del Atlantico, km 1.
☎922/731 562
A kilometre inland from Las Galletas and on a busy road, this place offers a mix of rooms, some with en-suite bathrooms, and all at reasonable rates. Be warned that the plumbing tends to

back up, though – a point worth bearing in mind if you're looking for an en-suite room. ❷

Pension Los Vinitos

C/de Venezuela 4, Las Galletas
☎922/785 803
The smarter of two simply decorated and reliable pensions in Las Galletas (the other is *Pension Cano*), the rooms here are a little less cramped and each has a private bath. ❷.

Ten-Bel

Map 10, G9. Avda del Atlantico, Las Galletas

Ⓣ 922/730 721
Ⓕ 922/731 259
Ⓦ www.tenbel.com

Despite now having a somewhat institutional, nostalgically 1960s, feel, this Belgian-masterminded holiday village has stood the test of time surprisingly well. The 4500-bed complex offers six types of apartment from simple studio flats to apartments sleeping up to seven people, most with balconies and housed in large concrete blocks scattered around the complex, some overlooking the sea. Communal facilities include tennis courts and a large salt-water pool by a tiny beach around which guests, lounge or take part in aerobics programmes. Most visitors book this accommodation from home as part of a package deal, but it can be booked on site in the office beside the neighbouring CC Ten-Bel. ❷.

The town and resort

A pleasant enough Canarian coastal town in its own right, **Las Galletas** mainly attracts visitors to its large adjoining resort area, the **Costa del Silencio**. As the nearest urban centre to this resort, the town has a small collection of modest shops, restaurants and cafés – many of which line the promenade that adjoins a small **harbour area**, itself a pleasant place for a short stroll. The main shopping area, however, is further inland, along the pedestrianized, **Calle Central**, one of a number of narrow streets lined with the nondescript modern buildings that make up the town centre. From here it's a short walk south to another, more pleasant, but considerably less lively pedestrianized area, the tree-lined avenue **La Rambla** that hems in buildings along the seafront. Here you'll find a small selection of restaurants overlooking a slender promenade and a narrow pebble beach, where the waves crashing along the rocky shoreline attract local surfers and body-boarders. The **beach** continues well west of town, though its length is interrupted by a large concrete sea defence, built to shelter fishing boats in the tiny harbour. The murky waters of the small man-made bay are home to a number of small fishing boats as well as vessels belonging to the town's numerous diving schools, all are watched over by the handful of sunbathers that regularly lie on the surrounding pebble beach.

The focal point of Costa del Silencio is east of Las Galletas along Avenida Tavio Alfonso, the main road through the resort. The main centres of activity along this stretch are three charmless commercial centres: **CC Trebol** and **CC El Chaparral**, opposite each other and beside Ten-Bel at the western end of the road, and **CC Coralmar Square**, at the eastern end. Each mall contains a similar collection of shops and services, from small supermarkets and travel agents to restaurants and bars.

Montaña Amarilla

Map 10, H8.

East of Costa del Silencio the development ends abruptly and the wild and rugged coastline affords a welcome break from the strip of development. It is the protected landscape around **Montaña Amarilla** that has prevented the eastward sprawl of the resort. The twisted striking landforms around its base border a sheltered bay where bathing ladders give access to clear waters. The short ascent of the hill itself is worthwhile for the view over both the resort and a rocky wasteland where magnificent cacti thrive.

Rasca nature reserve

For a longer hike, through a similarly dusty and wild landscape, head west out of Las Galletas, past its harbour to the little-visited **Rasca nature reserve**. It's 4km along the rocky coastline dotted with small thorny shrubs and cacti to one of the few landmarks in the reserve, a **lighthouse** (Map 10, E9), and a further 3km along a barren and beautiful, undeveloped stretch to the village of **PALM MAR** (Map 10, E8). Large-scale building development is currently under way around this village, filling the steep-sided valley with apartments and covering its pebble beach with sand – the beginnings of yet another large resort in southern Tenerife. Climbing north out of the Palm Mar valley, a steep path (the only real climb on this hike) leads up into the protected area around the peak of **Montaña Guaza** (Map 10, F7) and tremendous views over Playa Las Americás and Los Cristianos. From here the path begins a narrow rocky descent via a seafront promenade to Los Cristianos (see p.162) from where regular buses head back to Las Galletas. The entire hike (approx. 10km) takes around six hours and is devoid of shade and services, so be sure to come prepared.

Eating

Each restaurant listed in the *Guide* has been categorized as either inexpensive (under €6), moderate (€6– €10) and expensive (above €10) – indicating the price of an average main course.

Most of the restaurants in **Las Galletas** line the promenade, serving fresh seafood at moderate prices. A couple of good cafés also along here serve snacks and great ice cream – try the excellent rich, creative ice creams at *Valentio* La Rambla 22, by the harbour – though the bulk of the town's cafés are on the pedestrianized Calle Central inland.

Over on the **Costa del Silencio** almost all the restaurants are in the three commercial centres along Avenida

Tavio Alfonso; many of these are run by expats, with menus from northern Europe aimed squarely at the holiday-makers wanting familiar food.

Cafeteria Los Vinitos

C/Venezuela, Las Galletas.
Around the corner from the pension of the same name, this is one of a number of cafés sprawling over the town's only pedestrianized street and as good a place as any to head for snacks and light lunches. Along with the filled croissants, sandwiches, hamburgers and omelettes, there's also a good range of tapas and a selection of fresh-pressed juices. Inexpensive.

Carnaval

Paseo Maritima, Las Galletas.
A dimly lit and atmospheric place in a strip of otherwise functional seafood restaurants along the promenade. Salads, hamburgers and sandwiches are served for lunch, while the varied dinner menu includes numerous seafood options and unusual offerings such as ostrich. Moderate.

Colibri Playa

Paseo Maritima, Las Galletas.
Popular with locals, this basic, strip-lit restaurant on the promenade has one of the largest, least expensive selections of fish and seafood in town. The menu varies according to the day's catch, but portions are always generous. Inexpensive.

L'alpage

La Estrella 7, Las Galletas.
℡ 922/730 577
Excellent, unpretentious Swiss restaurant sporting heavy alpine-style furnishings and red-check table cloths. It's a bit of a trek out of town – 1km along Avenida del Atlantico, next to Pension La Estrella – but worth it for the wide range of wonderful fondue and rösti dishes. Closed Sun. Moderate to expensive

La Herradura

C/Candida Pena Bello 2, Las Galletas.
Restaurant and bar serving tapas and sandwiches below a

blaring TV. The large, though unimaginative, restaurant menu includes lots of meat and a few fish dishes along with a fairly comprehensive selection of pizzas. Inexpensive.

Old Brussels

CC Trebol, Costa del Silencio.
Stylish, dimly lit Belgian-run restaurant with an adventurous menu, offering unusual dishes such as springbok and rabbit in dark beer. Moderately expensive.

Totem

CC El Chaparral, Costa del Silencio.
Popular and colourful restaurant, with interesting decor involving totem poles and intimate lighting. The menu includes some fish and meat dishes (including pork and veal medallions) as well as the inevitable selection of pizza and pasta. Moderate.

Drinking and nightlife

While the teeming nightlife associated with nearby Playa Las Américas is conspicuously absent in Las Galletas and the Costa del Silencio, a wide variety of bars serve drinks well into the small hours every night. Locals tend to congregate in the bars of **Las Galletas** to watch sport on TV and eat tapas. *Bar Paropo*, C/La Arena, is the pick of the bunch, here – small, smoky and atmospheric, its walls are covered in beer mats and diverse memorabilia and, unusually in town, the option of drinking at outside tables too.

Theme pubs predominate in the commercial centres of **Costa del Silencio**. If watching sport on widescreen TVs is your thing, then you'll find plenty of bars to choose from in CC Trebol. For something a little more stylish, try the *Peanut Disco Bar* in CC El Chapparal, one of a handful of bars, many of which quickly come and go, in the same centre. The area's single, low-key, disco, *Disco Lord* (closed Tues & Wed), also in CC El Chapparal, is nothing special, pumping out the usual array of chart music and hosting 60s and 70s nights. At the newer, eastern end of the resort, CC Coralmar Square is home to around a dozen, mostly British, bars that sometimes club together to provide live entertainment (such as mediocre cabaret) in a central courtyard.

Listings

Banks and Exchanges Several banks are clustered around the northern end of Calle Central, but it is an estate agent – Properties Nina C/La Arena (☎922/786449) – that generally provides the best rate in town.

Car Rental Trading post, La Rambla 8 (☎922/730 058).

Internet *Explorers internet c@fe*, Avda Tavio Alfonso 1 (Mon–Fri & Sun 1pm–1am; €4.6 per hour).

Laundry At CC Ten-Bel (daily 9am–11pm).

Post Office C/Luis A. Cruz, at the northern end of Calle Central.

Scuba diving Buceo Tenerife, C/Maria del Carmen Garcia 22 (☎922/731 015).

Taxi ☎922/390 924.

GOLF DEL SUR

Map 10, J8.

As the name suggests, golf is the main business in the **GOLF DEL SUR**, site of two courses and proposed locations for a further three. In fact there's little else here, save for a modest, unfinished commercial centre, **CC San Blas**; containing a few bars, restaurants and car-rental outlets, it serves as a focal point for the sprawling streets of low-rise apartments and several acres of ongoing construction.

GOLF DEL SUR

Most of the holiday **accommodation** here caters for high-spending golfers, who can choose from the *Hotel Occidental Tenerife Golf* (☎ 922/738 566, ℱ 922/738 889; ➐) and the *Hotel Aguamarina Golf* (☎ 922/714 378, ℱ 922/715 875; ➐). Both are by the sea and offer four-star facilities including pools, exercise rooms and restaurants, but are currently surrounded by building sites. Accommodation in the rest of town consists of inexpensive, low-rise self-catering apartments catering to the package-holiday industry. Independent travellers should contact the Los Cristianos based *Apolo Services* (☎ 922/790 251; ℱ 922/797 026; ℮ apoloprop@arrakis.es), who can organize studios or apartments here from €211 a week.

EL MÉDANO

Map 10, M7.
Best known for its long sandy beaches and breezy conditions, allowing great year-round windsurfing, the small town of **EL MÉDANO**, 7km east of the Golf del Sur, has developed into a laid-back resort for sporty types. As a pioneer of tourism in the region, the town has not escaped the on-going building boom, yet it has managed to retain a pleasant easy-going atmosphere thanks to some thoughtful development and its continued popularity with Tenerifian's, many of whom have holiday homes here.

The central **Plaza Principe de Asturia**, which joins a boardwalk spanning the length of the large, natural main beach is lined with shops selling clothing and watersports paraphernalia to the windsurfing crowd that congregate here; and the presence of health-food shops and places running yoga courses also help to give the place a trendy, bohemian feel. Despite the presence of several large **beaches**, however, it's best not to have your heart set on sun-

bathing, since the local winds that make this place so popular for surfing often create sandstorms that make it an
uncomfortable and chilly business. On these days it's worth
hiking to the two nature areas around **Montaña Pelada**
and **Montaña Roja** that flank the town's east and west
sides respectively.

In the week before Easter El Médano gets particularly
lively, filling with young islanders who come here to party
and whose tented villages spring up on the beach, joining
the large camper vans of the windsurfing community.

Arrival and information

Public **buses** from Los Cristianos and the airport drop passengers off at the town's tiny harbour. A helpful **tourist
information booth** (Map 14, B6. Mon–Fri 9am–1pm &
4–7pm, Sat 9am–1pm; ☏922/176 002) is located on the
north sie of Plaza Principe de Asturia.

Accommodation

Package-holiday needs are catered for by a few large hotels,
and aside from these – which rarely have vacancies for independent travellers – there's little else in the way of catered
accommodation here. There's only one pension, but
plenty of inexpensive small-scale apartment complexes in
town. Longer rental periods (over two weeks) in these
apartments are usually rewarded with significant reductions
in price. Only some of the locals running apartments in
town speak English.

The nearest **campsite** *Oasis* (☏922/770 414; €2 per
tent, plus €2 per person), is near the hamlet of Ciguaña
Alta just north of the airport (signposted off a small road off
the northern side of the airport motorway junction). It is
well-presented, with its own pool and friendly owners, and

EL MÉDANO

has good views, but its relative isolation – about 3km from the nearest public transport, though only 4km from the international airport – make it far from ideal for most tourists.

HOTELS

El Médano
Map 14, C7. Playa de El Médano
ⓣ 922/177 000
ⓕ 922/176 048
ⓦ www.medano.es

Offering accommodation largely to package tourists, this 1960s hotel, built on stilts over the sea, was one of the first hotels in southern Tenerife. Though rooms have been renovated since, the hotel is no longer the seat of luxury it once was, but still offers a satisfactory standard of accommodation in a superb central location. Many of the rooms have excellent views. ❺.

Playa Sur Tenerife
Map 14, A8. Playa El Médano.
ⓣ 922/176 120
ⓕ 922/176 337
ⓦ www.hpst.litech.net

Modern hotel offering accommodation mostly to package tourists in a leafy site just east of the centre at the far end of the boardwalk. Each of the seventy rooms is elegantly furnished with traditional Spanish furniture and the hotel has all the usual four-star facilities, though the pool is somewhat disappointing. Various outdoor activities such as hiking trips are organized for guests. ❼.

PENSIONS

Hostal Carel
Map 14, C4. Avda Principes de España 22.
ⓣ 922/176 066

Recently renovated pension on the edge of the town centre, beside the main approach road. Singles and doubles available, some with private bathrooms. ❸.

EL MÉDANO

APARTMENTS

Bungalows Ker Tulakito
Map 14, A7. La Gaviota 17.
☎ 922/177 083
Small group of pretty, well-equipped bungalows, with excellent views over the bay from this cliff-top vantage point, five minutes walk from the town centre. Each bungalow has its own garden and terrace area and sleeps up to four. The friendly owner speaks English. ❺.

Durazno Sur
Map 14, C5. Avda Principes de España 1.
☎ 922/176 958
ⓕ 922 176 299
Unusually spacious, simply equipped apartments, many of which have massive balconies overlooking the busy main plaza and the sea. Most sleep up to three people, but there are some reasonably priced singles too. English spoken. ❹.

Esmeralda Siona
Map 14, A4. C/Tenerife 10.

☎ 922/176 946
Roomy apartments in a charmless modern block a couple of minutes walk from the town centre. All come with a well-equipped kitchen, TV and balcony – though the views from these are onto the street and neighbouring blocks. Sleep up to six. ❹.

Marazul
Map 14, B5. Corner of Plaza Principe de Asturia and C/Evaristo Gomez.
☎ 922/177 159
ⓕ 922/177 277
Very centrally located block containing several plain and uninspiring apartments. Most are small and slightly gloomy, though a couple are more spacious and bright with views over the central plaza and sea. All apartments sleep two people and the management speaks English. ❺.

Playa Grande
Map 14, C6. Hermano Pedro 2.
☎ 922/176 306
ⓕ 922/176 168

EL MÉDANO

Swish, modern apartments with Scandinavian-style furnishings overlooking the main plaza. Sleeping up to four people, they all have telephones, satellite TV and a balcony. There's also access to a pleasant roof terrace. There are particularly good discounts on stays of four weeks or more here. €300 per week.

The town and around

El Médano centres on **Plaza Principe de Asturia** (Map 14, C6), a multilevel plaza surrounded by restaurants and cafés and bordering the large main beach. It also marks the start of a boardwalk that heads west along the coast above the warped sandstone rocks that line the beach and lead to an area reserved for windsurfers to assemble their equipment before launching off into the reliably good winds here. West of the plaza is the town's second main square, **Plaza Roja** (Map 14, F7). A coastal road leads from here around a flat headland to a line of quiet beaches five minutes walk further east, where prevailing winds whip up waves for surfers and bodyboarders, making the beach too windy for sunbathing.

Two striking hills of warped and twisted volcanic rock flank the town at either end of the coastline. To the west the 171-metre high **Montaña Roja** (Map 10, M8) is the centre of a nature reserve protecting a dune ecosystem. One path through this area leads to the summit while another rounds the hill on its inland side. The latter leads to a massive, beautiful, windswept and shadeless **Playa de la Tejita** (Map 10, L8). To the east, along a dirt road that flanks the coast, is the magnificent crater of **Montaña Pelada** (Map 10, 96), shaped by the influx of seawater during a volcanic eruption. A **hiking trail** begins from a sheltered sandy bay on the west side of the mountain – a favourite with nudist sunbathers – and leads steeply up to the crater rim, from where there are good views along the coast and over the couple of tiny, quiet beaches below. You can follow a trail around the crater rim, returning back down the steep west side, or descend on its northern side to link up with a track that leads east to a wind farm, Parque Eólico (see p.197). The hike is about a three hour return trip and is detailed in a free booklet available from the tourist office. It's also fun to explore the area by mountain bike on trails that require little off-road experience.

Eating, drinking and nightlife

Each restaurant listed in the *Guide* has been categorized as either inexpensive (under €6), moderate (€6– €10) and expensive (above €10) – indicating the price of an average main course.

El Médano has a good selection of cafés, restaurants and trendy bars for a town of its size. Most are clustered around **Plaza Principe de Asturia** and **Plaza Roja**, and beside the long wooden boardwalk that heads west out of town. However, a hectic nightlife is largely absent here, consisting mainly of windsurfers relaxing after a hard day of hanging onto their sails.

Though some of the restaurants in El Médano serve fish and seafood none have the excellent reputation of those in the small fishing village of **Los Abrigos** (Map 10, K8), 6km west of El Médano. This village has developed a reputation as an excellent place to eat local fresh fish and its small seafront is crammed with restaurants. Here, *Vista Mar* has a large selection and good reputation, particularly for its excellent grilled seafood assortment. *La Langostera*, as the name suggests, is a good place to eat lobster as well as offering a good value set meal. For more gourmet presentation

EL MÉDANO

try *Bencomo*, but to keep things cheap and simple *Yaisara* is the best bet – and offers a good range of salads too.

BARS AND CAFÉS

Brasil Tropical

Map 14, D6. Paseo Galo Ponte. Snazzy cocktails served in a lively tropical-style bar, just off Principe de Asturia. Open till 2am, this is usually one of the last places in town to close.

Flashpoint

El Médano Beach.
Trendy café with a shady terrace overlooking the part of the beach reserved for windsurfers. Serves excellent breakfasts, and filled rolls and pizzas to crowded tables in the afternoon. In the evening the bar takes over, serving drinks and snacks until midnight.

RESTAURANTS

El Médano

Map 14, C7. *Hotel El Médano*, Plaza Principe de Asturia. Though the salads, meats and vegetables at this nightly buffet are far from exciting, the views over the sea could hardly be better, and the prices are very reasonable. Inexpensive.

Pescador

Map 14, B5. C/Evarvisto Gómez Gonzalez 15.
Popular with locals, this restaurant serves reliably good, fresh fish and seafood dishes at tables decked with cheerful green cloths. Closed Tues. Moderate.

Piemonte

Map 14, B4. C/Gran Canaria 7. Tucked away in a basement on the edge of the town centre, this stylish Italian restaurant decorated in pastel tones with art on the walls, offers a large menu of top-quality pizza and pasta dishes. Closed Wed & Sat afternoon. Moderate to expensive.

Playa Chica

Map 14, E7. Paseo Marcia Garcia.

EL MÉDANO

Good tapas and fine views over the bay from the downstairs terrace make this a popular place for an inexpensive meal; the restaurant upstairs is also good value, serving many of the usual fish and meat dishes. Closed Mon. Inexpensive.

Yaiza

Map 14, C5. C/Iriarte 12.
Elegant restaurant serving creative gourmet food. The menu includes interesting fish dishes, such as sole in saffron sauce, and various choice cuts of meat including pork and beef fillets, but there are no vegetarian options. Closed Thurs. Expensive.

Listings

Banks and exchanges Caja Canarias, the Plaza Principe de Asturia.

Car Rental Rent a Car Médano, Paseo Galo Ponte (☎922/177 062 or 649 464 195); Avis in the hotel Playa Sur Tenerife (see p.192).

Internet Inforred, C/Inglaterra 3 (€3 per hour); WebBar on Plaza Roja (€4 per hour).

Laundry Elios, Plaza Roja (☎922/178 067).

Sports equipment Fun Factory El Cabezo, in the Hotel Atlantic Playa (☎ 922/176 273; @funfactory@teleline.es) sells, rents and stores a wide range of watersports equipment, plus hiking and biking equipment.

Taxi Just north of the plaza, or call 922/390 924.

PARQUE EÓLICO

Map 10, N6. Mon–Fri 10am–5pm, Sat & Sun by appointment; €6, under-12s and students free; Ⓦ www.iter.rcanaira.es
The land immediately east of El Médano and Montaña

Pelada has been designated for industrial use, with huge, empty roads laid in anticipation of as yet unrealized demand. For visitors, this area is only of interest for the innovative wind farm and renewable energy centre, the **Parque Eólico** – follow signs from the motorway for the Granadilla industrial area (*Pol. Industrial Granadilla*). The centre offers visitors informal and insightful tours (1hr 30min) that include a short film on the reasons against using fossil fuels and a trip along an ecological walkway lined with exhibits demonstrating principles behind solar and wind power at both domestic and industrial scales. The island government has sponsored the institute's research and provided subsidies to ecologically responsible households as part of its commitment to reduce global carbon dioxide emissions. The hope is that this wind farm will provide around 16 per cent of the island's energy needs, but ultimately the centre acknowledges that large wind farms are a rather unwieldy form of harnessing energy on a large scale and that this is best done on the household level. To illustrate possible methods of doing this, 25 "bioclimatic dwellings", using and producing energy in the most efficient and sensible manner, are planned on the site and should make visiting the centre more interesting, as will the planned visitors' centre.

PORÍS DE ABONA

Map 1, H7.

East of the Parque Eólico, the rocky coast is lined with small fishing and commuter villages, most comprised of a fairly ugly collection of houses occasionally including a small bar and often rudimentary bathing facilities, though the sea here is often too rough for swimming. The main town on this stretch of coast is **PORÍS DE ABONA** around 12km north of the wind farm. Many of the apartments in town serve as weekend homes for families from urban areas in the north, so the place has a sleepy feel outside major holidays. It boasts a short promenade as well as a couple of pleasant, sheltered and little-used sandy beaches and a handful of **restaurants**. Of these, the large pastel-coloured *Restaurant Casablanca*, Ctra General (☎ 922/164 296; closed Mon) is particularly recommended; it makes and sells its own cheese and wine, and serves excellent, if expensive, paella as well as hosting regular live folk music.

The undeveloped headland **Punta de Porís** just south of town features a picturesque lighthouse perched on rocks.

PORÍS DE ABONA

The southern interior

I n the green hills overlooking the hot and dusty southern coast, the towns of the **southern interior** were originally developed as farming land. Reliable sources of fresh water meant that this was one of the earliest areas to be developed following Spanish occupation of the island. Farming remained the principle occupation here from that time until a generation ago, when the mechanization of the industry, impossible on these narrow terraces, led to foreign imports undercutting local prices and left the local economy flagging. Luckily, at about the same time the arid coastal fringes of the island were being developed for sun-seekers from northern Europe, so these farming communities had another way to earn their keep in servicing these new resorts. Administrative towns such as **Adeje**, **Arona** and **Granadilla** have become comparatively wealthy on the back of this industry and have expanded, as have smaller settlements between, leaving little of the island's southern

---
Map 10 covers southern Tenerife.

ACCOMMODATION PRICE CODES

Throughout the *Guide*, accommodation has been graded according to price, based on the cost of the cheapest double room in high season – but excluding the time around Christmas and New Year, when rates can rocket. In the case of apartments that sleep more than two, the price for the smallest available unit, as described in the body text, is given; where apartments are available by the night, the price refers to the cheapest two-person apartment. Where singles – which are usually more than half the price of doubles – are available, this has also been mentioned. Travellers wanting to stay a week or more may find that nightly rate can be reduced a little.

❶ up to €12		❺ €48– €60	
❷ €12–€24		❻ €60– €84	
❸ €24–€36		❼ €84– €120	
❹ €36– €48		❽ over €120	

slopes free of housing. Development only thins higher up, where the pine trees take over around the traditional village of **Vilaflor**, Spain's highest settlement.

There are no particular attractions here other than the quaint villages themselves, and few restaurants or places to stay. Primarily, the area is of interest for a handful of **hikes**, many with tremendous views over the coast.

ADEJE

Map 10, D3.

Though its location and its centre are pretty enough, most of the administrative town of **ADEJE** is bland and sprawling. However, thanks to profits from servicing the coastal resorts it is generally quite well turned-out and a couple of historic buildings in the old town – the **Casa Fuerte** and

ADEJE

Iglesia de Santa Ursula– are interesting enough. But the real reason visitors come here is to join the hiking trail up the **Barranco del Infierno** (Map 10, E3), the deepest gorge in the Canaries.

The village, prey to frequent Arab attacks, was also sacked by Sir Frances Drake in 1586, so fortification has played an important part in the development of Adeje. The sturdily fortified hacienda, **Casa Fuerte** stands as testimony to the village's remarkable defensive structure. The Casa Fuerte is not open to visitors, however. The one accessible sight in the village is the simply decorated sixteenth-century **Iglesia de Santa Ursula** at the top of the main road, Calle Grande.The building's white-washed walls and simple *Mudéjar* wooden roof protect a copy of the famous Virgin of Candelaria (see p.94).

Uphill of the old cannon that guards the Casa Fuerte and beside the panoramic terrace of the restaurant *Otello* (closed Tues) the path up the side of the impressive, steep-sided **Barranco del Infierno** begins. The four-hour return trek along the ravine affords dizzying views down the valley and passes through several distinct vegetation zones – from semi-desert to willow and eucalyptus forest. The rather puny eighty-metre waterfall at the farthest end of the trail is, however, something of a disappointment, but the upper reaches of the hike are dramatic enough, requiring a slippery scramble along the shady, steep-sided gorge and making sturdy footwear and an extra layer of clothing advisable.

Practicalities

Adeje is a short ride from Las Américas on **bus** #416 (36 daily; 30min; €0.80). Two simple pensions provide the only **accommodation** in town: *Rambala*, C/Grande 7 (☎922/780 071; ❷), and the more basic *Rochil,* Corpus Christi 29 (☎922/780 252; ❷). Adeje has a reputation for

ADEJE

good upland Canarian **food**, particularly garlic chicken, the only dish available at restaurants such as the inexpensive *Oasis* 5, C/Grande (closed Wed), where the chicken is served with salad and fries to crowded tables on the tree-lined main road. For more choice and a little ambience, try *Sol en Canarias*, C/Piedra Redonda 6 (9am–12pm, closed Sat), downhill from the Casa Fuerte, which offers a good range of moderately priced Canarian dishes, including the house speciality, grilled meat and braised rabbit in garlicy *Salmorejo* sauce.

ARONA

Map 10, F4.

The pretty streets of **ARONA**'s tiny centre are good for a short stroll and the modest, typically Canarian, seven-teenth-century **Iglesia San Antonio Abad** at its heart is also worth a peek, but the town is primarily of use as a good base from which to make the hike (4hr return) to the thousand-metre high flat-topped summit of the **Rogue del Conde** (Map 10, E4) for rewarding views over south-ern Tenerife and La Gomera. For the large part, the shade-less route up Conde follows a steep, loose path along an old pack-road – developed to allow cultivation of the plateau on the top of the hill – though the irregularly spaced painted waymarks occasionally deviate from this. To find the trailhead, leave the plaza in front of the church by the road that runs uphill to the left and cross the main road onto an unmarked road. After a couple of bends this road straightens, leaving town in the direction of the mountain. Turn left at a statue of Jesus and right at C/Vento 30. Here, painted trail markers follow a route that immediately crosses a gorge and then heads up the left-hand side of the hill, the path getting steeper and steeper until it reaches the summit.

ARONA

Practicalities

Bus #480 connects Arona with Los Cristianos (36 daily; 45min; €1). There are a number of tapas **bars** in town, but for a proper **restaurant** meal try *El Patio Canario,* C/de Dominguez Alfonso 4 (closed Sun). Run by a Belgian-Canario family, the restaurant sources its dishes from both culinary traditions. The food is good and the prices moderate. If you have your own transport, another option is a rustic restaurant by the road to Ifonche, west off the Arona–Vilaflor road. *Refugio* (℡922/725 894; closed Wed, Sat & Sun) has a small, though relatively expensive, range of tasty home-made dishes and fantastic views over the southern coast from the patio. It also offers **B&B** (❺) and is run by keen hikers and paragliders, happy to advise (in English) about local routes and conditions.

EAST TO GRANADILLA

A minor road heading east from Arona's church plaza leads via San Lorenzo, San Miguel and a handful of smaller settlements scattered along the way to **Granadilla**. Many of the roadside houses flanking this road are positioned to take advantage of the excellent views across the southern part of the island and a couple of interesting projects – a sculpture garden at **Mariposa** and an orchid nursery, the **Centro de las Orquideas**, just outside San Lorenzo – both started by German expatriates – combine interest with great views.

Mariposa

Map 10, F4. Free. Guided tours, by prior appointment, €12.
Ⓕ 922/725 140.

The would-be artists' and thinkers' colony of **MARIPOSA** is 2km east (not signposted) of Arona. The philosophy behind the project, begun in 1992, was to create an environment conducive to the creation of ideas, where artists and academics could retire to develop new lifestyles. While this engaging private project has failed to receive the expected support from sponsors, the help of a number of resident artists has turned part of the area into a **sculpture garden**, tastefully interspersing various pieces of art with splendid vistas over the southern coast. One of the most interesting parts of the garden is a short tunnel exhibiting a number of artefacts found while working it. To gain access to the garden, call at the house with the blue door opposite the gardens and ask for Uli. Alternatively, you could arrange a **guided tour** by faxing ahead.

Centro de las Orquideas

Map 10, G5. Mon–Sat 10am–5pm; €6, under 12s €3; ℗ 922/765 566.

Around three kilometres east of Mariposa and signposted just above San Lorenzo on the road to San Miguel (found by following a paper-chase signpost system through a residential area) is a small orchid nursery. The **Centro de las Orquideas**, though little more than a large greenhouse, has 65 varieties of orchid in over two thousand colours. Of the hundred thousand plants on the site, most are grown for sale locally, the centre even supplying the Loro Parque near Puerto de la Cruz with its extravagant needs (see p.108). A small shop sells specimens in crush-proof packaging from around €12. Though there's not much to the centre, the staff are enthusiastic horticulturists, keen to field questions on orchids and other flowering plants.

The centre's excellent little **café** serves large slices of torte on a terrace with outstanding views over the southern coast.

Granadilla

Map 10, K3.

The bustling administrative market town of **GRANADIL-LA** acts as a focal point for the surrounding towns and villages. Off the busy main road that cuts through the workaday town centre is its quainter heart, where elegant townhouses line quiet side streets. One such house, the *Hotel Rural Senderos de Abona* (☎922/770 200, ⊕922/770 308; ❸), a refurbished nineteenth-century post house beside a plaza and the Iglesia San Antonio, offers stylish accommodation. Facilities include a tiny pool and a **restaurant**, the *Terrero*, where the ambience of the old stable in which it's set is more interesting than its mediocre, but moderately priced Canarian cuisine. You can stay in town for less expense at the *Pension Dos Hermanos*, Avda Fundador Glez (☎922/770 735; ❷), at the junction with the Vilaflor road; the clean and simple rooms here are en suite.

VILAFLOR

Map 10, H1.

High above the coast and nestled near the very top of the mountain towns of southern Tenerife, lies the handicraft centre and one-time spa town of **VILAFLOR**, Tenerife's highest parish. With incredible views from the base of the grand forest of Canarian pines that all but encircles the Parque Nacional del Teide (see p.211), pure upland air and local springs, it's easy to see how the town's charming old brick-and-tile houses once attracted those looking to improve their health. And though it is rather short on facilities today, the town still makes for a tranquil and practical upland base for hikers exploring local pine forests and the nearby national park – all this at less than an hour's drive from the glut of facilities on the coast.

THE CANARIAN PINE

The biggest specimens of the large and sturdy **Canarian Pine tree** (*Pinus Canariensis*), a plant vital to the ecology of the island, can be found just above Vilaflor by the road to Teide. The first, downhill of a roadside stop, has a trunk circumference of 9.3 metres, making it the fattest tree on the island – the other, the tallest on the island, is just over the road. The size of both is impressive, but no more so than many of the oversized characteristics of this species: pine cones the size of babies' heads, foot-long needles and hugely thick, robust bark. The lengthy needles act to trap moisture from the clouds that regularly shroud these heights – introducing vital water into the island's otherwise arid ecosystem. To stop other species from taking advantage of this service, the needles are also designed to degrade slowly, which, along with their acidifying effect on the soil below, prevents little else growing and helps assure the Canarian Pine's primacy in the forest. Where needles have been removed – they are sometimes collected as litter for farm animals or as packaging material for dainty tropical fruits – the balance is upset and other species take hold. Ultimately, though, the Canarian Pine is likely to maintain its dominance thanks to thousands of years of volcanic training – these pine trees are unique to the species in having evolved a thick bark that amazingly protects the tree's heart from fire. It is not uncommon to see badly scorched trees with cinder branches and needles sprouting healthy new branches.

The town's main street, Calle Santo Domingo heads up to a large plaza centred on the plain but imposing seventeenth-century **Iglesia de San Pedro**. A number of handicraft shops around here make it a good place to look for gifts, particularly woodcarvings and lace. If you're serious about buying lacework, you should also look in the tiny shop, Artesania Delfina, on C/Santo Domingo itself, where you can often watch the painstaking process of lace being made. From the plaza it's a short, steep, but worthwhile walk up a road to the viewpoint, **Mirador San Roque** above town (just west of the road to Teide), which provides a spectacular view over the slopes of southern Tenerife. Beside the viewpoint a cluster of buildings makes up the **Parque San Roque** (July–Sept daily 9am–6pm; €3), which includes a museum of Guanche life. The museum is rather short on exhibits, however, relying on wall charts, and occasional, corny live re-enactments, to give an insight into the lives of the native islanders.

Practicalities

Bus #482 (3 daily; 1hr 15min; €83) grinds up the hairpin main road from Las Américas and Los Cristianos to Vilaflor en route to the Parque Nacional del Teide.

As you might expect of a former spa town, there are plenty of **places to stay** in Vilaflor, and good **restaurants** at all of them, mostly serving typically hearty upland Canarian fare such as the thick vegetable stew, *escaldón*. *Pension German*, C/Santo Domingo 1 (☎922/709 028; ❸), has the least expensive rooms (some with private bathroom), as well as some of the best value food in town. The *Hotel Rural El Sombrerito*, C/Santa Catalina 15 (☎922/709 052; ❸), is a cleaner, more comfortable and generally much smarter option. Rooms here are all en suite and some have a balcony onto the quiet main street. The basement contains a rustically furnished bar and restaurant, decorated with artefacts from the adjoining tiny museum and handicraft shop. The restaurant (closed Fri) offers breakfast, lunch and dinner to visitors as well as residents. Just outside the centre of town, and split from it by the road to Teide, the *Hotel Rural Alta Montaña*, Morro del Cano 1 (☎922/709 000; ❺), is a stylish mini-resort with both double and single rooms available, all en suite. The garden here features a swimming pool and sun lounge area in front of splendid coastal views. Prices include breakfast.

El Mirador (☎922/709 135), the town's best **restaurant**, just below the viewpoint for which it is named, isn't too pricey, considering the grand views and the quality of the Canarian and international cuisine available. Half a dozen **bars** scattered around town, usually exclusively frequented by locals, serve drinks until late and offer inexpensive, straightforward snacks and meals around the clock.

PAISAJE LUNAR AND THE BARRANCO DE LAS ARENAS

Two small areas of tall, thin and smooth, rock columns, the **Paisaje Lunar**, located 9km east of Vilaflor, form the highlight of a good two- to three-hour hike.

The dirt road to the trailhead is marked by a wooden sign on a bend in the road to the Parque Nacional del Teide not far above Vilaflor. From here it's a two-hour walk, or half-hour drive to the trail proper. Note that this dirt road is a rough one and will give your car a good workout – so, if you're in a rental car, you may want to look at the small print first to see if your insurance covers you for this.

Marked by white-painted rocks, the hike begins on a narrow woodland trail, but the trees soon thin out to reveal good views of Tenerife's southern coast 17km below and the outside of the ridge-like rim of the vast Las Cañadas crater 2km above (see p.211). In about an hour you should arrive at the first of the columns, eroded stone whose wide bases support tapering pillars with delicate looking, top-heavy tips. At the nearby second group of columns, green-painted rock markers lead you along the uphill trail to the black lunar-style landscape of the **Barranco de Las**

Arenas then back to the start of a downhill trail which briefly follows the course of some water-pipes before bearing left to cross an area of volcanic ash. The white trail-markings, irregularly spaced along this stretch, resume beyond here and the path leads down to a children's summer camp and the dirt road back to Vilaflor.

Parque Nacional Las Cañadas del Teide

Set inside a massive volcanic crater at the centre of the island, the **PARQUE NACIONAL LAS CAÑADAS DEL TEIDE** protects a bleak and sun-baked volcanic desert. Used as a set for the film *Star Wars*, it is vaguely familiar to the 3.5 million visitors who come here each year to explore the harsh landscape and ascend **Pico del Teide**, the colossal volcano at its heart. A single east–west road crosses the park and along it are numerous roadside stops which provide good views over the inhospitable **lava and pumice plains**. Some also give access to **hikes**, passing through cool, thin and pure park air while crossing warped and gnarled rock.

Map 15 covers the Parque Nacional del Teide.

Enjoying national-park status since 1954, Teide is of considerable interest to naturalists for its large proportion of **endemic species**, but to the layperson the small tenacious shrubs and plants that manage to survive in this harsh environment are of no real interest. If you come in May or June, however, there are some spectacular exceptions to this rule: the resilient **Teide violet** adds a pretty scattering of colour among the lava and pumice, while **Tajinaste rojo**, a two-metre high conical spike and an impressive skeleton, comes into bloom with spectacular maroon flowers.

There is no especially good or bad **time to visit** the park and streams of visitors come year-round. Most generally only make a couple of roadside stops before making a beeline for Teide's cable car, so hikers soon find themselves in relatively quiet areas. Given the park's delicate ecosystem, however, it's important to observe the various park rules governing visitor behaviour. Most, such as not littering or picking plants, are fairly common sense, but note also that it is forbidden to remove stones (particularly from around the upper reaches of Teide), stray from marked paths and camp anywhere within the park.

Geological history

At only 3 million years old, the area protected by the national park is in the youngest part of Tenerife; one which joined up the older volcanic ranges to the north, west and south to form a large island backbone, the **Cumbre Dorsal**, that stretches west from the park. Volcanic activity continued in the centre of the island, reaching a peak around 300,000 years ago in a volcano of spectacular proportions whose sixteen-kilometre wide crater now forms the boundary of today's park. Exactly what geological event destroyed the volcanic mountain that once stood here is unclear. Subsequent volcanic activity and thousands of years of more subtle erosive forces has made it difficult to judge. Perhaps an enormous explosion blew its top off, or caverns forming underground as lava and gases escaped may have caused the whole mountain to cave in. The crater rim is still clear in the south of the park where the steep-sided mountain of **Guajara** is its highest point, but is buried to the north by the majestic bulk of **Pico del Teide**.

Near Guajara and beside the classy, state-run Parador Hotel, are **Los Roques de García**, a line of bizarre twisted rock formations which stand as tribute to the erosive forces that have helped shaped the park. These rocks are thought to be the boundary of two basins produced by material being eroded away from either side of this landform. Both these basins would be filled with more disfigured rock if this hadn't long since been buried by rivers of lava and small pumice pellets spewed up from Teide. The resulting vast and inhospitable lava and pumice plains that dominate this landscape are known as **Las Cañadas**, from which the park gets its name.

Park Practicalities

There are four main routes up to the park, one from each corner of the island, and though it is easiest by far to get here by **car**, there are several **buses** daily from Las Américas and Los Cristianos and from Puerto de la Cruz calling at the Parador Hotel in the south of the park, the base of the cable-car up Teide itself, and the visitors' centre.

The main park **visitors' centre** (Map 15, H2. Daily 9am–4pm; ☎922/290 129) is at the eastern end of the park, about 1km southwest of a El Portillo. It has displays on the geological history of the area, its flora and its fauna. As well as selling topographical maps and providing rudimentary leaflets about the generally well-marked hikes in the park, the centre also organizes free **guided hikes** of varying difficulty – from easy four-hour trips to two-day expeditions of the summit of Teide. There's a second centre (same hours) beside the Parador Hotel on the south side of the park; this concentrates almost exclusively on the park's human heritage (see p.216). Lastly, two tiny booths with unpredictable opening hours, field general enquiries and distribute leaflets: one is located at the junction of the roads from the west and the south, the other at the junction of the roads from the east and north.

Since camping is prohibited in the park, there are only two **places to stay** here. The first is a simple refuge, 500m below the summit of Teide. At 3270m, **Refugio Altavista** (Map 15, E3. ☎922/239 811; ❷; closed Nov–Feb) is around thirty minutes' walk below the cable-car terminus; although it can sleep up to fifty people, it is often filled to capacity and reservations are advisable. There are some cooking facilities here, but water can be in short supply at busy times, resulting in the closing of toilets and washing facilities; you should always bring your own drinking water in any case. When the refuge is closed there is a free no-frills bunkhouse open next door. It contains a dozen beds and blankets as well as windows that rattle all night. Despite the blankets, you'd be well advised to bring a good sleeping bag since temperatures frequently drop below freezing, particularly in winter. Offering considerably more comfort, but at a price, is the one hotel – the stylish, state-run **Parador Hotel** (Map 15, E6. ☎ & ⒻⒻ 922/386 415; ❼) is beautifully located beside Guajara and Los Roques. It has a small pool and large and expensive restaurant. The **restaurant**, which looks out onto Teide, serves good Canarian cuisine and a particularly good local stew (*puchero*), but has a rather sterile atmosphere. The complex also contains an overpriced **snack bar**, beside the main entrance. The only other restaurants in the park are a number of bus-tour favourites in El Portillo. There are snack bars here, and at both ends of the cable car too.

APPROACHING THE PARK

The **road from the west**, the least sinuous and so fastest route up to the park, begins its ascent near Santiago del Teide and climbs through a comparatively thin belt of pines. Most of the island's recent volcanic activity was at this side of the peak and before the road rises out of the belt of trees it passes just south of an area of solidified lava flows from the island's most recent (1909) eruption of **Montaña Chinyero**. Beyond the trees the road rises (with great views over the Teno range and the island of La Gomera behind) to cut through a vast, stunningly impenetrable area of lava frozen into twisted and forbidding shapes. The origin of this lava wasteland is indicated by a conveniently placed roadside stop and information board beside a good view of the side vent, **Las Narices del Teide** (Teide's nostrils), from which twelve million cubic metres of lava spewed over a three month period in 1789. The vent is technically part of **Pico Viejo** (3134m), a peak in its own right that rises out from the side of Teide itself.

From the south a busier road climbs to the national park via the pretty upland village of Vilaflor (see p.206) and through impressive stands of Canarian pines, including the island's biggest specimen. The many bends in the road expose good views over southern Tenerife and La Gomera and a couple of roadside stops make for good photo opportunities.

Visitors coming **from the east** are likely to take the relatively long and impressive route along the **Cumbre Dorsal**, the mountain backbone of the island. Climbing quickly from the congested urban areas around La Laguna, the road ascends beyond **La Esperanza** to pass through some of the largest continuous pine forest on the island. Almost straight away there are great views over Santa Cruz and the Anaga mountains below, and having entered the

MAN IN THE PARK

Though the **Guanches** divided the rest of Tenerife into king-doms, the area around Pico del Teide was communally used for summer pasturing. The daring adventures of **goatherds** on the slopes of the volcano are solely the stuff of legend, howev-er, as the slim pickings on the slopes themselves kept the goats away and the goatherds steered clear too, believing *Guayote*, the devil, lived inside, his foul moods leading him to spit out fire and lava.

Superstitions concerning the peak appear to have been passed on to **Spanish settlers** on Tenerife who continued to pasture goats, but avoid the peak, so it wasn't until the nine-teenth century that the first documented ascent of Teide was made, by visiting scientists and the earliest tourists. By the early twentieth century **ascending the peak** had become an important part of the tour of Tenerife. From around the same time, successive **scientific surveys** of the area revealed that alongside the many striking geological features a rare and deli-cate ecosystem existed and in 1954 the area was awarded **national-park status**, the remaining goatherds were banished and visitor freedom was regulated.

Despite the protection that the area is now afforded, it is still a major draw to **tourists**, and the greatest strain on the park's fragile ecology is the rising numbers of visitors that come to the park each year. Today, access is strictly controlled, with only 150 visitors a day permitted onto the summit of Teide.

peaceful forest, there are a number of viewpoints at which travellers ritualistically stop. The first of these, the **Mirador de Ortuno**, is placed to admire views over vast areas of forest on the north side of the island and Puerto de la Cruz. Further along, the **Mirador Cumbre Dorsal** is a grand place to see the ridge itself in the context of the towering Teide and the lush Orotava valley. Moving west down the

Cumbre Dorsal road, views open up to the south, exposing the craggy valleys above Arafo and Güímar. The trees thin here, a barren volcanic landscape taking over as the route passes the **Izaña Observatory**, home to the Instituto Astrofisica de Canarias (Ⓦ) where clear dark skies have attracted astronomers since the mid-nineteenth century.

The busy **road from the north**, having twisted itself around countless hairpins on a rough road through the Orotava valley, rises into the dense vegetation and large pine forests on the damp side of the island. Views back down the densely populated valley reveal a network of terraces and hamlets; though often the combination of forest and low cloud (particularly in the afternoon) largely obscure views along this approach road.

GUAJARA

Map 15, F6.

Part of the ancient crater rim that runs alongside the park boundary, **Guajara** (2717m) stands over 700m above the crater floor, from where it looks more like a series of cliff faces than a mountain. Though a fairly strenuous five-hour return trip, with a steep climb and a loose descent, the **hike up** is one of the best walks on the island. The path climbing across its sheer north face has excellent views over the whole national park and is a good perspective from which to make out the flow of the most recent lava tongues on the slopes of Teide. On a clear day the views of the island of La Palma, seen on the way up, form part of a summit panorama that includes La Gomera, El Hierro and Gran Canaria along with large parts of Tenerife's southern coast.

The **trail** begins just a few metres south of the Parador Hotel beside a sign depicting park footpaths. The narrow track soon ends in a T-junction, where a left turn follows a path that curves to the right before meeting a road. (There are parking spaces here too.) Crossing the road, the reasonably well-trodden trail heads straight up, marked by occasional paint spots. Around 500m beyond the road the path bears left and begins to steepen as it crosses a cliff face at its base to lead out onto the rim of the crater. From this point the path steepens further, leading up at the foot of a row of cliffs that mark Guajara's northern face. The path climbs up in front of these cliffs, then passes over them (follow the irregular and faded paint markings carefully to find the quickest way to the summit), past a triangulation point to the summit and a large wind shelter. The **descent** is to the east of here – paths to the south lead in the direction of Vilaflor and Paisaje Lunar, but to return to Las Cañadas continue along the line of the crater rim. This path, which is steep and loose with small pumice rocks, heads down to a saddle just over a kilometre away where it is crossed by another path. From here you have two options. Head north around 500m back downhill to reach the crater floor and follow the wide track along the base of Guajara back to return to the Parador Hotel. Alternatively, heading right at this junction will take you south to Paisaje Lunar (see p.209), near Vilaflor, in around three hours.

LOS ROQUES DE GARCÍA

Map 15, E6.

In the centre of the park, **Los Roques de García**, a line of huge, bizarrely eroded, top-heavy rocks, stands proud in an otherwise flattened landscape. Most visitors to the national park stop here, but few make the rewarding two-hour circular hike around the rock formation, which is well worth the effort for its imposing views of Los Roques themselves and the more recently solidified streams of lava nearby. Even at peak times, when the car park is bursting with visitors, you're unlikely to encounter more than a couple of other walkers on the loop.

HIKING IN THE PARK

Despite being restricted to a few established routes, **hikers** will find plenty of good trails of massively varying difficulty in the park. Though the visitors' centre at the eastern end of the park – and numerous private operators – can arrange guided hikes, most visitors strike out alone.

Even on hikes near the park's heavily visited areas you quickly leave any crowds behind. The best short hike in the area loops around the varied and engaging rock formations around **Los Roques de García**. The ascent of nearby **Guajara** is equally rewarding for its views over the park. Though much more strenuous, the obvious challenge for fit ambitious visitors is the ascent of **Teide**, from the summit of which you can see the entire archipelago.

Bear **climate** in mind if you are planning to make any of these hikes. Though the high altitude makes the park relatively chilly, the absence of cloud and shade make sunscreen and plenty of water essential. The altitude also means there are lower concentrations of oxygen here. On most hikes you're unlikely to notice this, though you'll get out of breath more easily and end up walking more slowly, but on ascents of Teide, mild **altitude sickness**, in the form of a headache or dizziness, is common. Slowing the pace is usually enough to solve such problems but if this doesn't work then making your descent is the best option.

Formed from magma that has been forced through near-vertical underground cracks, Los Roques are **volcanic dykes** which have solidified into walls of rock. This cooled magma, much harder than the surrounding rock, has been left standing proud while the softer material around it has eroded away.

The same process, here with the softer rock forming a horizontal layer near the base, created the precarious look-

LOS ROQUES DE GARCÍA

ing, top-heavy **Roque Cinchado** at the centre of the group. The subject of hundreds of postcards, this rock, with Teide as its background, has become a near obligatory photo opporutnity for park visitors. Unfortunately, during the day the crowds tend to hamper a good shot of the rock, but by sunset, when the light is at its best for photos and people mostly absent, the rock's grandeur and rich brown colour can be appreciated in peace.

The **hike** around Los Roques begins by heading out of the car park in the direction of Teide, starting an anti-clockwise loop that allows the steep loose slope to the car park at the end to be climbed rather than descended. The route follows a well-trodden path to the northernmost rock in the line and then dips down to follow a rougher trail back down the other side of the landforms. Finally, beside the spectacular geometric patterns of the massive rock monolith "**La Catedral**" the trail returns steeply back to the car park.

PICO DEL TEIDE

Map 15, D3.

The steep slopes of the massive **Pico del Teide** (3718m), one of the highest volcanoes in the world, rise from the flat Las Cañadas plains to form one of the most enduring symbols of the island. It has long been an irresistible pilgrimage for thousands of visitors and the need for its protection was pivotal in encouraging the creation of the surrounding national park. Most visitors use the **cable car** to ascend, but for the determined few, the intensely gruelling **hike** up via Montaña Blanca offers a satisfying and relatively quiet alternative.

Access to the summit of Teide is by permit only. See box on opposite page.

THE SUMMIT PERMIT

Only **150 visitors a day** are allowed up to the eight-metre wide crater rim on the summit of Teide and the tiny sulphurous vents that surround it. Permission needs to be obtained from the **ICONA park administration** in Santa Cruz (C/Emilio Calzadilla 5; Mon–Fri 9am–noon; ☏ 922/290 129). Permits are free but are only issued to those visiting the offices in person with their passports and a photocopy of the photo and details page. You need to book the time you'll be visiting the top, but it's still generally OK if you turn up outside this time, though you may have to wait if there are quite a few people on the summit. If there's snow on the peak it's closed to visitors.

The cable car

Map 15, E4. Daily 9am–4pm; €18 return, €11 one-way; ☏ 922/694 038; Ⓦ www.teleferico-teide.com

The ride up Teide by **cable car** is not one for those with vertigo, but for those with a head for heights, the eight-minute near-vertical, thousand-metre climb affords spectacular views back down the side of the mountain and around Las Cañadas. Passengers are deposited at a station 200m below the summit of Teide, from where a couple of easy walks have been laid out for the best views of the park and island.

The first walk leads east to the **Mirador La Fortaleza**, which has excellent views over the Orotava valley, the second leads west to another viewpoint which overlooks the 800-metre-wide crater, Pico Viejo. Permit holders can, of course, make the short steep **climb to the summit** of Teide (around 30min).

Visitors are only allowed to spend an hour up here, and though this rule is not strictly policed, the cold biting winds and short length of the available hikes usually pre-

PICO DEL TEIDE

vents too much lingering. From the cable-car station itself, there are good views of Gran Canaria, La Palma, La Gomera and El Hierro on a reasonably clear day, and on really good days you can also just about see Lanzarote and Fuerteventura.

High winds, snow and occasional maintenance can close the cable car at short notice for days at a time; if in doubt, call ahead to check that the car is running. In summer, it's also worth getting here before 9am, as substantial queues soon build up.

Hiking up Teide

The **hike** up Teide takes around four hours, with another three hours needed for the descent, so you'll need to set off early to avoid the heat of midday Many hikers save their joints the strain of the descent, however, by catching the cable car. Potentially, the crowds brought up by the cable car could lessen the satisfaction of accomplishing the gruelling trek up, but actually they make little difference since the trail doesn't arrive at the busy cable-car area until the very last section. In any case the permit system means that you're likely to be alone on the actual summit.

There is only one permissible route up the peak, beginning at a roadside car park at the base of **Montaña Blanca** (2740m), 4km east of the cable car station. The route up the slopes of this mountain are well graded and wide, making a good two-hour return hike in itself. The route up takes in beautiful vast swathes of beige pumice gravel dotted with huge dark, lava boulders, their shape earning them the name *Huevos de Teide*, or Teide eggs. The mountain's smooth rounded summit is a particularly good place to enjoy the sunset (after which there's just enough time to get back down before dark) when the immense, triangular shadow of Teide covers the valley floor.

HUMBOLDT'S ASCENT OF TEIDE

One of the first recorded ascents of Teide was made by the German scientist **Alexander von Humboldt** in 1799. Though his account conveys a great deal of struggling against the elements, it is difficult not to find a touch of humour in the interactions between his party and the local guides: "Unfortunately the laziness and ill-will of our guide soured our ascent. The(ir) indolence … was despairing; they sat and rested every ten minutes and threw away our carefully collected obsidian and pumice stones when our backs were turned … it became evident that none of them had ever been on the peak."

Other than Jorullo in Mexico, Humboldt felt Teide was the hardest volcano he had climbed. He talks of the freezing cold experienced whilst squatting overnight at 2900m under an overhang without tent or coat (presumably due to the inexperience and indolence of his guides). No doubt this encouraged the decision to press on to the top at 3am by the light of flaming torches. The party eventually gained the summit at 8am "stiff with cold, while our feet burnt in our boots (from the heat of the volcano)". Nevertheless, this didn't deter Humboldt from lowering himself into the 35-metre deep crater to investigate its sulphurous emissions. On the descent hardships continued, this time due to the continued shenanigans of their guides, who had not only drunk the small supply of wine that the explorers looked forward to, but had also broken the water bottle. This left the party without water, which was in any case in short supply for the duration of the twenty-one hour round-trip.

From the summit of Montaña Blanca, the trail becomes rougher, narrow and steep as it zigzags its way up the solidified lava flows on Teide's flanks. There are no real landmarks in this desolate landscape and few distractions from the gruelling climb, so the **Refugio Altavista** (see p.214),

PICO DEL TEIDE

an hour and a half's hike beyond Montana Blanca, is a welcome sight, even if you don't intend to stay. From the *refugio* it's about a further hour and a half straight climb to the top through a similar craggy and desolate area, though the grade of ascent begins to ease. After around twenty minutes a short detour is possible (marked by a pile of stones) to a cave, the **Cueva del Hielo**. A slippery metal ladder leads down into the small icy cavern where numerous stalactites grow.

From the turnoff to the cave it's another thirty minutes' walk to the **Mirador La Fortaleza**, which overlooks the Orotava valley and is joined to the top cable-car station by a well-graded stone path. Those with permits can ascend the peak's summit from the cable-car area, those without have to satisfy themselves with a hike to the other viewpoint overlooking Pico Viejo.

Those who want a **longer trip** or want to leave their vehicle in a more secure spot might want to start an ascent of Teide from El Portillo on the park's eastern edge (Map 15, H1). Several trailheads start here, including one from the visitors' centre, and converge on the one climbing Montaña Blanca. This desolate trail adds around two hours to each leg of the journey and crosses vast areas of pumice gravel, interspersed by hardy bushes. The extra four hours put the summit out of reach of a comfortable day trip, so is best done as a **two-day trip**. Since camping is forbidden in the park, this longer trip necessitates staying at the *Refugio Altavista* (see p.214).

La Gomera

LA GOMERA, the tiny disc of an island 28km off Tenerife, has a forgotten, laid-back air about it that even Tenerife's most remote corners can't match. Bisected by deep impenetrable ravines that radiate out from its centre, and covered in lush laurel forests, it is the greenest and least populated island in the Canaries.

Like Tenerife, Gomera can broadly be divided into a cool, wet, lush north and a sunnier, drier, less fertile south. It's around 10 million years older than Tenerife, however, during which time volcanic activity has been largely absent – the **landscape** here is one sculpted by erosive forces rather than spectacular volcanic events. Aside from forming the sheer ravines that dominate the scenery and the spectacular rock monoliths that stud the island, erosion has also meant that the peaks at the island's centre are fairly unimpressive by Tenerife's standards. At less than half the height of Teide, Gomera's summits are inside rather than above the cloud base, giving rise to a misty, dense and ghostly **laurel forest**, one of the world's most ancient woodlands.

The absence of major beaches – and, consequently, resorts – makes it a great place to come to get away from

Map 16 covers La Gomera.

ACCOMMODATION PRICE CODES

Throughout the *Guide*, accommodation has been graded according to price, based on the cost of the cheapest double room in high season – but excluding the time around Christmas and New Year, when rates can rocket. In the case of apartments that sleep more than two, the price for the smallest available unit, as described in the body text, is given; where apartments are available by the night, the price refers to the cheapest two-person apartment. Where singles – which are usually more than half the price of doubles – are available, this has also been mentioned. Travellers wanting to stay a week or more may find that nightly rate can be reduced a little.

❶ up to €12
❷ €12–€24
❸ €24–€36
❹ €36– €48
❺ €48– €60
❻ €60– €84
❼ €84– €120
❽ over €120

the crowds and take in the scenery on any one of many splendid **hikes**. If time is tight, however, it is well worth taking in the island in a **day trip**, as most of the 20,000 annual visitors do. The classic route heads anti-clockwise from the island's small, sleepy capital, **San Sebastián**, up into the cool damp **north**, where the climate has been as successful at encouraging substantial banana plantations around **Hermigua** and **Vallehermoso**, as it has at discouraging tourist resorts from taking hold. In the **south**, warmer weather has encouraged visitors to cluster around a few small sand-and-pebble beaches. The local population, traditionally eking out a living farming poor soil on difficult terrain has eagerly embraced visitors, building numerous small apartment complexes, particularly in the popular and traditionally bohemian destination **Valle Gran Rey**.

Holidaymakers in this valley tend to divide their time between lazing on beaches and heading up into the hills and the thick laurel forest of the **Parque Nacional de Garajonay**, which encompasses most of the centre of the island and has been deemed a World Heritage site by UNESCO. Further east along the coast and with the sunniest weather on the island, the uninspiring fishing village of **Playa de Santiago** has also constructed a smattering of tourist accommodation.

Getting there and getting around

For a laid-back holiday "away from it all", consider renting on the island's **casas rurales** – refurbished former farmhouses. Available by the week (from €200), they need to be booked in advance, which is best done by calling central reservations on ☎ 922/144 101.

As yet, there are no regular services to La Gomera's new domestic airport, so most locals and travellers alike find there way to San Sebastián, the island's capital, on the frequent, **daily ferry service** from Los Cristianos in Tenerife – some of these ferries also go on to La Palma and El Hierro.

The island is served by three public **bus services**, which leave from the ferry terminal with an additional stop at the bus station on Via de Ronda. The first heads up to Valle Gran Rey via Chipude (Linea #1; 2–4 daily; 1hr 40min; €4), the second runs to Playa de Santiago (Linea #2; 2–4 daily; 1hr 10min; €4), and the third goes to Vallehermosa via Hermigua (Linea #3; 2–4 daily; 1hr 30min; €3.5).

Though the bus network is neither extensive nor services frequent, the buses are not only a good and inexpensive way of getting around, but also the most practical way of making a **hiking tour** of the island. In acknowledgement of this useful service, bus drivers are happy to stop anywhere en route to drop passengers off, though they will usually only pick up from recognized stops. To fill in where and when buses don't run, **taxis** are a useful and relatively affordable alternative for those travelling in groups – fares from San Sebastián to Valle Gran Rey are around €36; to Vallehermoso €24; to Hermigua €18.

For more leisurely touring, the **rental car** is the most practical and affordable option and there are several rental companies in San Sebastián, Playa de Santiago and Valle Gran Rey. Some even have a couple of branches and allow one way rentals at no extra charge. Charges start from around €25 per day, including unlimited mileage and full insurance. In Valle Gran Rey **mountain bikes**, **scooters** and **motorbikes** can also be rented.

SAN SEBASTIÁN

Map 16, M6.

Map 17 covers San Sebastián in detail.

Sandwiched between imposing steep-sided headlands, the busy transport hub of **SAN SEBASTIÁN** was the first Spanish settlement on the island and has grown to be far and away La Gomera's largest town, though with a population of 5000 and a waterfront that runs to just 400 metres, it's hardly hectic or huge. Central to the functional little town's role as the island capital is its good sheltered **harbour**, home to many yachts and docking point for ferries from Tenerife. The harbour was also party to La Gomera's most famous hour, on September 6, 1492, when Christopher Columbus led three small caravels out of the bay on his first voyage west to the Americas.

Over the years the harbour has drawn the attentions of other seafarers, including English, French, Portuguese and Dutch pirates. Gomerans became well used to doggedly defending their patch, fleeing to caves in the hills with their possessions and fighting fiercely from there; as a 1599 Dutch raiding party found: "…Canaria is by interpretation, dogs kinde, for they ran as swift as dogs, and were as tyrannicall and bloudthirsty as the ravening Wolfe…". Losing over a hundred men in skirmishes further up the valley, the Dutch contented themselves with setting the town ablaze. English pirates had even less luck; Sir Francis Drake's attack of 1585 was successfully repulsed, as was Charles Windham's in 1743, as is celebrated in murals in the town's major church.

The harbour mostly turned itself to less dramatic events after this, as San Sebastián busied itself with the island's agricultural **exports**, first silk and rum and later cochineal dyes. But when the boom and bust cycles of these monocultures hit the island's economy, the port was host to tearful good-byes as many of the islanders left for South America.

There is still something of a rural atmosphere in San Sebastián, and though most visitors tend to see it as a noisy transport hub, high-tailing to quieter parts of the island as soon as bus timetables allow, there are plenty of attractions here and these days the little place is emerging as a **good base** in itself. Away from the cliques of tourists in Valle Gran Rey it is a fine place to retire to after a day in the mountains, with plenty of bars and restaurants. If you only have a couple of days on the island and no car, you'd do well to base yourself here, from where all the island bus services radiate.

Arrival and Information

From the ferry terminal it is a short walk past the yacht harbour to the main **Plaza de las Américas** (Map 17, D6)

SAN SEBASTIÁN

and the smaller adjoining **Plaza de la Constitución**. Both plazas face the promenade and main beach and are at the heart of the functional little town. Behind them, two narrow roads, **Calle Ruiz de Padrón** and **Calle del Medio** house the bulk of the town's accommodation, bars and restaurants. The town's **tourist office** (Map 17, D5. Mon–Fri 9am–1.30pm, Sat & Sun 10am–1pm; ☎922/140 147) is in the old Customs House, on the corner of C/del Medio and Plaza de la Constitución.

Accommodation

With the exception of the luxury state-run *Parador Nacional* and one apartment block on the cliff above town, **accommodation** is clustered in the area around the plazas. A large number of private apartments supplement the list below and many of these can be good value, starting at €25 a night for two, with rates dropping for stays of more than two nights. You may be met at the harbour by touts trying to let these, otherwise keep a look out for signs in shops and bars.

HOTELS

Garajonay

Map 17, D6. C/de Ruiz de
Padrón 17
☎922/870 550
Big four-storey hotel in the
centre of town, with 56 clean
and simple, pine-furnished,
en-suite rooms; a lift and
reception that's opened round
the clock. The hotel usually

has vacancies and can also offer
some singles and triples. **❸**.

Parador Nacional

Map 17, F6. Lomo de la Horca
☎922/871 100
🅕922/871 116
Graceful four-star Canarian-
style mansion high above
town with breathtaking views
over it, the valley and out to
sea towards Tenerife. Despite
being built in the 1970s the

rooms have a rustic and slightly uncomfortable feel to them. Even so the hotel is consistently full and reservations generally need to be made several weeks in advance. **❼**.

Torre del Conde
Map 17, C6. C/Ruíz de Padrón 19
☎ 922/870 000
🖷 922/871 314

New central hotel with simple elegant rooms, including some singles, all with TVs and air-conditioning. Many also have balconies and some overlook the park containing Torre del Conde as does the high rooftop terrace which is equipped with sunloungers. Prices include breakfast; full- or half-board deals are also on offer. **❺**.

PENSIONS

- - - - - - - - - - - - - - - - - - - -

Hostal Colombina
Map 17, B4. C/de Ruiz de Padrón 83
☎ 922/871 257

Functional, clean and quiet

property with friendly owners and a pleasant roof-terrace with views over town. Being five minutes walk from centre of town, there is often room here when elsewhere is full. Rooms come with bath and there are some triples and good value singles, too. Reception is open daily 7.30am–1pm & 4pm–7.30pm. **❹**.

Pensión Colón
Map 17, C4. C/del Medio 59
☎ 922/870 235

A collection of simple, clean and tastefully decorated rooms – though those with balcony look out onto a noisy road, and those without are windowless, dark affairs. Some rooms have their own bathrooms and there are singles and triples available too. If there is no-one in reception, ring at the green door for attention. **❷**.

Pensión La Gomera
Map 17, C5. C/del Medio 33
☎ 922/870 417

Despite the great first impressions — a huge wooden gate and a lush courtyard garden – the dark, cramped rooms in this pension are in need of renovation. A good standard of cleanliness reigns throughout though, including in the shared bathrooms. Of the five rooms one sleeps three, another four and the rest are doubles. ❷.

Pensión Victor Leralta

Map 17, D5. C/del Medio 23
℡ 922/870 207 or 607/517 565
Collection of dingy rooms with rough whitewashed walls behind a bar in a charming old Canarian house. The two rooms above the bar, one sleeping three, face the street, are particularly noisy and have very thin walls. Some rooms have their own bathrooms, most share. ❷.

Residencia Hespérides

Map 17, C5. C/de Ruiz de Padrón 42
℡ 922/871 305
Clean, basic, good value pension in the thick of the things. Rooms have sinks but share bathrooms. There are some cheap singles beside a roof terrace, too. Ring at the door on the first floor for attention. ❷.

APARTMENTS

Canaris

Map 17, D6. C/Ruíz de Padrón 3
℡ 922/141 453
New well-run apartment block with roomy, well-equipped, modern apartments near the plaza, some with views over Torre del Conde. Both the apartments and studios sleep two; the studios are particularly good value. ❷.

Garcia

Map 17, D5. C/del Medio 27
℡ 922/870 652
Ugly multistorey house where most apartments are let to locals. Of the basic units reserved for holiday lets, many have sea views – and there is a roof terrace available to all. Lets are for a minimum of three nights and can sleep three. €100 for three nights, €200 per week.

Miramar

Map 17, E5. Orilla del Llano 3

☎ 922/870 448
Above town beside the *Parador Nacional* complex, these smart pine-furnished apartments are peacefully beyond the noise and bustle of the town centre and face away from a busy road nearby. Units can sleep three, with the third person on a sofa-bed. Lets are for a minimum of three nights. If there's no answer try Bar Curva next door. €110 for three nights, €210 per week.

Around Town

Other than the sturdy little medieval fort, **Torre Del Conde**, in a park near the promenade, all the town's most interesting buildings are to be found along the Calle del Medio. These include a number of elegant wood houses and the town's main church, **Iglesia Nuestra Señora de la Asuncion**. Townspeople try to link many of these buildings with the visit of Christopher Columbus. In fact links are at best circumstantial, and in any case most old buildings in San Sebastián have been destroyed and rebuilt several times following the repeated sackings of the town by pirates. Even so, a wander around the old streets gives an insight into the town's history and probably won't take much more than an hour. A stroll along the promenade overlooking San Sebastián's main **beach** leads to the harbour and a headland, around which is the town's second, more secluded beach.

Torre Del Conde

Map 17, C6. Tues–Sat 10am–1pm; free.
The first building of any note to go up in town was the stocky **Torre Del Conde**, built in 1447 as a strategic fall-back whilst the conquest of the rest of the island slowly continued. It proved useful, serving just this purpose when Beatriz de Bobadilla, the wife of the murdered governor

SAN SEBASTIÁN

●

Hernán Peraza, barricaded herself in this citadel in 1488 until help arrived (see p.236). Today the fort contains probably the definitive collection of maps and etchings charting Gomeran history. Maps from 1492 show how, at the time when Columbus was striking out into unknown waters, most of the Gomeran interior still remained uncharted – and would remain so until the seventeenth century. A copy of the 1743 demand by English naval officer Charles Windham, ordering that San Sebastián give up arms and surrender, is also here – along with the defiant reply of Diego Bueno, representative of the citizens of San Sebastián, and a print of the subsequent British retreat.

Customs house
Map 17, D5.

Overlooking the Plaza de la Constitución, on the corner of Calle del Medio is the large, classy, seventeenth-century **customs house**. Currently housing the town's tourist office, a couple of the rooms are given over to displaying information about Columbus's voyage to the Americas. A few scale models of the three ships he took are part of this display, but the most famous link, in the courtyard of the building, is the Pozo de la Aguada, the well from which Columbus took his water supplies to consequently "baptise" the New World.

Iglesia Nuestra Señora de la Asuncion
Map, D4.

Before setting off on his voyage, Columbus is said to have visited the town's main church, **Nuestra Señora de la Asuncion**, for a final session of prayers. Construction of the building started in 1490 and since this project took twenty years to complete, it's difficult to imagine quite what it would have looked like in 1492. In any case, a 1618 attack by Algerian pirates destroyed all but its basic structure, so today's building dates mostly from the seventeenth century – a brick-and-lime, mostly Gothic-style construction, with some Baroque elements, particularly in the carvings of the impressive **wooden altars**. A large faded mural on one wall of the church depicts the successful repulse of Windham's naval attack on the island, cause for great celebration for a town no doubt weary of rebuilding after pirate attacks. The archway to the left of the main entrance is the **Puerta del Perdón** which the Guanches were invited to step through for a full amnesty after an uprising in the hills in 1488. Hundreds came, only to find they had been tricked, and consequently were executed or sold as slaves.

Casa de Colón and the Ermita de San Sebastián

Further down Calle del Medio a quaint, wooden-balconied seventeenth-century house at no. 56 has been called the **Casa de Colón** (Map 17, C4. Mon–Fri 9am–1pm, 4.30–7.30pm, Sat 9am–1pm; free). Built over a hundred years after his death, it would of course have been impossible for Columbus to have actually stayed in this building. Even so, maps of the voyage, some pieces of Peruvian pottery, and small rotating exhibitions of contemporary Gomeran art provide a few diverting minutes here. A short way further along this same street is the tiny **Ermita de San Sebastián**, the island's first chapel, built in 1450. Like all buildings in San Sebastián the chapel was not spared by pirates, and has been destroyed at least three times. Recent restoration has returned the building to its original basic form. One of the few decorations are fourteen iron crosses on the wall, representing the Stations of the Cross.

The beaches

The plazas at San Sebastián's centre overlook the bay, the harbour and a pleasant long promenade beside the longest sandy **beach** (400m) on the island. **Playa de San**

SAN SEBASTIÁN

●

BEATRIZ DE BOBADILLA

Although La Gomera's most famous association is with Christopher Columbus, its most infamous is with the aristocratic Beatriz de Bobadilla, by reputation a vicious medieval nymphomaniac, and by all accounts – including a portrait in the Parador Nacional – a great beauty.

Beatriz first came to the attention of Isabella of Castille, the queen of Spain, as one her husband Ferdinand's mistresses. Fearful of how this beautiful woman might manipulate her husband, Isabella took a fairly instant dislike to Beatriz and contrived to have her banished to La Gomera, the outermost island of the Spanish empire, by having her married off to Spanish aristocrat Hernán Peraza the Younger, who was equally out of favour being suspected of murdering another noble.

Isabella's judgement of the pair seems to have been borne out by their ruthless treatment of the native population, leading to uprisings and Peraza's death in 1488. The episode began as the result of a love tryst between Peraza and a Guanche princess, Yballa, in a cave in the hills, during which the princess's Gomeran suitor surprised the couple and ran Peraza through with a lance. An island-wide rebellion followed in the wake of this event, forcing Beatriz to hole up in the Tore del Conde in San Sebastián and send for the governor of Gran Canaria, Pedro de Vera, who came to brutally crush the rebellion. Hundreds of Gomerans were coaxed from the mountains by promises of complete amnesty, to be summarily put to death or sold as slaves. De Vera even went to the extraordinar-

Sebastián (Map 17, C8), originally a pebble beach, is now sandy through regular dredging of the harbour, when sand from the sea floor is sprayed onto the beach (for the sea to wash back again). Playa de la Cueva (Map 17, G6), a smaller sandy beach, less disturbed by the Tenerife ferry, is a

ily cruel extent of massacring his own resident Gomeran population, around three hundred people, on Gran Canaria. The only slight justice for Gomerans came once Isabella learned of the situation, landing Beatriz with a huge fine, and stripping Pedro de Vera of his post as governor.

Four years later, still ruler of La Gomera, but now single, Beatriz played host to Christopher Columbus. In her company, he delayed his first journey to the New World in 1492 for over a month, giving rise to much speculation about the pair. The fact that San Sebastián was not even the best-equipped Canarian port (Columbus sent one ship to Gran Canaria for repairs) suggests that the lady's companionship was a large part of Columbus's motivation. Rumours of a liaison grew and on subsequent trips Columbus would add to the circumstantial evidence, interrupting both his 1493 and 1498 journeys on the island. In 1498 he was disappointed to find that Beatriz had married Alonso Fernández de Lugo, the conqueror of Tenerife, so that on his final 1502 voyage Columbus didn't even bother to weigh anchor in San Sebastián.

Meanwhile, ruling La Gomera from Tenerife, Beatriz, became increasingly paranoid about her position there. In response to rumours of a plot to oust her from power, she had the governor and a townsman, who was alleged to have talked of her loose ways, put to death. These and other irregularities were now the last straw for Isabella, who sent for Beatriz to attend the royal court to explain herself. Within days of taking up residence at court Beatriz was found poisoned in bed. Few efforts were made to carry out an inquiry into the death.

five-minute walk beyond the yacht harbour and along a short road that leads around the headland at the harbour end of the promenade (or a short tunnel that leads through it from just beside the road).

BEATRIZ DE BOBADILLA

Eating

Each restaurant listed in the *Guide* has been categorized as
either inexpensive (under €6), moderate (€6– €10) and
expensive (above €10) – indicating the price of an average
main course.

A fair selection of **bars** and **restaurants** serve simple, inexpensive Canarian dishes, tapas and international fast food at
the centre of town. In addition to the places listed below,
there are plentiful **cafés**, most of them scattered around the
two adjoining plazas in the town centre, which make a
good place for coffees, cakes, ice creams and snacks. Some
stay open late, serving drinks until around 2am.

Breñusca

Map 17, D5. C/del Medio 11
Wood-furnished bar serving
good basic Canarian food –
try the tasty cress soup,
chunky stews such as *rancho
canario* or the spicy rabbit in
salamorejo sauce. There's a
good selection of meat and
fish and the restaurant opens
from 9am – serving omelettes
for breakfast. Closed Sun.
Inexpensive.

Casa del Mar

Map 17, E6. Avda Fred Olsen 2
℡ 922/871 219
Photos of ships and boats line
the walls of this brightly light

restaurant that serves the
largest selection of fish and
seafood on the island. The
friendly owner prepares most
of the dishes and does an
excellent fish stew (*cazuela*),
involving *gofio* and lots of
herbs, that takes almost an
hour to prepare. The good
food and moderate prices
attract locals as well as
visitors. Open for lunch and
dinner, but closed Sun.
Moderate.

Cubino

Map 17, E5. C/de la Virgen de
Guadelupe 2.
Small, rustic, but brightly lit

bar and restaurant just off the main square serving typical Canarian fare. Main courses such as the solid tuna steak and grilled chops cost less than €6. Order *papas arrugadas* to dip in the great home-made *mojo*. Inexpensive.

La Casa Vieja
Map 17, C5. C/de la República de Chile 5.
Small simple bar where the TV blares football and you can get fresh tapas off a chalkboard menu listing dishes such as octopus, rabbit and goat. Inexpensive.

La Tasca
Map 17, C5. C/de Ruiz de Padrón 34
Multilingual menus indicate a mostly tourist clientele in this old, dimly lit Canarian house. Even so, prices are pretty reasonable and there are lots of fish and meat dishes to choose from. Most are simple dishes such as garlic chicken

with chips, or a great mixed salad involving lettuce, tomatoes, onion, artichoke, asparagus, beans, olives, carrots and paprika. Try the excellent spicy Mexican tomato soup to start. The restaurant also has a good wine selection. Open evenings only. Inexpensive to moderate.

Marqués de Cristano
Map 17, D5. C/del Medio 24
☏ 922/870 022
Classy restaurant in a restored eighteenth-century house. The superb selection of tapas is served in a pleasant courtyard, while the restaurant above serves Canarian food with a decidedly gourmet twist: rabbit in marmalade; lobster with melon and mint; and garlic shrimps. The restaurant opens for lunch and dinner and often puts on live music on Saturdays. Closed Sun. Expensive.

Drinking and Nightlife

Other than the few bars gathered around the plaza, there is little nightlife in San Sebastián. One fun **bar** on the Plaza de la Constitución is *Bar RP*, a sociable place to sample thirty-five varieties of beer until 2am (closed Sun). After 2am options are limited to the rather mediocre **disco**, the *Discoteca Fin Fan*, C/de la Virgen de la Guadalupe 7 (€6 cover), that's never busy before this time, but blares chart music until 5am. The other option, but also only busy at weekends, is a new semi-outdoor venue *Discomera* at the west end of the seafront promenade.

Listings

Banks and exchanges Several banks have branches in town. Caja Canarias, Plaza de las Américas 8, is conveniently central with an ATM.

Books Junonia, Avda de Colón 24, has a small selection of books in English and good hiking maps of the island. It also sells and develops photographic film.

Car rental Hertz, Avda Fred Olsen (☎922/870 439); La Rueda, C/del Medio 19 (☎922/870 709, ☏922/870 142; ⓦwww.autolarueda.com).

Hospital Hospital El Calvario (☎922/870 450) on the west side of town. In an emergency, call ☎112.

Internet El Cambijú, a bar on Plaza de la Constitución has a terminal for Internet use (€4 for 30min).

Laundry Lavanderia Hecu, C/del Medio 76.

Pharmacy Farmacia Devina Creus Rey, Plaza de la Constitución 14 (☎922/870 905) is the English-speaking one of four pharmacies, between them providing a 24-hour service (details posted on the door of each).

Police Policia Municipal (☎922/870 062) offices are in the town hall on Avda Fred Olsen. The Guardia Civil barracks

(☎922/870 255) are out of the town centre on the highway to Valle Gran Rey. In an emergency call ☎062.

Post office The main office is at C/de Medio 60 (Mon–Fri 8.30–2.30pm, Sat 9.30–1pm; ☎922/871 031).

Scuba diving The German-run Little Diving School, C/Ruiz de Padron 50 (☎922/141 135, ©Kleine.Tauchschule@mail.infocanarias.com).

Taxis At the harbour or at the rank beside Plaza de las Américas. To book, call ☎922/870 524.

Travel agents Tamaragua Tours, Plaza de la Constitución (☎922/141 056) organizes island tours and hiking trips in the national park for around €21 per person for a two- to four-hour hike.

Around San Sebastián

There are **good hikes** with rewarding views conveniently close to San Sebastián. A couple of hikes can be done straight out of town, but it's worth using the public bus service to get a bit further to see some of the island's most spectacular spots, most of which are on this side of the island.

The short, steep climb up to the Parador Nacional hotel on the headland to the east of town is an obvious excursion that doesn't take long and is a good way of getting your bearings. On the headland directly opposite stands the **Sagrado Corazon de Jesus**, an imposing seven-metre high statue of Christ and a worthwhile two-hour hike. It's reached via a rough track (follow a path to the right of the diesel power station on the west side of town), or you can take either the Valle Gran Rey or Playa de Santiago bus up to the nearby road to significantly shorten the hike.

Both these buses continue further up the hairpin road to **Degollada de Peraza**, a spot associated with the murder of the island's governor in 1488 and now home to **Bar Peraza**. From Bar Peraza, hike 100m further west along the road to a viewpoint, from where a steep, but well-marked path leads through groves of palms and orange trees and past vineyards to **La Laja**. There's a small shop and telephone in the village, which is connected to San Sebastián, a pleasant three-hour hike away via a minor road down the idyllic Barranco de Villa. Another route up to the huge volcanic plug of **Roque Agando** climbs out of town past more palms, rudimentary stone houses and terraces growing potatoes and vegetables. The climb is mostly shaded by pine and eucalyptus, where scorch signs of the large 1984 fire are still visible. The route passes a stone refuge **Degollada de Tanque**, whose pine needle-covered floor can provide a basic place to sleep three. With the splendid backdrop of the Roque de Ojila, it's also a good place to picnic. The path climbs back up to the road, to a memorial to those who died in the 1984 forest fire, just below the Roque Agando, where buses to San Sebastián stop.

NORTHERN LA GOMERA

Thanks to Atlantic trade winds regularly clouding the skies above the damp lush valleys of northern La Gomera, these are the most fertile areas of the island. Bananas are still grown in large quantities, particularly in **Hermigua**, and most of the tiny population on this side of the island is involved in agriculture. Despite the picturesque nature of valleys here, the lack of reliable sunshine has kept tourism to a minimum. The north only plays host to a few **hikers**, enjoying hikes along the steep cliffs of the coastline, particularly around **Vallehermoso**, not minding that the sea off the north's small pebble beaches is generally too dangerous to allow bathing.

Hermigua

Map 16, I3.

Scattered the length of a pretty ravine, and fed by water from La Gomera's only stream, **HERMIGUA** is in the island's lushest valley. The presence of a relatively plentiful supply of water here has encouraged prolific **banana cultivation** to dominate the valley's landscape for over a century. However, there's not much to keep visitors, unless they are using this as a base for hiking trips to the national park, and the sea at its northern end is generally too rough for bathing.

Though buildings seem fairly evenly scattered along the length of the valley, Hermigua broadly divides into a lower and upper village. The centre of the upper village, **VALLE ALTO**, the original heart, is marked by the sixteenth century **Iglesia de Santo Domingo** (rarely open) beside a convent of the same name. Nearby, in a pretty, renovated house a handicrafts workshop, Los Telares, sells crafts and occasionally puts on demonstrations, though mainly for bus parties. Lower down the valley the village of **VALLE BAJO**, has as its centrepiece a small plaza beside the modern church Nuestra Señora de la Emancipatión. Another small collection of buildings is further down the valley, by the large **pebble beach**. Huge Atlantic rollers and strong undercurrents mean that the only spot to swim here is in the large **sea-water pool**.

Practicalities

The San Sebastián–Vallehermoso **bus** passes through the valley four times a day each way, stopping by both churches. A couple of small shops, bars, two banks (with ATMs) and a petrol station serve basic needs. There are also a few functional places to stay and a couple of reasonable restaurants in the valley.

In **Valle Bajo** there are a couple of places **to stay**. Five rooms are offered in the former clinic turned pension, *Clínica*, Ctra General 72 (Ⓣ & Ⓕ 922/881 040). A sociable place and well set up for groups (up to eight people) as there's a communal kitchen, eating area and pleasant little garden. Rooms must be rented for a minimum of three days (€60, €126 per week). Nearby and also German-run, *La Casa Creativa*, Ctra. General 56 (Ⓣ & Ⓕ 922/881 023; ❹) offers well-equipped studios and apartments, sharing a pleasant terrace and small pool, and can offer full-board deals involving its wholefood **restaurant**. As well as having the most hilariously translated English menu on the island, the moderately expensive restaurant does a good job of creatively blending German wholefood fare and Gomeran cuisine.

Further **down the valley**, overlooking the shingle beach, is *Apartamentos Playa* (Ⓣ 922/880 758, Ⓕ 922/880 276; ❷), a collection of clean basic **apartments** sleeping two and run by the neighbouring bar Los Prismas. On the road just above them, *Pension Piloto* (Ⓣ 922/144 120; ❷) also has pretty views of the sea, but more basic rooms sharing bathrooms. The neighbouring *Bar Piloto* (closed Sun) serves good inexpensive **bar food** to three small tables that look out to sea. Though the menu changes daily, it often serves fresh tuna with tasty salads and a good home-made mojo. Good breakfast options include filled rolls, aniseed bread and fried eggs and bacon. Just above *Bar Piloto* and with the same sea views, *Restaurant El Faro* (closed Wed & June), does more substantial **meals** including a great fish paella that needs pre-ordering (same morning at the latest) and a good fresh fish and cress stew. It also offers meat dishes such as lamb with *papas arrugadas*. Down beside the beach and the sea-water pool, *Bar El Pescante* offers a small menu of tapas and fish dishes to tables on a terrace. The bar is only open from June to September, when it plays pop music to young Hermiguans and a handful of holidaymakers.

Around Hermigua

Whereas the sea off Hermigua's own beach is rarely safe enough for swimming, the quiet, pretty, black sand-and-pebble beach **Playa de la Caleta** (Map 16, J3), about an hour's walk (6km) east, is usually a better bet. A little restaurant, open on fair days between April and October, serves grilled fresh fish, mostly caught by fishermen living in a couple of nearby huts. The dirt road to Playa de la Caleta begins near the plaza in Valle Bajo and heads east up a steep road to the top of a headland, from where it descends into a valley.

Heading west, the road to Vallehermoso passes the seventeenth-century picture-book village of **AGULO** (Map 16, I2), 5km from Hermigua; a small maze of cobbled alleys and whitewashed houses huddled on a rock platform below dramatic cliffs. A short walk around its pretty, quiet streets is well worthwhile.

Further west along the main road there is the turn-off to La Palmita and the national park visitors' centre (see p.261).

EL SILBO: THE WHISTLING TONGUE

Devised to overcome the difficulties that steep terrain posed to communication, a remarkable whistling language, **El Silbo**, was invented by the Guanches to relay messages between valleys. The whistles require two fingers to be inserted in the mouth, while the other hand shields and modulates a sound that is loud enough to be heard up to 4km away. Over time different dialects have even developed – northern islanders' whistles are slower and more accentuated. Today Gomerans are more likely to pick up the telephone than whistle and the language is restricted to performances for visitors and at fiestas, though in an attempt to keep the language alive, El Silbo is now a compulsory subject for Gomeran school children.

NORTHERN LA GOMERA

Further along the main road from this junction, the tourist restaurant *Las Rosas* (daily noon–3pm) serves mediocre food amid regular demonstrations of the whistling language, El Silbo, to tour groups, but the views over the coast are wonderful. From Las Rosas the road winds its way 13km to **Vallehermoso** through traditional farming hamlets and thousands of neat, well-kept terraces.

Vallehermoso

Map 16, F2.

The setting of **VALLEHERMOSO**, whose name means beautiful valley, is without doubt picturesque, with the eponymous town nestling between the steep drops of surrounding ridges, and the precariously towering volcanic monolith **Roque Cano** rising 250m above it. Much of the surrounding countryside makes for first-class **hiking**.

Focal point for the town is the **Plaza de la Constitución**, a small plaza inside surrounded by bars, shops, banks (with ATMs), a post office, a medical centre and a petrol station. Heading north from here, it takes thirty minutes to walk to the sea. The tempestuous surf that barrels against the **rocky beach** generally rules out bathing, in any case not encouraged by the often gloomy weather on this side of the island. Undeterred however, the local community has, for around five years, been building a large bathing pool to be surrounded by various services – a project that seems destined to become a white elephant.

The climb onto the **Cumbre de Chijeré** ridge west of the beach forms part of an excellent, varied four-hour return **hike**, with incredible views in every direction. First ascending a steep-sided gorge up to the ridge a few hundred metres shy of the beach, between three houses, the trail, soon marked by blue arrows and red dots, zigzags its way steeply up the rocky arid slopes. Views from here take in the

NORTHERN LA GOMERA

rugged line of cliffs, usually pounded by a turbulent sea on this side of the island, with Teide in the background. As the path reaches the top of the ridge the view opens to a landscape of ochre rock eroded into swirling shapes. A dirt road, which leads as far as the viewpoint on the tip of the ridge nearby, runs inland past a tiny neat chapel. Once the chapel is out of sight, follow a narrow track off to the right, through woods with more great views over the cliffscape to the west. The columned Los Organos cliffs are below here, but can only be viewed by boat (see p.253). The path rejoins the main track at another chapel, where a short way further on another narrow track turns off to the east, snaking its way through dense Laurasilva forest, then descending through terraces, back into the centre of Vallehermoso.

Practicalities

The **bus** from San Sebastián stops near the Plaza de la Constitución, the town's most popular meeting point. *Bar/Pension Amaya* (☎922/800 073; ❷), dominates the plaza's social life and is consistently busy serving coffees, basic food and tapas. It also rents both basic rooms sharing bathrooms or more luxurious options featuring a private bath, TV and fridge. Another option, just south of the plaza, is *Casa Bernardo*, C/de Triana 4 (☎922/800 849; ❷), whose friendly, relaxed owners speak English and offer clean and simple singles and doubles, along with use of a communal kitchen. Two apartments on the roof here are also good options, but require a three-night minimum stay. A little further down the same street *Hostal Vallehermoso*, C/Triana 9 (☎922/800 283; ❷), has five rooms sharing a bathroom and kitchen. The landlady lives at C/Mayor 11 just north of the plaza, where she runs the textile shop.

The town's most elegant **accommodation** option is provided by the *Hotel de Triana* (☎922/800 528, ☎922/800 128; ❺) a short walk further down Calle Triana. The en-suite singles and doubles come with TV, phone and fridge and share a roof-top terrace with excellent views over town. One of the few places **to eat** in town, *Restaurant Triana*, C/Triana 27, serves basic food such as chicken and chips, Spanish omelette and vegetable soup. Try the daily specials posted on a blackboard.

VALLE GRAN REY

Map 16, B6.

Map 18 covers Valle Gran Rey in detail.

Always referred to as though it were a single town **VALLE GRAN REY** is actually a deep gorge carved out of the island's ancient rock containing a number of villages along its length. What visitors usually mean by Valle Gran Rey is the collection of villages near the sea, where the valley fans out into a small fertile delta, filled with banana plantations and surrounded by forbidding basalt cliffs. More tourist infrastructure and more tourists are concentrated here than on the rest of the island put together – though by Canarian standards it remains a minor resort. There's not much to do here, but the relaxing sand-and-pebble beaches and a collection of pleasantly low-key bars and restaurants are a good base for a laid-back holiday or, as is the case everywhere in La Gomera, sensational hiking.

In the late 1960s the valley became the destination of choice for many German hippies and drop-outs. As their numbers have dwindled, their place has been taken by a multitude of generally left-wing German students and professionals seeking an "alternative" beach holiday – away from the package destinations elsewhere in the Canaries. But though most of the upper valley is terraced for agriculture, the comparatively large earnings from tourism have

VALLE GRAN REY

been irresistible to locals who have built lots of small apartment blocks to accommodate visitors near the sea. These are concentrated in five villages, separated by small banana plantations and tenuous building restrictions that prevent them melting together.

At the point where the mouth of the narrow valley opens out into a delta, clustered houses have clawed their way up a cliff to form **La Calera**. Steep stairs and winding alleys connect old buildings enjoying great valley and sea views. The biggest and busiest of the three resorts, **Vueltas** is built around the valley's harbour and still retains some of the feel of a small harbour village, despite all the newly erected, small-scale apartment buildings. On its western side new building work has created nondescript housing and tourist accommodation in two areas known as **Borbalán**, along the road to La Calera, and **La Puntilla**, along the seafront. **La Playa**, a ten minute walk further west alongside a large pebble beach, is also a collection of newer buildings, clustered around a relatively modest beach where a short busy promenade creates an easy-going seaside atmosphere.

Arrival and information

Buses from San Sebastián stop in La Calera, Vueltas and La Playa. If leaving the valley by bus, it's worth hiking to La Playa to be sure of a seat. The valley's **tourist office** (Mon–Sat 9am–1.30pm; ☎922/805 458) is in La Playa, on the road that runs parallel to the promenade.

Accommodation

A couple of **hotels**, a handful of **pensions** and over a hundred small-scale **apartment buildings** are scattered around the three main villages in Valle Gran Rey. Prices for the last two are similar, though apartment owners will tend to look for at least week-long lets. **La Calera** tends to be a quiet destination favoured by families; **Vueltas** attracts those wanting nightlife; and **La Playa** – also with its fair share of nightlife – is well positioned for the best beaches, if lacking in a traditional atmosphere.

Hunting around between the many, frequently unmanned, apartment buildings is a tiring business, requiring some patience. To avoid this, it's worth contacting one of the **apartment agencies** at least three weeks in advance – longer for stays over Easter or Christmas. *Servicos Integrados La Gomera* (℡ & ℻ 922/805 866, Ⓔ risac@mx3.redestb.es) is based beside the bus stop in La Calera can offer a large number of apartments all around the valley; *Manuel Trujillo y Trujillo* in La Puntilla (℡ 922/805 129) has around thirty apartments, most in La Puntilla, Vueltas and some in La Calera; and *Viajes Gran Rey*, also in La Puntilla (℡ 922/805 480, ℻ 922/805 293) can organize apartments all over the valley.

HOTELS

Argayall: Place of light
℡ 922/697 008
ⓦ www.argayall.com
New Age centre fifteen minutes walk from Vueltas in an isolated spot by the beach. A big activity programme includes meditation workshops, reiki, yoga, African dance and drumming. Both singles and doubles are available and prices includes

vegetarian full board. Reception is open 10am–1pm, but closed Tues. ❼.

Gran Rey
Map 18, D5. La Puntilla
℡ 922/805 859
℻ 922/805 651
ⓦ www.hotel-granrey.com
New, large waterfront hotel is the valley's most luxurious accommodation; facilities include tennis courts, a pool and a large roof terrace. En-suite rooms have air-

conditioning and TVs. There are some singles available and prices include breakfast. ❼.

PENSIONS

Cocha
Map 18, E3. La Calera
☎ 922/805 007
Elegant, hotel-quality lodgings in the first place in the valley to rent rooms to foreigners. Views from the sociable patios are superb and the pension also runs a couple of functional apartments nearby. ❸.

Candelaria
Map 18, F8. Vueltas
☎ 922/805 402
Simple, busy pension on one of the backstreets of the old port with a large sociable sundeck and good sea views from the roof. There are rooms of various sizes, styles and prices – plus some basic apartments (from €130 per week) – some with private bathrooms. ❸.

Casa Bella Cabellos
Map 18, F2. La Calera

☎ 922/805 182
Restored old Canarian home with dark-wood balconies surrounded by lush vegetation. Run by an amenable old lady, this place has simple doubles, a studio and a four-bed apartment on offer. The house is a bit off the beaten track on the old village road. ❷.

Las Jornadas
Map 18, C3. La Playa
☎ 922/805 047
Excellently positioned in front of the beach, above a large restaurant. The large sociable roof terrace overlooking the sea is the highlight of the pension, whose simple rooms (some tiny) share grubby bathrooms. ❷.

Lola
Map 18, inset. La Playa
☎ 922/805 148
Ⓦ www.teide.net/emp/lola
Unattractive modern three-storey block over a restaurant of the same name houses small rooms, some windowless, and seven apartments. ❷.

VALLE GRAN REY

APARTMENTS

Avenida

Map 18, E8. Vueltas
☏ 922/805 461
Four-storey apartment block
in a splendid waterfront
position, with sea views from
all balconies. Apartments are
equipped with kitchenettes
and sleep two. ❸.

Bello

Map 18, inset. La Playa
☏ 922/805 008
Spacious, well-equipped,
modern apartments with
balconies beside the
promenade. Some overlook
the beach, others face a wall
of an apartment block only
yards away and are
consequently less expensive
(but darker). All apartments
sleep two. Enquire at Bar
Yaya below. ❹.

Casa Domingo

Map 18, C3. La Playa
☏ & Ⓕ 922/805 143
Bright, clean, pine-furnished
apartments close to the beach
with sea views in a four-
storey house surrounded by
banana groves beside the road
to La Calera. Most
apartments are permanently
let to locals, the rest rented
out to tourists. They sleep
two or four. ❸.

Yenay

Map 18, F8. Vueltas
☏ 922/805 471
Large basic block with
standard apartments, studios
and a couple of basic
windowless rooms. The roof
terrace is on one of the
largest buildings in town, so
has great panoramic views.
❷.

Beaches and Activities

A number of small **beaches**, all in walking distance of each
other, are dotted along the length of the coastline from the
north side of La Playa to well south of Vueltas. The commercial attractions of the valley are few, restricted to **boat
trips** from Vueltas searching for whales and dolphins and

viewing the northern cliffs Los Organos, and a **tropical orchard** offering tours. But its easy to spend a pleasant day wandering along the coastline and around the alleys of Vueltas and La Calera, before going on to explore some of the great **hiking** the valley has to offer.

Beaches

The best, and consequently busiest, beach is the one at **La Playa**. At its eastern end, by the laid-back restaurants and bars of the promenade, this is a black sandy affair, while further west – it stretches to La Puntilla – it is covered in fist-sized pebbles. From La Playa, a dirt track leads north to the most popular nudist beach **Playa del Inglés**. There are sharp rocks scattered around the sand here, beneath crashing waves, and great care is required to avoid them. The size of the surf and strength of ocean undertows regularly suspend bathing here.

Bathing is much more reliable around Vueltas. Just north, in La Puntilla, the placid, shallow waters of a small cove, dubbed the **baby beach**, entertains paddling toddlers, while **Playa Vueltas**, by the harbour is usually suitable for all – though occasional oil leaks from the harbour's boats are off-putting.

Boat trips

Boat trips depart from the harbour at Vueltas every day, the standard six-and-a-half-hour trip done by both the *Siron* (Tues–Sun 10.30am; €30; ☎922/805 480) and the *Tina* (daily 10.30am; €30; ☎922/805 699) heads out to the impressive, geometric-columned cliff face **Los Organos**. The 175-metre wide and 80-metre high wall of six-sided basalt columns, weathered to different heights, are said to resemble a church organ. The boats also stop so passengers can have a swim off a small beach only accessible by sea. Food is provided. You may also get to see dolphins and

VALLE GRAN REY

whales. Neither boat will run during rough seas. For specifically **whale-watching trips**, or to arrange tailor-made yachting trips, enquire at the Bait and Tackle shop (closed Sun) just inland of the plaza in Vueltas. The latest sea-life sightings are listed here and you can arrange sailing trips around the island (€45) and to Heirro and La Palma (€48) as well as deep-sea fishing trips.

South along the coast

A dirt road leads south of Vueltas along a base of a cliff face, to a large pebble beach beside which is a track up the Barranco Argaga. The tropical orchard **Argaga tropicfruitgarden** (Tues & Fri 10am–6pm; €9; ☎922/697 004, @personales.mundivia.es/schrader_La Gomera/), is a five-minute walk up this track. Originally just developed by enthusiasts as an organic garden for fruits and flowers, visitor curiosity has led to the orchard being opened for frequent, pleasantly informal tours. These concentrate on sampling around a dozen of the exotic fruits grown here, accompanied by the salient information on their cultivation. Tours are usually in German but can be given in English on request. Above the gardens, the incredible steep narrow gorge **Barranco Argaga** is an amazing sight and well worth a short hike up to investigate. Hiking its length and up to Chipude to catch the bus back is one of the hardest, but most memorable day hikes on the island.

Clambering further south along the pebble beach, at the base of the Barranco Argaga, a narrow track leads around some rocky headlands to **Playa de Las Arenas**. The series of coves here is home to a collection of hippies, who refer to it as rainbow beach and have painted a rainbow on the rock at its entrance. Expatriate Germans settling in the Valle Gran Rey know this as the *Schweinebucht* (bay of pigs) – expressing their feelings about its residents, not the 1960s Cuban missile crisis. The beaches are also popular with nudists.

Hiking in the valley

Striking out on foot, the most obvious local excursion is the three-hour return **hike up La Merica** (Map 16, C5), the magnificent headland above La Calera, for excellent views over the valley and out to sea. The well-trodden track starts from the high road at the furthest end of La Calera from the sea, marked by a large wooden sign. After winding up precipitous, treeless, volcanic cliffs, views improving all the time, the path branches off to a viewpoint near the top – marked by a windsock. The steepness of the headland here puts La Playa almost vertically below. Views north of the headland reveal an inaccessible and uninhabitable collection of steep gorges. This hike can also form part of an excellent half-day hike (approx. 4hr) from Arure at the head of the valley. By taking the bus up to this village you can head east to a trail that follows the stunning ridge south, alongside views over knife-edge cliffs to the accompaniment of goat bells, back to La Calera.

Eating

The local **restaurant** scene includes plenty of excellent-value dining options, most specializing in traditional, basic Gomeran food, typically fresh fish, with *papas arrugadas* and good home-made *mojo*. The bulk of the cafés in the valley are by the promenade in La Playa, a good place to sit and watch the world go by or enjoy the sunset.

Each restaurant listed in the *Guide* has been categorized as either inexpensive (under €6), moderate (€6– €10) and expensive (above €10) – indicating the price of an average main course.

VALLE GRAN REY

CAFÉS

Café Der Anderen Art
Map 18, E8. Vueltas.
Small trendy café in the centre of town with good continental breakfasts. Also serves cakes and crêpes all day.

Carlos
Map 18, E3. La Calera.
Café with tiny outside terrace overflowing with people watching the valley's busiest road, while they sample the good ice cream and freshly pressed fruit juices.

Casa de la Playa
Map 18, C3. La Playa.
Consistently busy, large, shady terrace beside a banana plantation on the edge of La Playa – the place to hang out at sunset. Serves good snacks and bocadillos along with ice-cream, shakes and fresh-pressed juices. Closed Sun.

Tambara
Map 18, E8. Vueltas.
Small bar with great views over the sea. Spots on the tiny patio are hard to come by, but the interior, decorated with Turkish mosaics, is also pleasant. The tapas are good, though the sandwiches seem over priced, as are the mediocre cocktails. Open 5pm-1am, but closed Wed.

RESTAURANTS

El Baifo
Map 18, inset. La Playa
℡ 922/805 775
Excellent Malaysian restaurant that makes the most of local supplies of fresh fish to offer a good break from the usual Gomeran cuisine. Vegetarians will be pleased with a selection of dishes. Closed Fri & July. Moderate.

El Mirador
Map 18, F3. La Calera
Large restaurant high up along the cobbled alleys of the old town is a good place to start or finish the day with great valley views (except on windy days, when plastic sheeting protects the terrace). Breakfasts include eggs,

bacon, omelettes and bocadillos and a good selection of fresh juices. The tapas and salads make for a good light lunch, while dinner sees the usual fish and meat options, served with *papas arrugadas* and excellent home-made *mojo*.

El Puerto
Map 18, F8. Vueltas

Strip-lit harbour-side restaurant whose formica tables are a favourite with local domino players and local fishermen enjoying a drink. Food is suitably basic, the €6 menu of the day typically including salad, a tuna steak and ice cream. The grilled fish platter for two people is the restaurant's speciality and an excellent choice. Inexpensive.

La Plaza
Map 18, E3. La Calera

Basic bar with no ambience and air laden with frying smells on the main road by the taxi rank. Popular despite this for its low prices and large portions of food like rabbit and chicken *en salsa*. Inexpensive.

La Salsa
Map 18, F8. Vueltas.

Bright, cheery, trendy restaurant with bold colour schemes and great vegetarian food. The varied menu includes tacos, Thai curry and tofu dishes. Though a bit pricey by local standards it's well worth it for the big portions of creative food. Closed Fri. Moderate.

La Terraza
Map 18, inset. La Playa

Large enclosed terrace visited exclusively by holidaymakers, this place specializes in big, good-value portions, including large pork chops with *papas arrugadas*, pizzas and paella. Closed Mon. Inexpensive.

Las Jornadas
Map 18, C3. La Playa

Well-liked landmark restaurant on the beach front and below the pension of the same name. Large portions of home-made food include a massive Spanish omelette, a tasty saffron-rice paella and a superb grilled chicken breast. Check for the fresh dishes of

VALLE GRAN REY

the day on the blackboard. Closed Tues. Moderate.

Mirador de Palmaerjo
Head of Valley
☎ 922/805 868

Restaurant and viewpoint, designed by Canarian artists César Manrique, with dizzying views of Valle Gran Rey beside the road that snakes down into it from the hills. A training ground for young chefs, the food is gourmet variations on old Canarian favourites. Well worth a stop on the way back from hiking in the uplands, but only if you have access to a car or taxi. Book ahead to get one of a handful of tables with the unobstructed valley views. Open Tues–Sat. Moderate to expensive.

San José
Map 18, inset. La Playa.

Small dimly lit restaurant serving some of the best Canarian food in the valley. Everything on the menu is reliably good, with superb fresh fish and fantastic *mojo*. There are plenty of good wines on offer, too, and the service is particularly friendly. Moderate to expensive.

Drinking and nightlife

By Gomeran standards the nightlife in Valle Gran Rey fairly rocks with several busy bars open until 2am. The majority of the trendiest places are in **Vueltas** – *Bar La Tasca* (Map 18, F8), primarily a tropical feel cocktail bar is a reliable option from around 10pm; the trendy stylish *Cacatua* (Map 18, F8), the most popular bar in the valley, further down the same street gets going a bit later and also serves good cocktails. There are some good, cosier options in **La Playa**, including the pub-style *Tasca La Gomera* (Map 18, inset), with its pleasant tiny outdoor terrace. The valley's only **disco** *Hubalupo* (Map 18, inset. Tues–Sat 11pm–5am), despite opening early, doesn't really get going until 1am and only really fills up on weekend nights. For a traditional

Gomeran evening look in at *El Bodegón* (Map 18, inset. Closed Sun), where local men have gathered to play folk music.

Listings

Banks and exchanges Caja Canarias has a branch with an ATM near the bus stop in La Calera. There are more banks and ATMs in Borbalán and La Puntilla.

Bike rental Bike Station La Gomera in La Puntilla (☎ & ℻ 922/805 082), rents out beach cruisers and mountain bikes from €5 per day; for €9 they also provide a shuttle up to La Laguna in the heart of the national park. Alofi Rentals in La Playa (☎922/805 554), also rent out bikes (from €5 per day) as well as a range of scooters and motorbikes (from €14 per day).

Books El Fotógrafo, on the promenade in La Playa, has a range of hiking maps, books and excellent postcards.

Car rental Autos El Carmen (☎922/805 029), near the harbour in Vueltas; Avis in La Puntilla (☎922/805 527); Auto La Rueda in La Playa (☎922/805 197); Hertz in Borbalán (☎922/805 527).

Hospital The nearest is in San Sebastián. In an emergency call ☎122.

Internet Internet Viva in Vueltas and Gerado's Café in La Playa both charge around €4 per hour.

Language courses i.d.e.a. in La Calera (☎ & ℻ 922/805 703; ⓦ www.laGomera.net/idea) offers two-week tuition for €150.

Laundry Lavanderia Waltraud, La Playa (Mon–Sat 10am–3pm).

Pharmacy Celina Chinea Hocar, on the main road in Borbalán; also near the Medical centre in Las Orijamas, above La Calera.

Police There is no police station in Valle Gran Rey, though the local Policia Municipal can be contacted on ☎922/805 000.

Post office Behind the petrol station in La Calera (Mon–Fri 9am–1pm, Sat 9am–noon).

Scuba diving Fisch & Co (9am–1pm, but closed Fri; ☎922/805 688; ⓦwww.lagomera.net/tauchen) opposite the tourist office in La Playa.

Travel Agents La Paloma (☎922/805 685) in Vueltas, can help with flights, bus and boat tours. They can also change money and have a fax service.

PARQUE NACIONAL DE GARAJONAY AND AROUND

Map 16, F4.

One of the world's most ancient forests, the mass of moss-cloaked laurel trees in the **PARQUE NACIONAL DE GARAJONAY** is La Gomera's most outstanding attraction. As many as four hundred species of flora, including Canary willows and Canary holly, and sixteen varieties of laurel flourish here among swirling mists. Atlantic trade winds barrelling against the island and condensing into cloud cause these mists and supply enough moisture for plants to thrive, producing a dense, light-blocking canopy and encouraging moss and lichen to smother everything.

Up until the end of the tertiary period, around two million years ago, when ice ages wiped it out, laurel forest covered most of the Mediterranean region. This climate change had less of an effect on the Canaries, allowing last remnants of this dense forest to survive on damper islands such as Tenerife and La Gomera. When humans first arrived in La Gomera most of the island was covered in laurels, but logging has since restricted it to a relatively small upland area, protected since 1978 as a national park and registered as a World Heritage site by UNESCO.

Hikes in the cold, damp, atmospheric forest often head up the island's highest peak, **Garajonay**, where, when it's not too cloudy, great views spread over the dense tree canopy below and beyond to neighbouring islands. Some of the thickest and darkest forest is further north near the hamlet of **El Cedro**, home to the park's only (very limited) accommodation options. More readily accessible places to stay are just outside the park in the main upland town of **Chipude**, a good base for park exploration, and near the impressive mesa **La Foraleza**, a good short hike and once an important Guanches spiritual site.

Arrival and information

Buses linking both Valle Gran Rey and Playa de Santiago with San Sebastián stop at Pajarito, a fork in the road, before turning south to Chipude. This is the most convenient place to get off to access the park and is very close to Mount Garajonay.

The **park information centre**, Centro de Visitantes del Parque Nacional de Garajonay (Map 16, H2. Tues–Sun 9.30am–4.30pm; free; ☏992 800 993), is well outside the park, near Agulo in the north of the island. Though not served directly by bus it's only a 2km uphill hike to the centre from the restaurant Las Rosas beside the main road, where the bus stops. The centre has a few displays on the park and a supply of maps and books, though there's little information in English. For much better guidance ask the centre staff about their free weekly guided hikes. You can buy hiking **maps** at the information centre, though there's a better range available in the bookshops of San Sebastián and Valle Gran Rey.

Among the scattering of fine old Canarian houses in the centre are a couple of **craft workshops** where craftsmen can sometimes be watched making pottery, musical instruments such as tambourines and castanets and baskets. A diverting little museum of folk history, also on the site, describes the stages in the production of goat's cheese and reconstructs a traditional Gomeran home.

Beside the centre, and with the same opening hours, is the rustic *Restaurant El Tambur*, which serves fresh and simple Gomeran **food** such as excellent watercress soup, garlic mushrooms and potatoes stuffed with fish.

Garajonay

Map 16, F5.

The most obvious excursion in the national park is the hike to its highest point, which offers superb views over the surrounding the dense tree canopy, when the summit isn't cloaked in mist. On a clear day you can see the islands of Tenerife, La Palma, El Hierro – and sometimes even Gran Canaria from here. It is named for Gomera's answer to Romeo and Juliet, Gara and Jonay, a Gomeran princess and a humble peasant boy from Tenerife who visited his princess by paddling over on inflated goatskins – or so the Guanche legend goes. Neither family were keen on the couple's relationship, but their love ran far deeper than their differences in status, and so, determined never to be parted, they clambered to the top of Garajonay and ran each other through with lances of laurel wood – settling instead for death in this last passionate and dramatic act.

To **climb the peak**, head up from Pajarito, the road junction where the bus stops, from where the route is signposted (1hr return). You can vary the route by returning down a steep loose trail along a ridge at the northeast side of the peak to arrive at the small roadside car park by **Alto de Contadero** (Map 16, F5), the start of a great trail that heads down to El Cedro and Hermigua. East along the road, this route heads back to Pajarito, west along it there is soon a turnoff onto a wide track (part of a confusing network that requires a map) that roughly parallels the road to lead to **La Laguna Grande** (Map 16, F5), a large shallow former crater. The crater is home to a popular picnic spot and a **restaurant** (Tues–Sun 9am–6pm); often busy with day trippers from Tenerife, this restaurant serves good stews and some excellent *mojo*. Just beyond here is one of the most interesting trails in the park, one that clambers through dense laurel forest before meeting up with a trail that leads back to Garajonay – via numerous crossroads that need to be negotiated with the aid of a map.

El Cedro

Map 16, H4.

A rural hamlet set amid lush cultivated terraces and dense laurel thickets, overlooking the Hermigua valley, **EL CEDRO** is the national park at its best; a good place to stop on longer hikes, or, as the only place to stay in the park, a destination in itself. Connected to a minor road at the eastern end of the national park via a driveable dirt road, El Cedro is at the meeting point of several excellent hiking trails, through some of the densest, darkest laurel forest on the island.

One stunning **trail to El Cedro** descends through premium laurel forest from Garajonay, via Alto de Contadero (see Garajonay, above) and past the small *Mudéjar*-style chapel Ermita de Nuestra Señora de Lourdes, takes around two hours to reach the village. From here the trail descends down the ravine at the centre of town to become one of the island's prettiest hikes, with great panoramas over the lush Hermigua valley a further two hours below. The distinct path passes a small waterfall (part of La Gomera's only stream), a couple of dams and an old *gofio* mill – the grindstone is still here. It crosses the stream several times along the way, before turning into banana plantations (by a couple of tin-roof shacks) and arriving in Hermigua.

Another **route to El Cedro** works its way up from the head of the Hermigua valley and includes the possibility of an exciting hike through a 575m underground **water tunnel** – not for the claustrophobic, nor for those without a torch. To reach the head of the trail, take the bus that runs between Hermigua and San Sebastián and ask to be dropped off at the El Rejo junction. From here head a little further down the main road towards Hermigua, then climb up a track that leads past a chapel to a minor road. The route crosses this road, arriving at the water tunnel, which took 26 years to chisel by hand, was once used to transport water between valleys to help irrigate Hermigua's thirsty banana plantations. An alternative route runs from the start of the tunnel over the hill to El Cedro.

In El Cedro *Bar La Vista* (☎922/880 949) serves good, hearty Gomeran **food**, in lovely outdoor surroundings, offers simple **rooms** (❷) and runs a small **campsite** (€2 per site) – the island's only one – and the only place you can legally pitch in the park.

Chipude

Map 16, E5.

Up until two hundred years ago **CHIPUDE**, served by the bus between San Sebastián and Valle Gran Rey, was La Gomera's largest town. Today only the relatively large sixteenth-century **Iglesia de la Virgen de la Candelaria**, dominating the central plaza, hints at the former importance of the town. Beside it, a couple of bars serve basic **food** and provide **accommodation**, but there are no shops in town. *Bar Pensión Sonia* (☎922/804 158; ❷) on the plaza offers excellent, hotel-quality en-suite rooms, sometimes playing host to large hiking parties. Large dishes of *gofio* stand on tables in its restaurant, ready for the good, if basic, food, off a menu that's limited to one soup and one main course every night. *Bar Navarro* (☎922/804 132; ❷) next door is not quite so good value, but still a friendly place to stay or eat tapas.

La Fortaleza

Map 16, E6.

Once a place of considerable spiritual significance to the Guanches, and still the most impressive landmark in the uplands, the mesa **Fortaleza** makes a superb two hour round trip from Chipude (an hour trip from the road at its base). Starting out along the road to La Dama, the start of the track up the side of the hill is obvious, beginning by the roadside. As the track ascends, its improbable path up the final steep sections are unclear, but once there it's easy to find the route up – which is steep and in places involves a scramble and a head for heights. The top of the hill is almost uniformly flat and for Guanches was an important place of retreat and worship. Remains of stone circles were found here along with bone fragments, suggesting sacrifices. The views over Chipude, the national park and El Hierro are excellent, but winds usually don't encourage you to linger long before heading back down the only path up.

El Cercado and Las Hayas

North along the bus route to Valle Gran Rey from Chipude, is the small village of **EL CERCADO** (Map 16,

E5), where traditional **pottery** (*Alfarería*) – made without a wheel and rubbed with red earth before glazing – is still crafted in a couple of workshops where you can sometimes catch the potters at work. Further up the road **LAS HAYAS** (Map 16, E5) is best known for the superb, reasonably priced, vegetarian wholefood cuisine of *Bar La Montaña*. The **restaurant** specializes in stews made from almost completely home-grown ingredients – the picking of which is often part of the lengthy preparation time – best spent sampling the goats' cheese, salad and distinctively local house wine. Almond cake garnished with palm honey is a fine, typically Gomeran, finish to the meal.

PLAYA DE SANTIAGO

Map 16, I9.

The second largest resort on the island, **PLAYA DE SANTIAGO** is still first and foremost a small harbour town with few restaurants and a virtual absence of nightlife. Other than several large pebble beaches and the island's sunniest weather, there's not much to keep you here – even the local hikes are dull by Gomeran standards.

Santiago comprises a number of smaller settlements in a broad valley, of which the sea-side **Playa de Santiago** is the most significant. Here the Avenida Maritima, a relatively busy seafront road housing the town's business district, including its few bars and restaurants, looks out onto the harbour, a huge sea defence wall of unattractive concrete blocks and, to the east, a pebble beach. Inland of this pebble beach, and separated from it and the Playa de Santiago by a large banana plantation, is **Laguna de Santiago**, a small functional village clinging onto the side of a steep hill where the handful of apartments offering accommodation have great rooftop views of the valley. Above the village, and overlooking the entire valley from its cliff-top vantage point, is the gigantic self-contained five-star resort-hotel **Tecina**.

East beyond the massive headland on which the Tecina sits are a number of bays with three main **pebble beaches**. Each is a fairly considerable half-hour hike from the other, via a driveable dirt road. The closest beach to the Tecina tends to attract the hotel's guests along with locals. The next beach along has a less mainstream scene – attracting mainly nudists. The caves at the back of this beach used to house a sizeable hippie community, moved-on by a concerted police campaign in the 1990s that eventually led to the caves being filled in. As a result a number of the community moved east to the next beach along, which at low tide can be accessed via a rock arch over the sea.

The island's only surviving **dragon tree** (see p.127) is about an hour's return trip west of the highway near **Alajeró**. The San Sebastián–Playa de Santiago bus stops near the trailhead opposite the turn-off to Imada. Follow the track here downhill in the direction of Agalán, then follow signs to Camino de El Drago.

Arrival and information

Four **buses** a day link Playa de Santiago with San Sebastián, leaving from in front of the Hotel Tecina and from the little Plaza at the centre of Avenida Maritima. The **tourist office** (Mon–Fri 10am–2pm; ☎922/870 281) is a couple of hundred metres east along from here along this seafront road.

Accommodation

Considering Playa de Santiago offers so little to do, it has quite a good selection of **accommodation**, ranging from the cheapest pensions on the island to the most expensive luxury hotel. Along the Avenida Maritima, in **Playa de Santiago** itself, an inviting floral jungle in the forecourt announces *Pension del Carmen* (☎922/895 028; ❷). Small basic rooms (some without windows) furnished almost solely by two sagging beds, and shared bathrooms with poor plumbing are all that's on offer here. *Pension La Gaviota* (☎922/895 135; ❷) beside the plaza is definitely preferable, though slightly more expensive, offering some en-suite rooms with a small balcony. Enquire at the restaurant below.

Another pension *Casa Lolita* (☎922/895 232; ❶), the cheapest on the island and blessed with fine views thanks to its location in **Laguna de Santiago** has mattresses on the floor of the "student" rooms and windowless doubles sharing a bathroom. Nearby, the modern *Apartamentos Negrin* (☎922/895 282; ❷) are much more appealing, sleeping up to three and offering roof terraces with good bay views. The apartments are in three separate blocks, avoid Negrin one at the hairpin in the road – Negrin two and three are less exposed to traffic and so quieter.

Spread out on the cliffs overlooking the ocean at the eastern side of town, is the grand **Hotel Jardín Tecina** (☎922/145 850, ☎922/145 851, ⓦ www.fredolsen.es; ❻), built and run by Norwegian shipping magnate Fred Olsen, who operates ferries around the archipelago. The self-contained resort includes over four hundred rooms, five pools and restaurants, four bars and extensive sports facilities. All facilities are open to the general public, including a scuba-diving centre that operates from the premises. Prices include breakfast and dinner. Olsen also owns the extensive *barranco* Valle Benchijigua, a valley of banana plantations off the road to San Sebastián, where simple self-catering rustic **bungalows** can be rented (☎922/145 864; ❹).

Eating

Most of the modest little **bars** and unpretentious **restaurants** in Playa de Santiago are scattered along the seafront. *Bar El Paso*, by the plaza is popular with locals, serves huge portions and has some spectacular photos of the 1999 storms, when the sea tore through the town. *Pizzeria Avenida* is another cheap option, with a big selection of good pizzas, as well as steaks and fish. The best restaurant in town is *La Cuevita* (closed Sun), in a candlelit natural cave at the harbour end of Avenida Maritima. The massive selection of fish and meat includes fine steaks and the particularly good local fresh fish *vieja*, served with a salad garnish and *papas arrugadas*. The restaurant also offers a big and unusually imaginative dessert selection. Up beside *Hotel Tecina*, with excellent views over the harbour and bay, *Restaurant Tagoror* serves good tapas and has a large wine selection but otherwise its moderately expensive food, the usual cross-section of fish, meat, paella and pizza, is nothing special.

Boat trips on the *Siron* to Los Organos (€36) start from Playa de Santiago on Tuesdays, Thursdays and Sundays at 9am. Tickets can be purchased at *Bar Info* just east beyond Avenida Maritima

---

CONTEXTS

History

Though bound with Spanish history and the collective heritage of the Canary isles, both Tenerife and La Gomera have their own distinctive histories. Their **early history** is, however, shrouded in mystery, for despite vague references in Classical literature, it was only when European slave raiders began to land on the Canaries in the fourteenth century that accounts of the **natives** began to filter through to the Old World. At the dawn of Europe's era of great exploration, the culture and origins of these Stone Age inhabitants perplexed outsiders, and only recently are conflicting scholarly theories about them being resolved – with links to ancient **Berber tribes** being the most likely hypothesis.

By the end of the fifteenth century **Spanish conquistadors** had claimed and conquered the entire archipelago for Spain, beginning a period of settlement in a pioneer society that wiped out the indigenous culture and created an island economy based on farming and trade. Prevailing winds put the Canaries right on trade routes to the New World making them an important last stopping point before an Atlantic crossing, a pattern that **Columbus** started when he paused in La Gomera before, unwittingly, discovering America.

People and goods as well as ships moved through the ports, helping to forge strong cultural and economic links with South America. Crops discovered there, such as sugar cane, cotton, tobacco, cochineal and bananas would be introduced to Tenerife as monocultures, often suffering boom-bust cycles which led to regular bouts of **mass migration** of Canarians to South America in search of work. But sooner or later many of these migrants returned to their native islands, reinforcing cultural ties with the Americas and weakening the sense of a communal identity with the distant Spanish mainland, its people and the politics of Madrid. Today the Canary islands have a large amount of political autonomy within the Spanish state, and the islanders will generally call themselves Canarians rather than Spanish. But despite this rift at the level of the nation-state, the Canaries are being tied ever more closely with the rest of Europe by **tourism**, which brings millions of visitors to the island from northern Europe every year and has encouraged large numbers of others to emigrate here, too.

First references and contact

The earliest known references to the Canary Islands are thought to have been in some of **Plato**'s writings (428–348 BC) where he refers to Atlantis, a continent sunk beneath the ocean floor in a cataclysmic event which left only the highest mountains above the sea. Subsequent Classical writers built on this notion, creating a legendary garden of Eden and even identifying the islands as **Elysium** – the place where the virtuous would go in their afterlife, an assumed source of the tags Fortunate Islands or Blessed Islands that have sometimes been used to refer to the Canary islands. But though this early body of Classical writing seems to suggest references to the **Macronesia islands** (the Canaries, Azores, Cape Verde and Madeira), there is no evidence that either the Phoenicians or Greeks ever landed in the Canaries.

The first real, if questionable, evidence of contact between the islands and the outside world came four hundred years after Plato's writings. In an account of a fleet serving **King Juba II**, the Roman client king of Mauritania, it would appear that the ships might well have weighed anchor on one of the Canary islands, probably Gran Canaria, in 40 BC, though many of their observations of the island seem inaccurate. However, fragments of amphorae found on some of the islands suggest at least a fleeting Roman presence at some point and certainly, by the time the Greek geographer **Ptolemy** (c. AD 100–160) drew his well-respected map of the world the islands were included on it – the western tip of El Hierro marking the edge of the known world.

The first reliable account of European contact came in the early fourteenth century, when the Genoese captain **Lanzarotto Malocello** was blown off course in 1312, landing on – and ultimately lending his name to – the island of Lanzarote. Making the most of his accidental visit, the captain whiled away twenty years on the island before returning to Europe, causing a Portuguese–Italian mission to set out in 1341 and finally confirm the island's place on the world map. News of the discovery quickly spread, and it was not long before the curiosity of missionaries and slave raiders was aroused, precipitating regular visits by both throughout the rest of the century.

The Guanches

Despite relatively frequent European contact throughout the fourteenth century, the first accounts of the native islanders, known as **Guanches**, stem from the fifteenth cetntury. These describe tall, powerfully built Scandinavian-looking people with blue eyes and long fair hair. The Guanches in the south of Tenerife were said to have been dark-skinned, while those in the north considerably paler. While accounts describe a comparatively uncivilized people with Stone Age technology dressed in animal hide and living in caves, visitors also seemed remarkably impressed by the natives. At a time when the concept of the "noble savage" was becoming fashionable, observers could not resist ascribing legendary abilities to the handsome race. Their agility and prowess was described in detail, their ability to be consistently accurate with lances at ten paces and stones at a hundred commended. Guanches were said to be able to run over rough ground catching a goat by its hind legs, and many giants were reported among them, including one individual allegedly fourteen feet high with eighty teeth.

Archeologists have since drawn a clearer picture of the Guanches, who were indeed tall by the standards of time – men around 1.70m, women 1.57m – with a life expectancy of around 32 years, and common malformations resulting from a small genetic stock. The natives were **technologically primitive**, with no knowledge of the wheel or metallurgy. In fact, by standards of most Stone Age cultures, even stone appears to have been poorly crafted and little developed and horns and animal bones were more commonly used to make tools. The ancient Canarians subsisted largely by **hunting** and **gathering**, occasionally fishing, and engaging in a little **farming** – growing barley, wheat and pulses – but without the aid of a plough. They had domesticated dogs and pigs as well as goats and sheep. At the time of conquest, there were estimated to be around 200,000 sheep, but the Guanches had no knowledge of using their wool for weaving, dressing instead in a **tamarco**, a large goatskin fastened with fish bones and thorns – fashioned to cover a woman's chest and feet – which was also used as a shroud after death.

But probably the most intriguing feature of the Guanches' culture is that they had virtually no knowledge of **seafaring** and virtually no contact with other islands in the archipelago, let alone the African or European mainland. Not only is this a retarded state of development for an island race, but also a puzzling one, since presumably the natives must have arrived from somewhere by boat.

Origins

Among the **theories of the origin** of the Guanches there have been some that maintain they were a rogue and rebellious **Berber tribe**. Their tongues having been cut out, they were cast out to sea in boats without oars by Romans, before finally landing on the islands, later unable to communicate their origins to their children. Various theories were also put forward that maintained it was **Vikings** who had settled the islands, leaving behind their racial characteristics, or that the islands had been colonized solely by people from the Iberian peninsula in line with the prevailing direction of currents and winds to the islands. It seems likely now that there is an element of truth in each of these theories, and that in fact there were several waves of habitation after the first contact – thought to have been around 900 BC, the date of the earliest archeological finds on the islands.

These finds have been among evidence that has recently suggested that the Guanches were overwhelmingly of **Berber origin**. Other evidence has included similarities in ceramics, language, customs, traditions and culture. One particular line of archeological research, into the pyramids at Güímar, initially suggested a link with **Egyptian culture**. However, since the Guanches were considerably more primitive than the Ancient Egyptians, this line of enquiry has taken researchers back to Berber areas in the High Atlas mountains, where a cave-dwelling civilization existed that appears to have spread both east and west, spawning both the Guanche and Ancient Egyptian cultures. This theory is supported by similarities between Berber script, Guanche markings and Egyptian hieroglyphs – in fact, some inscriptions found in Tenerife appear to translate as **Zanata**, the name of a North African Berber tribe that was displaced from its territory around Maghreb during Roman occupation. The island of Fuerteventura is just about visible from the African continent 112km away, and the Berbers were capable sailors, who used large and relatively complex **reed boat designs** (as reconstructed by Norwegian archeologist Thor Heyerdahl; see p.95). These would have rotted away quite soon after the island's colonization, thus explaining the lack of knowledge of seafaring, since in any case there would have been little cause for the immigrants to return to the mainland.

Social structures and cultural practices

In contrast to their primitive technology, the ancient Canarians appear to have had a number of relatively complex **social structures and cultural practices**. Both Tenerife and La Gomera were divided into a number of *meneceyatos* (kingdoms) – the names of which survive as modern place-names, such as Anaga, Tegueste, Tacaronte, Taoro, Icod, Daute, Adeje, Abona, Güímar – whose peoples seemed to be commonly warring against one another. Each tribe consisted of three classes of society: the monarchy, a nobility and the rest of the population (mainly peasants, craftsmen and goatherds).

Only the **monarchy** seems to have been hereditary, and then only through the female line – although governance was not exercised by women, but by the men they chose to marry. An additional complication was that the title of *mencey* (king) did not pass directly from father to son, but first via the brothers of a former mencey. Only when the youngest brother died did the eldest son receive his title – in a ceremony that required the bones of the original mencey in the lineage to be kissed.

HISTORY

For the rest of the population, the rank of **nobility** was attained not through birth but as a result of personal qualities or actions, whose recognition in turn bestowed the right to grow hair long. The noble status was conferred after lengthy discussion among tribe elders who gathered beneath an ancient dragon tree (see p.127) to dispense justice and titles – impinging on the otherwise autocratic powers of the chief.

The role of **women** in Guanche society was a strong one, for the most part due to the matrilinear hereditary pattern that determined not only the transfer of titles in the monarchy, but also the transfer of possessions among the rest of the populace. Though a man would own belongings, on his death they would transfer to the children of his sister. Women could also take all kinds of jobs, and are known to have been priests, doctors, potters and even warriors. The status of women was also elevated by the fact that there were fewer women than men on the islands – thought to have been a result of the work of slave raiders and pirates. In consequence many took several husbands – who alternated between stints in the hills with their herds of goats and participating in married life on the coast. But at the same time it was customary, particularly in La Gomera, for the guest in a Gomeran household to be offered use of the wife – a facet of local culture that many conquistadors eagerly embraced.

Religion

The Guanches were a **religious** and deeply superstitious people, who worshipped a single God, **Achaman**, to whom animal sacrifices and libations were made in caves and whose physical manifestation was thought to be the sun. His opposite number was **Guayota**, a devil that dwelt in hell – **Echeyde**, within the crater of Mount Teide – and who punished misdeeds through volcanic eruptions. Other than the building of a number of flat-topped **pyramids** structures around the island (see p.95), the most significant Guanche religious practice appears to have been the **mummification** of their nobility (another link with Berber and Egyptian cultures), whose subsequent burial took place in caves with their possessions, including their *pintadera*, a person's unique wooden seal worn on a leather thong necklace and thought to be useful in the afterlife. Peasants were just burnt or buried.

The **mummification process** was carried out by a special caste of undertakers, who were shunned and lived apart from the rest of society. These undertakers would wash bodies in the sea, then dry them in the sun for two weeks, covering them in an ointment that consisted of various pulverized plants and included the sap of the dragon tree (dragon's blood), and removing internal organs which were replaced by bundles of plants that would soak up moisture from the corpse. Once properly dry, all orifices of the mummy would be sealed with beeswax, before it was wrapped in leather or basketry and propped vertically in a cave. Despite the existence of many parallels in the details of mummification with Egyptian techniques, the Guanche methods were in fact a good deal more primitive, with the result that the older mummies were found to have decomposed when the mass graves were explored in the eighteenth and nineteenth centuries. Many graves were plundered at this time, mummies being pulverized to be sold in European pharmacies as a medicine to improve longevity.

Spanish conquest

At the dawn of the great age of discovery and conquest of sophisticated civilizations around the world by European powers, it was surprising for Spain to be confronted with a Stone Age culture on its doorstep and at the same time to find itself struggling to bring that society under its control. Though the **Spanish campaigns** in the Canarian archipelago were not as bloody as later ones in the New World, the Guanches, who fought with little more than sticks and stones, did inflict several bloody defeats on the well-equipped conquistadors and it took almost a hundred years, the vast majority of the fifteenth century, to conquer the islands. La Gomera was one of the first of the Canary islands to fall under Spanish control, Tenerife the last.

La Gomera

Though a number of the Spanish aristocracy had been granted the title of King of the Canary Islands, it wasn't until 1402, when the French adventurer **Baron Jean de Béthencort** stepped ashore in Lanzarote to a friendly welcome, that the process of conquest formerly began. On his return to Spain, Béthencort was granted the title of King which encouraged him to make a return trip in 1404, when he secured Fuerteventura, El Hierro and La Gomera.

Despite his apprehensions and cautious landing on **La Gomera**, Béthencort actually met little resistance on the island. Friendly natives approached fearlessly, apparently happy to see him. They even tried out some Spanish they had picked up when a previous Spanish landing party had attacked the islanders, lost the fight, but somehow secured a peace with the victors that involved an exchange of gifts and cordial farewells. So Béthencort managed to claim La Gomera in an unlikely and harmonious way, that left him surprised, but also with only the most tenuous power over the island.

The balance between congenial local relations and the Spanish hold over La Gomera completely reversed in the following century. Relations began to become strained under the island's first governor **Hernán Peraza the Elder**, who – although managing to Christianize two of the four island tribes – caused a rift between the Spanish and the Guanches living in the impenetrable mountains of the island's interior. Peraza assessed his position accurately when he had the tough little fort, **Torre Del Conde**, built in San Sebastian in case of trouble. This was put to good use forty years later, during an island-wide rebellion in 1488 that cost the life of Peraza's grandson, **Hernán Peraza the Younger**, and forced his wife the beautiful **Beatriz de Bobadilla** (see p.236), to hole up in the fort until help arrived. The rising was crushed with undue cruelty to the locals, with many Guanches being executed or sold into slavery. Thereafter an uneasy peace was kept on the island, which was soon to be famously graced with the presence of an as yet relatively unknown **Christopher Columbus** in 1492, on his way west to find a shorter route to India.

Tenerife

Despite a couple of notable attempts to colonize **Tenerife**, when Columbus sailed past it was still in the hands of the Guanches. It wasn't until the year following Columbus's departure (1493) that the campaign that would ultimately conquer the island began.

On May 1 of that year, the Spanish conquistador **Alonso Fernández de Lugo** landed with a thousand men at a beach near what is now Santa Cruz. At first, if after some heated discussions, de Lugo's party was left in peace by the Guanches. This was partly because the chiefs (*menceys*) of local tribes speculated that this large alien force could turn out to be a powerful ally against the tribes on the northern side of the island with whom they were constantly squabbling. They also calculated the odds of successful resistance to the invader to be low. Bolstered by the knowledge and forces of the three defecting tribes, de Lugo proceeded north, heading towards the rich and heavily populated

Orotava valley, where the charismatic **Mencey of Taoro Bencomo** spearheaded a carefully prepared resistance.

On May 13, 1493, the Guanches, who up until then had consistently withdrawn, sprang a trap on the Spanish as they marched west. In a confrontation known as the **Battle of Acentejo** – or La Matánza ("The Massacre"), after which the modern settlement is named – de Lugo experienced a crushing defeat. Three hundred Guanches and nine hundred Spanish perished in the battle – de Lugo himself escaped dishonourably by giving his red cloak to one of his soldiers, who was consequently mistaken for the leader and pursued and killed by the Guanches. The fiasco cost de Lugo all but a handful of his men and was all the more embarrassing in light of the primitive nature of Guanche weaponry – which consisted entirely of stones and fire-hardened spears for long-range assaults, and wooden clubs and thin, pointed-stone blades for hand-to-hand combat.

The small number of remaining Spanish retreated back to Santa Cruz and waited for reinforcements before confronting the natives again. Over a year later the army advanced again, this time crushingly defeating the natives on the flat land around La Laguna. This was unsuited to Guanche guerrilla tactics but good predictable terrain for the Spanish, and the Guanches lost almost twice as many men here as the Spaniards had done at Acentejo.

Another year passed before the third and **final major battle** between Spanish and Guanche forces, which occurred near the site of Acentejo (today marked by the town La Victoria) on Christmas day in 1495. Defeat seemed certain this time for the Guanches, whose population had been reduced by an epidemic of "**sleeping sickness**" (a combination of influenza and pneumonia and lethargic encephalitis) – against which the indigenous population lacked immunity, and that had killed over four thousand people in the Orotava valley alone. The last *mencey* of the powerful Taoro, **Bentor**, who had recently replaced Bencomo, is said to have committed ritual suicide in the face of defeat, proclaiming "I will never submit to another. I am born free and will live free." And with that, the Guanche resistance more or less petered out, with over 15,000 natives having been killed by war or pestilence.

Accounts suggest that the scale of death made prompt burial hard, so that having lost their masters, packs of **wild dogs** formed to feed on the corpses and became so used to human flesh that they would even attack the living. Only a tiny Guanche population of around six hundred remained, most of whom quickly integrated into Spanish settler society, with many forcibly entering into domestic service or being sold by de Lugo to pay debts arising from his military campaigns. No more than a handful of Guanches, to be known as **Guanches alzados** – rebellious Guanches, managed to continue their traditional ways in remote, mountainous areas.

Settler society and the development of agriculture

Having founded **La Laguna** and made it the island's capital, in 1498 **de Lugo** married the Governoress of La Gomera, **Beatriz de Bobadilla**, and settled down to the task of clearing the debts of his military campaigns, at the same time milking Tenerife of its agricultural potential. In return for his own financing of his expeditions, the Spanish monarchy permitted de Lugo to dispense land and water rights on the island, which he did to the benefit of his financiers. Many of these were **Italian merchants**, who moved into the island's capital and built grand town houses incorporating a variety of cultural influences. Distinctive woodwork from Muslim architectural traditions reflects the origins of many of the local craftsmen and many buildings show a distinct *mudéjar* influence, exemplified by the island's trademark ornate wooden balconies and the impressive *artesonado* wooden ceilings in many of the island's churches.

The introduction of sugar cane

Both de Lugo and the financiers that had bankrolled him pushed along the production of **sugar cane**, often selling land only on the condition that cane would be grown there, in an attempt to emulate the success of this crop on Gran Canaria. With the farming industry's overwhelming dependence on one crop, sugar-mill owners soon formed a capitalist elite, often charging heavily for processing, and creating tensions with farmers. A similar situation emerged between those who held water rights and sold them at a premium and the smallholders who relied upon this resource.

Tensions between islanders were further fuelled by cultural differences. While the politically most powerful people were Castilian, the bulk of the island's investors were Italian, the farm workers Portuguese, the bulk of the craftsmen Arab and the slaves Guinean – all in all an **explosive mix of cultures** in a fledgling frontier society which, as Spain's New World artery, had become a crucial victualling stop for galleons bound west, and a port of call for returning ships laden with gold and jewels. Opportunities for smuggling, fraud and piracy presented themselves and attracted numbers of fugitive criminals to the island.

The economic success of sugar cane proved to be relatively short lived. It became but the first of a series of monocultures the island embraced, only for them to be buffetted in and out of a number of boom-bust cycles by outside factors (in this case competition from the Antilles and Brazil). These in turn played havoc with the island's economy and forced many workers to **emigrate** to South America in times of hardship.

The wine industry

The production of **wine** – at its peak between 1550 and 1670 – became the predominant industry on the island once the sugar-cane industry went bust. The sweet rich **malmsey wine** (*malvista*), produced by twisting bunches of grapes by their stalks and leaving them to shrivel before pressing, copied many of the qualities of popular Madeiran wine, and became highly regarded particularly in England. A barrel of malmsey wine was even part of William Shakespeare's annual salary. However, by the end of the seventeenth century Canarian wine production had fallen foul of diseases that had begun to raise its price, and changing tastes that made it less desirable.

Cochineal farming

Tenerife's fortunes were at their lowest ebb in the lean eighteenth century, but as the nineteenth century progressed things began to improve again. In 1817, a university was founded in La Laguna. In 1822 Santa Cruz became the island's capital – a reflection of its success as a port, which was bolstered further in 1852, when it became a free port with the associated custom and tax advantages.

But the next real upswing in the economy of Tenerife resulted from the introduction and harvesting of a tiny bug, **cochineal**, whose body fluids were used to make red dye. The industry took off from the 1830s, but again the boom was short-lived, and by 1870 the invention of chemically based dyes put cochineal farmers out of business.

Banana plantations

Farmers would only have a relatively short, but painful, wait for the next great money-making cash crop, for in the 1880s **bananas** were introduced to the Canary Islands. A small species from Indochina, the dwarf Cavendish, was found to weather the islands' spring-like climate well and has been cultivated ever since. Its economic success took off largely thanks to the development of refrigerated shipping, but the trade was ruined by the disruption of merchant navies caused by blockades during World War I. The collapse of the banana trade was inevitably accompanied by a flood of **emigration** to South America, particularly to Cuba and Venezuela, where bananas were also being successfully cultivated. Crucially, the fruit could also be produced there more cheaply, partly due to the high cost of water on Tenerife. Unable to compete with the lower costs of production in South America, the Canarian banana industry has only survived by virtue of **subsidies** from the Spanish government, who also guarantee a market for the banana.

Birth of the modern state

By the end of the nineteenth century Tenerife's role as unofficial capital of the archipelago encouraged other economic activity and wealth, and it became less dependent on the shifting fortunes of its agricultural sector. Though its position weakened as power gradually shifted to Gran Canaria, in 1927 the division of the archipelago into **two administrative regions** – with Tenerife governing La Gomera, El Hierro and La Palma – again helped to strengthen its position. To the government on the Spanish mainland, however, the island was of course still considered a remote backwater, so it was to Tenerife that a young **General Francisco Franco** was transferred, under suspicion that he was plotting a coup, in the hope that this would put him at a safe distance.

But it was as military governor of the Canary Islands, and while residing on Tenerife, that Franco hatched the plans that led to the **Spanish Civil War**. In 1936 Franco launched his coup, and within days he left the islands, flying to the sympathetic Spanish foreign legion in Morocco from where he organized the march into Andalucia, sparking a war which grew into a major international conflict, claimed half a million lives and sent as many into exile.

There was actually little fighting in the Canaries, but within hours of Tenerife falling into Nationalist hands repression began. Left-wing politicians as well as trade unionists, teachers, writers and artists were herded into **Fyffes' banana warehouse**, near the present football ground in Santa Cruz, to be shot in batches. A spate of summary **executions** followed elsewhere on the island, including that of **Lieutenant Gonzalez Campos**, the only officer in Tenerife to oppose the uprising. The civil governor and staff were also executed for good measure, allegedly because the governor had shouted "Long live Libertarian Communism." But neither a known Libertarian nor a Communist, the reports of independent witnesses who actually heard "Long live the republic" are more likely to have been true.

The Canaries suffered from Spain's **post-war economic depression** with thousands of refugees fleeing clandestinely to South America, many perishing in unseaworthy vessels on the way. But ultimately the Franco era brought prosperity to the Canaries, as it did in Spain, and Santa Cruz developed into an internationally important staging post for long-distance shipping (a role it still maintains); fish processing began to emerge as a major industry and the island's increasingly diversified agrarian sector showed stability and some growth.

Today the island's **agricultural sector** has shrunk drastically and has been in a state of crisis for some years. While forty years ago over half its population worked in agriculture, now only one tenth of the islanders work the land. Both exports of crops and seafood have declined considerably, with actually around six times more food being imported than exported. But luckily the rise in the level of imports is due to the needs of Tenerife's latest profitable monoculture – **tourism**.

Travellers and tourists

Tenerife became a popular destination on **The Grand Tour**, the European circuit that became a fashionable pastime for the rich in the late nineteenth century. Various contemporary artists and writers brought back favourable impressions of Tenerife that particularly caught the imagination of the monied English seeking a pleasant place to spend the winter or seek spa treatments. The first widely distributed and well-received **guidebook**, written by the parochial and opinionated Olivia Stone following a tour of the islands in 1884, was the first of a spate of guides about Tenerife. The most succcessful was a straight-talking little volume packed with practical detail, advice and opinions written by A. Samler Brown who authored fourteen editions of the guide to Tenerife between 1889 and 1932.

While interest among the wealthy continued in the period after World War II, it was the introduction of **charter flights in the 1950s** – nonstop flights to Tenerife beginning in 1959 – that changed the whole structure of the island's tourism.

Once limited to a collection of rather exclusive hotels in Puerto de la Cruz, **tourist developments** spread like wildfire around the island in the 1960s. Attempts at replicating Puerto's success elsewhere began along the north coast, but pretty soon it was realised that what modern holiday-makers were really after was great weather. Before long **huge resorts** began to mushroom at the southern end of the island, where there had been little more than desert – but which today contains around three-quarters of the island's accommodation. Since its beginnings in the 1960s, **mass tourism** has continued to boom on the island, despite occasional recessions (particularly in the 1970s) and today Tenerife plays host to around 4.5 million annual holiday-makers – of which around a third are British, a quarter Spanish and a sixth German. The island now owes around two-thirds of its Gross National Product to tourism.

Though tourism has proved to be a crucially important money-spinner for the island, providing employment and encouraging a host of otherwise unimaginable infrastructural improvements, the **unregulated growth** of resorts, together with the hasty concrete extensions to service towns, is beginning to cause some concern. The local abstract artist **César Manrique**, who also enjoys a degree of international recognition, particularly championed efforts to preserve Canarian culture and architecture from the onslaught of faceless mass tourism. To some extent his campaign has borne fruit, encouraging hotel architects to build in more vernacular styles, but the problems associated with tourism run deeper than this, impacting on the **natural environment**, where they are harder to regulate or control. They include problems associated with processing waste, sewage treatment, regulating water supplies, providing energy and protecting delicate ecosystems – needs all too often overlooked in the past, in the scramble for easy, short-term financial gains.

Contemporary Tenerife

Soon after the death of Franco in 1975 and the restoration of Spain's monarchy in 1978, the Canaries became an **autonomous region** in 1982, which encouraged an introverted politics on the islands that has brought nationalist parties to the forefront and has even made them power brokers at a national level. Many islanders push for still greater **independence** from Madrid, and support parties with clear agendas of complete self-governance, such as the Unión del

Pueblo Canario (UPC). Graffiti demanding the withdrawal of *godos* (goths), meaning mainlanders or *peninsulares*, is common all around the islands.

Associated with these political demands is an emerging fashion for emphasizing links to possible **Guanche ancestry**, naming children with Guanche names, and promoting Guanche festivals, like the harvest festival of *Beñasmen* celebrated in Candelaria. Linked also is the recent surge in local support for traditional Canarian activities, such as the local take on wrestling, *Lucha Canaria*. Tourism has also helped to encourage the nurturing of traditional crafts and customs.

But at the same time as the rift between the Spanish mainland and Tenerife widens, the island's links with the rest of Europe are strengthening. Whilst this is partly because of an economy dependant on tourists from these countries, it is also because there has been a sharp increase in the number of northern Europeans settling here, since the Canary Islands became a **member of the EU** in 1992, enjoying a special status with low taxes, though no longer entirely duty free. Presently, out of a total island population of around 700,000, about 25,000 are expatriate foreigners officially resident here, the vast majority of which are British. It is estimated that about that number of foreigners again are not legally registered, or on longer stays that don't require registration.

The environment

Together with the Azores, Madeira and the Cape Verde Islands, the Canaries belong to the **Macronesian Islands**, which all show common features in flora and fauna, are all of volcanic origin and have similar topographic patterns.

As early as the late eighteenth century, naturalists became interested in the Canary Islands. The German geographer and naturalist **Alexander von Humboldt** spent some time on Tenerife, surveying the flora and fauna, which he wrote about extensively. In 1831, **Charles Darwin** set sail on *HMS Beagle* for a four-year surveying voyage of the world. One of his first stops in 1832 was to have been Tenerife, but when the ship was informed that it would have to spend twelve days in quarantine prior to landing, the captain decided to set sail again. Darwin noted in his journal "… we have just left perhaps one of the most interesting places in the world, just at the moment when we were near enough for every object to create, without satisfying, our utmost curiosity."

Geology

The Canarian archipelago is estimated to be 30 million years old, relatively young by geological standards, and of

volcanic origin, the result of magma oozing through cracks in the earth's surface. This occurred at a time when a series of mountain ranges, including the Atlas mountains, were being crumpled into shape by movements of the earth's crust, as the African tectonic plate pushed north against Europe. The resulting cracks and fissures created an opportunity for lava to spew forth and ultimately become islands. Like similar so-called hot spots, tectonic activity continues in the region, with a build-up of magma eventually spewing forth after the tectonic plate on which the islands sit, shifts – currently it is moving at a rate of 3cm a year. Less than a tenth of the island mass of Tenerife is above the ocean, the top of Teide around 7000m above the sea-bed proper.

Tenerife and La Gomera are among the younger islands in the group. **La Gomera** is around twenty million years old and was formed on the ocean floor, before being pressed upwards to form an island. The last volcanic activity here took place some 2.8 million years ago and its present landforms are as much the product of erosive forces which have sculpted the island since. Owing to the differing resistance of rock types to erosion, numerous volcanic plugs of harder material have been left standing around the island, now known as **Los Roques**.

Although the mountain ranges on the eastern and western tips of **Tenerife** (the Anaga and the Teno) are roughly the same age as La Gomera, most of Tenerife is much younger – giving rise to the theory that several separate islands were joined to form Tenerife around six million years ago. A second volcanic period of activity around three million years ago then built the **Cumbre Dorsal**, the backbone of Tenerife that leads east–west down the centre of the island. The highest point along this section is **Las Cañadas**, now protected as a national park and include the massive volcano **Teide**. This area is one of the youngest parts of the archipelago and still an active volcanic region. Eruptions have been recorded here several times since written records began in the fifteenth century, but luckily have occurred only in sparsely populated areas, and not without considerable prior warning. The most **recent volcanic eruption** on Tenerife occured in 1909, although the neighbouring island of La Palma recorded volcanic activity as recently as 1971.

Flora

With a high proportion of endemic species, the Canary Islands are to **flora** what the Galapagos Islands are to fauna and Tenerife even has over a hundred endemic species of its own. In addition the island has an incredible range of vegetation with almost every vegetation zone in the world represented on the island. In addition to the many native species, many plants introduced from elsewhere have also readily flourished on the islands (illustrated best by the lush and varied Botanical Gardens in Puerto de la Cruz). The mountainous nature of the island helps to cause this – since this provides a large range of ecological niches, but also because trade winds and a cold Canary ocean current act to cool the island's subtropical maritime climate, particularly its northern side, where there's often thermal inversion and consequently cloud cover above about 1000m. In contrast, the range and even numbers of birds and animals on the island are small and generally unimpressive.

The reason behind the high level of endemicity of the Canary Islands again lies in their **mild maritime climate**. This has meant that drastic climate changes occurring nearby, such as ice ages in Europe or the drying of the Sahara have been considerably tempered in their effects on the Canary Islands. As a result a large number of plant species endemic to Macronesia are also ancient species such as the

Dragon Tree (see p.127), one of eighty species that survived the Tertiary ice ages on Tenerife, but died elsewhere.

Four basic **ecological zones** have been identified on the island: a lower zone of arid scrubland; a laurel forest zone (absent from the southern side); a zone of pine forest; and finally a high mountain area.

The zone of **arid shrubland** is at its starkest in the dry dusty south of the island. Here succulents naturally dominate, with **cacti** growing where they can. The **prickly pear** is particularly abundant, though not a native plant, having been introduced for the cochineal bug industry in the nineteenth century. Now out of hand, it has become problematic, spreading invasively and competing with local flora.

Outside the dry southern area and up to altitudes of 600m the land becomes progressively greener and is used all around the island, as **farmland**. Farming is made possible using a huge network of irrigation tunnels dug deep into the island's centre and thanks to the painstaking construction of thousands of terraces. **Bananas** are the dominant crop on the island, although various vegetables, including potatoes and tomatoes, and fruits such as oranges and mangoes are also common

Above 600m, **forests** begin to take over. In the Anaga and Teno and on La Gomera, this is predominantly an ancient forest dominated by **laurel trees** – another refugee of the Tertiary-era ice ages. Elsewhere the dominant fauna is **pine forest**, consisting almost exclusively of the endemic **Canarian Pine** (see p.207). At the time of conquest, forest covered nine-tenths of Tenerife and La Gomera, but today, thanks to extensive logging, it only covers about a fifth.

Most of the area above the tree line in Tenerife is protected in the **Parque Nacional del Teide**. This tundra-style wilderness harbours only the hardiest of plants, and is

GREEN DOGS

The **native dogs of Tenerife** are thought to have preceded humans on the island. Their arrival, according to the veterinary faculty at La Laguna University, was by way of natural rafts consisting of fallen trees and bushes drifting down rivers after floods and storms on the African continent.

When, over 2000 years ago, explorers are thought to have landed on what is now Gran Canaria, they recorded being confronted by these beasts. So impressed were they by the beauty, obedience and intelligence of these slender, striped creatures, that a couple of puppies were taken back to their Mauritanian King, Juba II. The island group accordingly became referred to as the **islands of Canes** (dogs), which has since been corrupted to Canary Islands.

With the increase in the archipelago's interaction with Europe, more breeds were introduced to the island. In consequence, many of the dogs on the streets of Tenerife today are descendants of other breeds – from dogs of refuelling conquistadors to the Pekinese-style sofa dogs popular among the holidaying gentry around the turn of the century. Recently, a large variety of new breeds, popular with northern European ex-pats settling on the islands have also been introduced. However, the dog championed as the true Canarian dog is the Canary Mastiff Verdino, or **Green Dog**, so-called because of its pelt's greenish hue. It is claimed that the breed is about 2000 years old, and therefore the breed found here by Juba's explorers, even though its form – a squat, short-haired guard dog with a broad jaw – bears little resemblance to the descriptions of the dogs these explorers found.

mainly the domain of tough little shrubs, with the exceptions of the resilient pretty little **Teide violet**, and the impressive two-metre high flowering conical spike of the **Tajinaste**

Certainly there are numerous records of the existence of this breed at the end of the fifteenth century, when conquistadors secured Spanish possession of the islands. With their masters dead as a result of conquest, some Verdinos turned wild, attacking goats and occasionally even conquistadors. In consequence, a law of 1499 condemned many Verdinos to death, only allowing shepherds one dog each to help guard flocks. Judging by its continual publicity and by the number of fines imposed, this law must largely have been ignored. However, the Spanish continued in this policy, at one stage even paying a gold coin to anyone producing the head of a Verdino. These severe laws were eventually annulled eight years after their passing by the Spanish ruler Castellao, almost certainly under pressure from the Guanche princess with whom he was in love.

In the last few decades, as the northern European presence on the island grew, so did interest in using the Verdino in **dogfights**. Only when dogfighting became outlawed did cross-breeding with bull terriers and alsatians by British and German dogfighting enthusiasts no longer threaten the purity of the breed.

Today, some Verdinos still perform their tasks as **working dogs**, particularly on Fuerteventura where they tend to be leaner and faster, and consequently useful in shepherding activities. However, most are just kept as tenacious little **guard dogs** and **pets** and there is a growing interest in showing and breeding what is now one of the most enduring symbols of the Canary Islands. On Tenerife, the Club Español del Presa Canario arranges meetings and competitions around the island, particularly in the main square in La Laguna where pups change hands for about £300.

GREEN DOGS

rojo. Its likely that there were more such interesting endemic plants, but that these disappeared well before the Spanish conquest when the Guanches introduced goats into the area.

Fauna

Neither Tenerife or La Gomera are renowned for their **animal** life. Though there is evidence that at one time giant rats, metre long tortoises and even large lizards (similar to those on the neighbouring island El Hierro) used to roam here, it seems certain that, not having evolved to cope with predators, all three were easily hunted to extinction by the Guanches. So today the only wild animals you'll see on the island are likely to be **rabbits** and **hares** and a variety of **geckos** and **lizards** – some up to 25cm in length. But the islands are home to a much wider variety of **birds**, some difficult to see elsewhere in Europe, and up to two hundred different species have been seen on Tenerife. Of the more unusual birds swifts, blue chaffinches, Berthelot's pipits and trumpeter finches, quails, owls, and various birds of prey are all relatively common. Although there are few endemic birds on the island, a number of interesting sub-species have emerged, thanks to a separate evolutionary development from the main species elsewhere. Though probably not the reason for the archipelago's name (see box below), the **canary** does live in the forested areas of the island. In the wild the bird is naturally a sparrow-like colour and appearance (it only turns to the familiar eye-catching yellow in captivity) and so it's difficult to spot and easier to recognize by the distinctive song of male birds (females don't sing). The only form or fauna where there is a high level of endemicity on the island is among **insects**, in particular many unique butterflies. None of the endemic insects are however harmful – expect for a rare and shy centipede with a mean bite.

Due to the cool Canary current and the fact that the coast drops steeply and suddenly into the ocean there is relatively little **marine life** here. Nevertheless, in spite of these conditions, some 350 species of fish and 600 species of algae have been identified around the island. **Dolphins** can often be seen from the shore, playing in the surf, however, while **sharks** (none of which are dangerous) and **whales**, though not common, do visit the waters further from the shore.

Books

Of the rather limited collection of books on the Canary islands, few are wholly specific to Tenerife or La Gomera and even fewer have been translated into English. A good place to search for Spanish language books is on the Web site of Interbook (Ⓦwww.disbumad.es), a major Spanish online bookstore, offering over a million titles. For English language titles, most high-street booksellers should be able to help with the titles listed below, but if you are having difficulty finding a title, or are looking for something quite specific, try contacting Books on Spain, PO Box 207, Twickenham TW2 5BQ, UK (☎020/8890 7789; Ⓦwww.books-on-spain.com), an excellent source of new used and out of print books.

John Mercer, *The Canary Islanders: Their prehistory, conquest and survival* (Collins). Readable well-researched history of the Guanches and their introduction into Castilian society – though having fallen slightly out of date in the light of recent archeological finds.

Felipe Fernández-Armesto, *The Canary Islands after the conquest: The making of a colonial society in the early sixteenth century* (Clarendon Press). Thorough history of the development of the islands and the problems and issues the colony faced.

Carole Stewart, *Self-catering in Spain, the Balearics and the Canary Islands* (Croom Helm). Good handbook for all those seeking to explore Spanish and Canarian cuisine to the fullest – with recipes and shopping advice for self-caterers.

Tony Clarke and David Collins, *A Birdwatchers' Guide to the Canary Islands* (Perry). Definitive guide for twitchers visiting the Canaries.

Philip Ashmole, *Natural history excursions in Tenerife* (Kidston Mill Press). Detailed coverage of the island's flora and fauna, though poorly illustrated. Includes a number of recommended excursions and talks you through what you're likely to see on the way.

Language

As on other Canary Islands, **Spanish** is the language spoken on Tenerife and La Gomera, though it differs slightly from mainland Spanish in its vocabulary, the main differences are in pronunciation – which is closer to South American than European Spanish. Numerous **Spanish phrasebooks** are available, one of the most user-friendly being the *Rough Guide Spanish Phrasebook*. For teaching yourself the language, the BBC tape series *España Viva* is excellent. Cassells, Collins, Harrop and Langenscheidt all produce useful **dictionaries**; Berlitz publishes separate Spanish and Latin-American Spanish phrasebooks.

For non-native speakers the easiest difference to notice in the **pronunciation** of Canarian Spanish is the absence of a "lisp" on the the letter "c" before vowels – which is replaced by an "s" sound. Thus Barcelona, pronounced Barthelona in Spain, becomes Barselona. But in its most casual form, the Canarian pronunciation doesn't even really bother with "s" sounds at all, particularly where these come at the end of a word – so gracias becomes gracia; and buenos dias, bueno dia. Another easily noticeable peculiarity to Canarian Spanish is the use of *Ustedes*, a plural form of "you", used in place of *vosotros*. On the mainland the former is reserved mainly for formal occasions to afford respect towards the person addressed.

BASIC SPANISH WORDS AND PHRASES

Basics

Yes	*Sí*	Closed	*Cerrado/a*
No	*No*	With	*Con*
OK	*Vale*	Without	*Sin*
Please	*Por favor*	Good	*Buen(o)/a*
Thank you	*Gracias*	Bad	*Mal(o)/a*
Where	*Dónde*	Big	*Gran(de)*
When	*Cuando*	Small	*Pequeño/a*
What	*Qué*	Cheap	*Barato/a*
How much	*Cuánto*	Expensive	*Caro/a*
Here	*Aquí*	Hot	*Caliente*
There	*Allí, Allá*	Cold	*Frío/a*
This	*Esto*	More	*Más*
That	*Eso*	Less	*Menos*
Now	*Ahora*	Today	*Hoy*
Then	*Más tarde*	Tomorrow	*Mañana*
Open	*Abierto/a*	Yesterday	*Ayer*

Greetings and responses

Hello	*Hola*
Goodbye	*Adiós*
Good morning	*Buenos días*
Good afternoon/night	*Buenas tardes/noches*
See you later	*Hasta luego*
Sorry	*Lo siento/disculpéme*
Excuse me	*Con permiso/perdón*
How are you?	*¿Cómo está (usted)?*
I (don't) understand	*(No) Entiendo*
Not at all/You're welcome	*De nada*
Do you speak English?	*¿Habla (usted) inglés?*
I (don't) speak Spanish/Catalan	*(No) Hablo Español*
My name is . . .	*Me llamo . . .*

What's your name?	*¿Como se llama usted?*
I am English	*Soy inglés(a)*
Scottish	*escocés(a)*
Australian	*australiano/a*
Canadian	*canadiense/a*
American	*americano/a*
Irish	*irlandés(a)*
Welsh	*galés(a)*

Hotels and transport

I want	*Quiero*
I'd like	*Quisiera*
Do you know . . . ?	*¿Sabe . . . ?*
I don't know	*No sé*
There is (is there?)	*(¿)Hay(?)*
Give me . . .	*Deme . . .*
Do you have . . . ?	*¿Tiene . . . ?*
. . . the time	*. . .la hora*
. . . a room	*. . .una habitación*
. . . with two beds/double bed	*. . . con dos camas/cama matrimonial*
. . . with shower/bath	*con ducha/baño*
for one person	*para una persona*
(two people)	*(dos personas)*
for one night (one week)	*para una noche (una semana)*
It's fine, how much is it?	*Está bien, ¿cuánto es?*
It's too expensive	*Es demasiado caro*
Don't you have anything cheaper?	*¿No tiene algo más barato?*
Can one . . . ?	*¿Se puede . . . ?*
. . . camp (near) here?	*¿ . . . acampar aqui (cerca)?*
It's not very far	*No es muy lejos*
How do I get to . . . ?	*¿Por donde se va a . . . ?*
Left	*Izquierda*
Right	*Derecha*

LANGUAGE

Straight on	*Todo recto*
Where is . . . ?	*¿Dónde está . . . ?*
. . . the bus station	*. . . la estación de autobuses*
. . . the bus stop	*. . .la parada*
. . . the nearest bank	*. . .el banco más cercano*
. . . the post office	*. . .el correo/la oficina de correos*
. . . the toilet	*. . .el baño/aseo/servicio*
Where does the bus to. . . leave from?	*¿De dónde sale el autobús para . . . ?*
I'd like a (return) ticket to . . .	*Quisiera un billete (de ida y vuelta) para . . .*
What time does it leave (arrive in . . .)?	*¿A qué hora sale ? (llega a . . .)?*
What is there to eat?	*¿Qué hay para comer?*

Days of the week

Monday	*lunes*		Friday	*viernes*
Tuesday	*martes*		Saturday	*sábado*
Wednesday	*miércoles*		Sunday	*domingo*
Thursday	*jueves*			

Numbers

1	*un/uno/una*	12	*doce*	50	*cincuenta*
2	*dos*	13	*trece*	60	*sesenta*
3	*tres*	14	*catorce*	70	*setenta*
4	*cuatro*	15	*quince*	80	*ochenta*
5	*cinco*	16	*dieciseis*	90	*noventa*
6	*seis*	17	*diecisiete*	100	*cien(to)*
7	*siete*	18	*dieciocho*	200	*doscientos*
8	*ocho*	19	*diecinueve*	500	*quinientos*
9	*nueve*	20	*veinte*	1000	*mil*
10	*diez*	30	*treinta*	2000	*dos mil*
11	*once*	40	*cuarenta*		

INDEX

stay in touch

roughnews

Rough Guides' FREE full-colour newsletter

News, travel issues, music reviews, readers' letters and the latest dispatches from authors on the road

If you would like to receive roughnews, please send us your name and address:

62-70 Shorts Gardens
London, WC2H 9AH, UK

4th Floor, 345 Hudson St,
New York NY10014, USA

newslettersubs@roughguides.co.uk

IF KNOWLEDGE IS POWER,
THIS ROUGH GUIDE IS A
POCKET-SIZED BATTERING RAM

THE MILLION-COPY BESTSELLER

THE ROUGH GUIDE TO
The
Internet
Angus J. Kennedy

2001 EDITION · FOR PCs AND MACS

£6.00
US$9.95

Written in plain English, with no hint of
jargon, the Rough Guide to the Internet will
make you an Internet guru in the shortest
possible time. It cuts through the hype and
makes all others look like nerdy textbooks

ROUGH GUIDES ON THE WEB

Visit our website www.roughguides.com for news about
the latest books, online travel guides and updates, and
the full text of our Rough Guide to Rock.

AT ALL BOOKSTORES · DISTRIBUTED BY PENGUIN

ROUGH GUIDES: Travel

THE MINI ROUGH GUIDE TO

Menorca

Phil Lee

ROUGH GUIDES: Mini Guides, Travel Specials and Phrasebooks

Seattle
Sydney
Tokyo
Toronto

German
Greek
Hindi & Urdu
Hungarian
Indonesian
Italian
Japanese
Mandarin
  Chinese
Mexican
  Spanish
Polish
Portuguese
Russian
Spanish
Swahili
Thai
Turkish
Vietnamese

MINI GUIDES
Antigua
Bangkok
Barbados
Big Island of Hawaii
Boston
Brussels
Budapest
Dublin
Edinburgh
Florence
Honolulu
Lisbon
London Restaurants
Madrid
Maui
Melbourne
New Orleans
St Lucia

TRAVEL SPECIALS
First-Time Asia
First-Time Europe
More Women Travel

PHRASEBOOKS
Czech
Dutch
Egyptian Arabic
European
French

AVAILABLE AT ALL GOOD BOOKSHOPS

ROUGH GUIDES:
Reference and Music CDs

REFERENCE
Classical Music
Classical:
 100 Essential CDs
Drum'n'bass
House Music

World Music:
 100 Essential CDs
English Football
European Football
Internet
Millennium

**ROUGH GUIDE
 MUSIC CDs**
Music of the Andes
Australian
 Aboriginal
Brazilian Music
Cajun & Zydeco
Classic Jazz
Music of Colombia
Cuban Music
Eastern Europe
Music of Egypt
English Roots
 Music
Flamenco
India & Pakistan
Irish Music
Music of Japan
Kenya & Tanzania
Native American
North African
Music of Portugal

Jazz
Music USA
Opera
Opera:
 100 Essential CDs
Reggae
Rock
Rock:
 100 Essential CDs
Techno
World Music

Reggae
Salsa
Scottish Music
South African
 Music
Music of Spain
Tango
Tex-Mex
West African Music
World Music
World Music Vol 2
Music of Zimbabwe

AVAILABLE AT ALL GOOD BOOKSHOPS

100 Essential CDs

Eight titles, one name

ROUGH GUIDES

Sorted

ROUGH GUIDES

MUSIC ROUGH GUIDES on CD

YOUR GUIDES TO A WORLD OF MUSIC

'Rough Guides have long been noted for their excellent travel books. Take note, because their musical guides are equally thorough and enjoyable' *HMV Choice (UK)*

THE ROUGH GUIDE TO GLOBAL DANCE

Global Dance

MUSIC ROUGH GUIDE

world beat carnival: access all areas

Available from book and record shops worldwide or order direct from World Music Network, Unit 6, 88 Clapham Park Road, London SW4 7BX tel: 020 7498 5252 • fax: 020 7498 5353 • email: post@worldmusic.net

Hear samples from over 70 Rough Guide CDs at

WWW.WORLDMUSIC.NET

Will you have enough stories to tell your grandchildren?

Yahoo! Travel

Do You
YAHOO!
?

NORTH SOUTH TRAVEL

Great discounts

North South Travel is a small travel agent offering excellent personal service. Like other air ticket retailers, we offer discount fares worldwide. But unlike others, all available profits contribute to grassroots projects in the South through the NST Development Trust Registered Charity No. 1040656.

For **quotes** or queries, contact Brenda Skinner or Bridget Christopher, Tel/Fax 01245 608 291. Recent **donations** made from the NST Development Trust include support to Djoliba Trust, providing micro-credit to onion growers in the Dogon country in Mali; assistance to displaced people and rural communities in eastern Congo; a grant to Wells For India, which works for clean water in Rajasthan; support to the charity Children of the Andes, working for poverty relief in Colombia; and a grant to the Omari Project which works with drug-dependent young people in Watamu, Kenya.

Great difference

Email brenda@nstravel.demon.co.uk
Website www.nstravel.demon.co.uk

ATOL
75401

North South Travel, Moulsham Mill, Parkway, Chelmsford, Essex, CM2 7PX, UK

Rough Guides
on the Web

www.travel.roughguides.com

We keep getting bigger and better! The Rough Guide to Travel Online now covers more than 14,000 searchable locations. You're just a click away from access to the most in-depth travel content, weekly destination features, online reservation services, and an outspoken community of fellow travelers. Whether you're looking for ideas for your next holiday or you know exactly where you're going, join us online.

You can also find us on Yahoo!® Travel (http://travel.yahoo.com) and Microsoft Expedia® UK (http://www.expediauk.com).

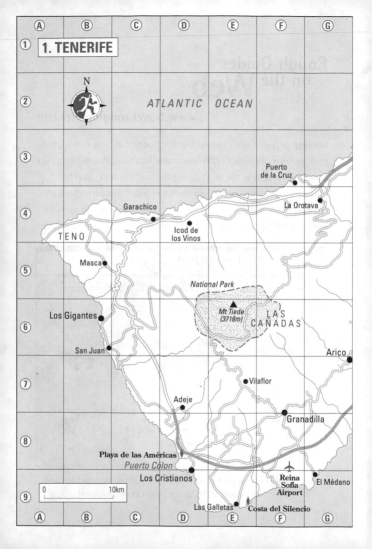

1. TENERIFE

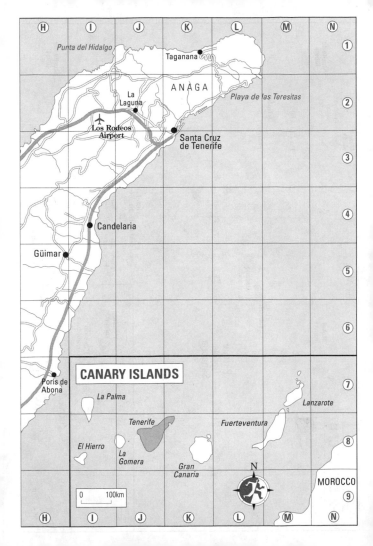

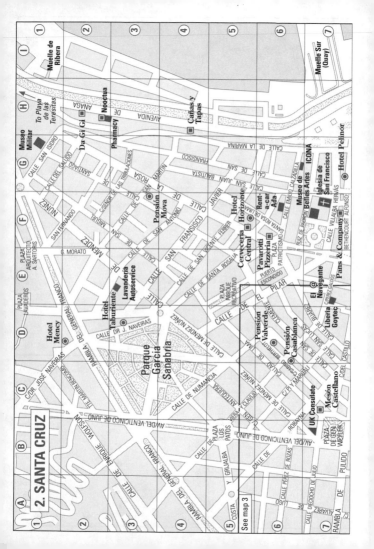

2. SANTA CRUZ

Muelle de Ribera

To Playa de las Teresitas

Museo Militar

Calle San Isidro

Calle del Saludo

G. Morato

San Fernando

Pensión Mova

Plaza Arquitecto A. Sartorius

Plaza Javaderos

Hotel Mency

Hotel Taburiente

Lavandería Autoservice

Parque García Sanabria

Da Gi Gi

Pharmacy

Calle de las Tribulaciones

Calle de San Antonio

Calle de San Vicente Ferrer

Calle de Santa Rosalía

Calle de Dr. J. Naveiras

Rambla del General Franco

C/Dr. José Naveiras

Calle de Enrique Wolfson

Calle de General Franco

Plaza de los Patos

Plaza de Gen. Weyler

Av. del Veinticinco de Julio

Avenida de Anaga

Noctua

Cañas y Tapas

Hotel Horizonte

Cervecería Central

Calle de San Martín

Calle de San Juan Bautista

Calle de San Francisco

Calle Emilio Calzadilla

Museo de Belles Artes

Rent-a-car Ada

Santa Rosa Olivera

Pavarotti Pizzeria

Plaza Patriotismo

Plaza Parque Recreativo

El @ Navegante

Pensión Valverde

Pensión Casablanca

Calle de Méndez Núñez

Calle del Pilar

Calle de El Clavel

Calle de Santiago Cuadrado

Calle de Imelda

Calle de San Clemente

Puerto Escondido

Librería Goytec

Pans & Company

Iglesia de San Francisco

ICONA

Hotel Pelinor

Muelle Sur (Quay)

Calle de la Marina

Ave de Ramón y Heras

Calle Villalba Hervas

Bethencourt Alfonso

Calle de San Francisco

Plaza Patriotismo

Mesón Castellano

Calle de Numancia

Calle de Antequera

Calle de Robayna

Calle de Juárez

Calle del Castillo

UK Consulate

Av. del Veinticinco de Junio

Calle de Pérez de Rozas

Calle de San Lucas

Calle de Clavel

Calle Pi y Margall

Calle de Costa y Grijalba

Rambla del General Franco

Pulido

Rambla de

Calle Diecinueve de Julio

Álvarez

Lugo

See map 3

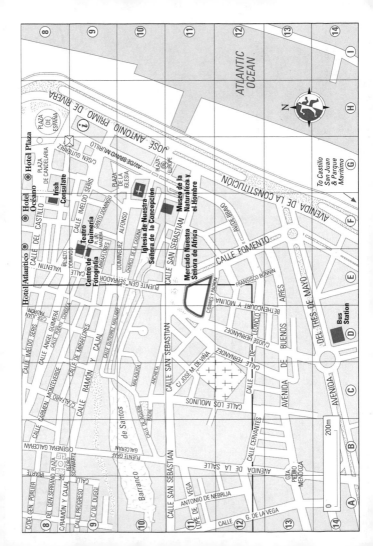

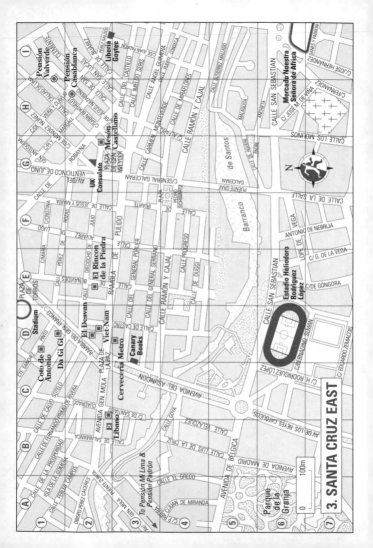

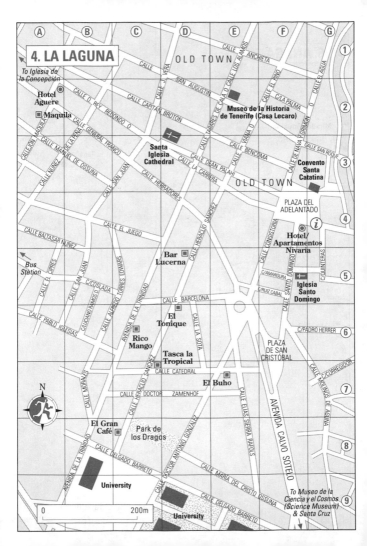

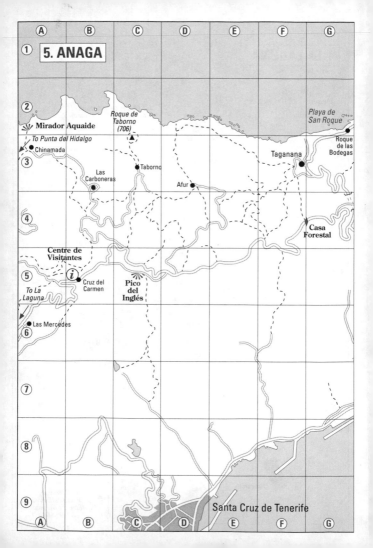

5. ANAGA

Mirador Aquaide

To Punta del Hidalgo

Chinamada

Roque de Taborno (706)

Las Carboneras

Taborno

Afur

Playa de San Roque

Roque de las Bodegas

Taganana

Casa Forestal

Centre de Visitantes

Cruz del Carmen

Pico del Inglés

To La Laguna

Las Mercedes

Santa Cruz de Tenerife

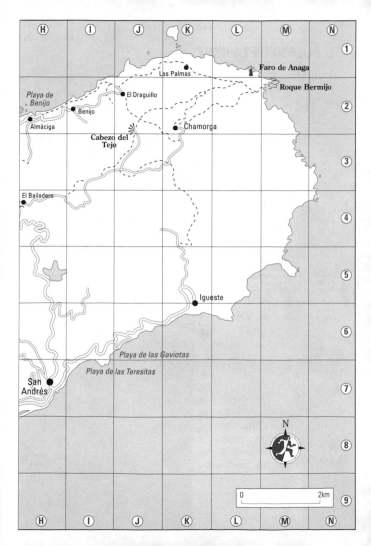

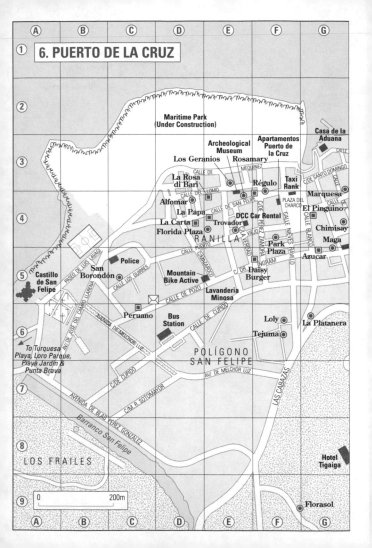

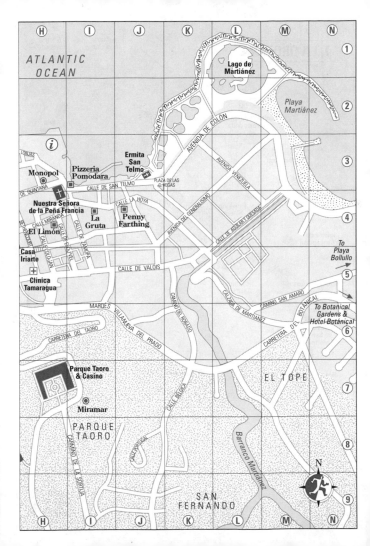

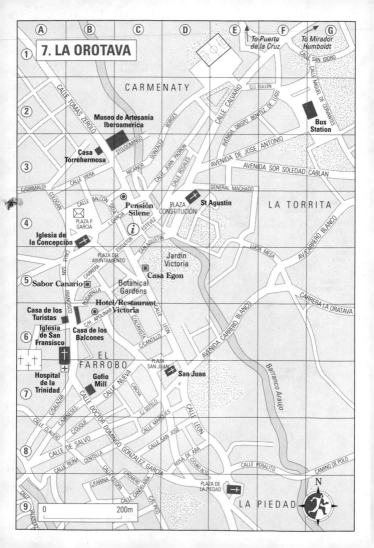

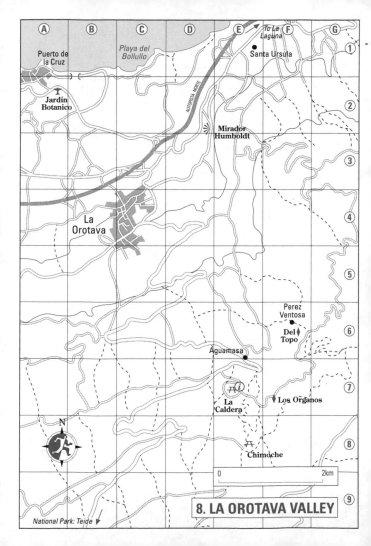

Puerto de
la Cruz

Playa del
Bollullo

To La
Laguna

Santa Ursula

Jardín
Botanico

AUTOPISTA NORTE

Mirador
Humboldt

La
Orotava

Perez
Ventosa

Del
Topo

Aguamasa

Los Organos

La
Caldera

N

Chimoche

0   2km

National Park: Teide

Ⓐ Ⓑ Ⓒ Ⓓ Ⓔ Ⓕ Ⓖ

①
②
③
④
⑤
⑥
⑦
⑧
⑨

8. LA OROTAVA VALLEY

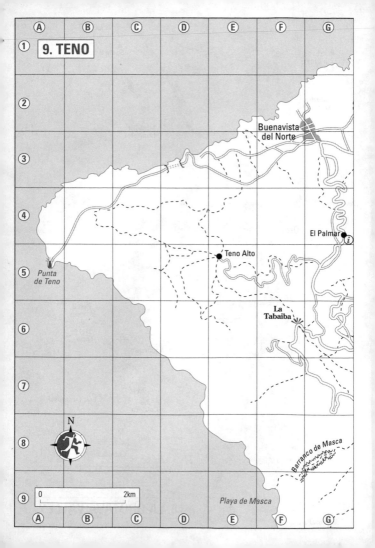

9. TENO

Buenavista del Norte

El Palmar

Punta de Teno

Teno Alto

La Tabaiba

N

Barranco de Masca

0   2km

Playa de Masca

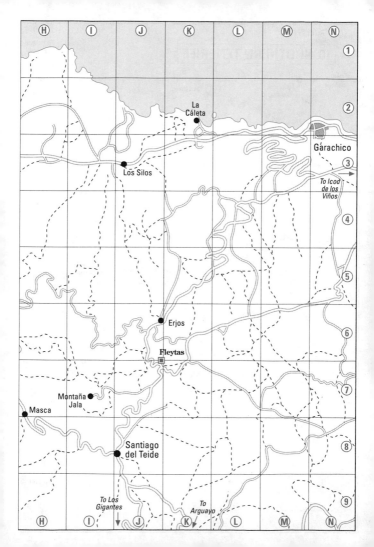

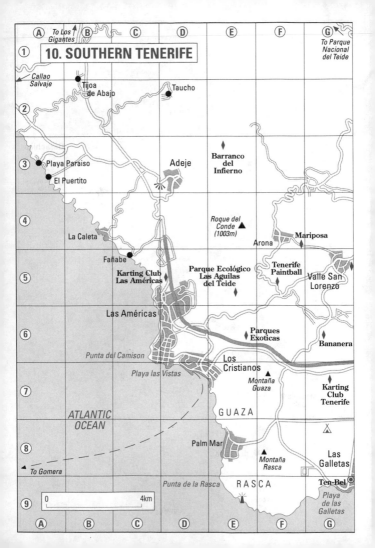

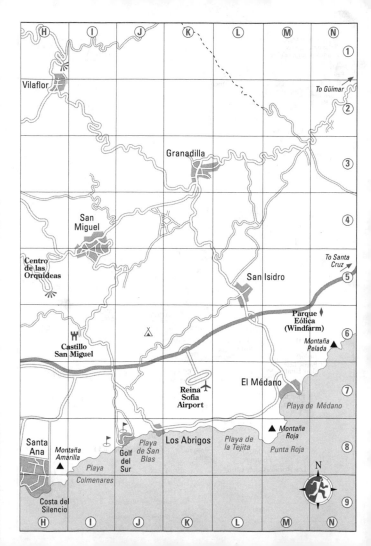

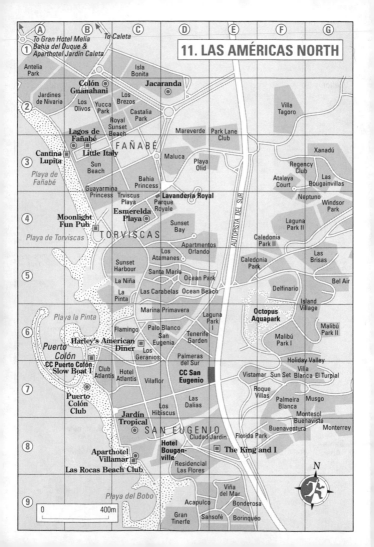

11. LAS AMÉRICAS NORTH

To Gran Hotel Melia
Bahía del Duque &
Aparthotel Jardín Caleta

To Caleta

Antelia Park

Jardines de Nivaria

Isla Bonita

Colón Guanahani

Jacaranda

Los Olivos

Los Brezos

Yucca Park

Castalia Park

Royal Sunset Beach

Mareverde

Park Lane Club

Villa Tagoro

Lagos de Fañabé

Cantina Lupita

Little Italy

FAÑABÉ

Sun Beach

Maluca

Playa Olid

Xanadú

Playa de Fañabé

Bahía Princess

Regency Club

Atalaya Court

Las Bougainvillas

Guayarmina Princess

Trviscus Playa

Lavandería Royal

Parque Royale

Neptuno

Windsor Park

Esmerelda Playa

Moonlight Fun Pub

TORVISCAS

Sunset Bay

Laguna Park II

Caledonia Park II

Playa de Torviscas

Apartmentos Orlando

Caledonia Park

Las Brisas

Los Atamanes

Sunset Harbour

Santa Maria

Ocean Park

Bel Air

La Niña

Delfinario

La Pinta

Las Carabelas

Ocean Beach

Island Village

Marina Primavera

Playa la Pinta

Flamingo

Palo Blanco San Eugenio

Laguna Park I

Octopus Aquapark

Malibú Park II

Puerto Colón

Harley's American Diner

Tenerife Garden

Malibú Park I

Los Geranios

Palmeras del Sur

Holiday Valley

CC Puerto Colón
Slow Boat 1

Club Atlantis

Hotel Atlantis

Vilaflor

CC San Eugenio

Vistamar

Sun Set

Villa Blanca

El Turpial

Puerto Colón Club

Roque Villas

Palmeira Blanca

Musgo

Jardín Tropical

Los Hibiscus

Las Dalias

SAN EUGENIO

Montesol

Buenavista

Monterrey

Aparthotel Villamar

Hotel Bouganville

Ciudad Jardín

Florida Park

The King and I

Buenaventura

Las Rocas Beach Club

Residencial Las Flores

Playa del Bobo

Viña del Mar

N

0   400m

Acapulco

Bonderosa

Gran Tinerfe

Sansofé

Borinqueo

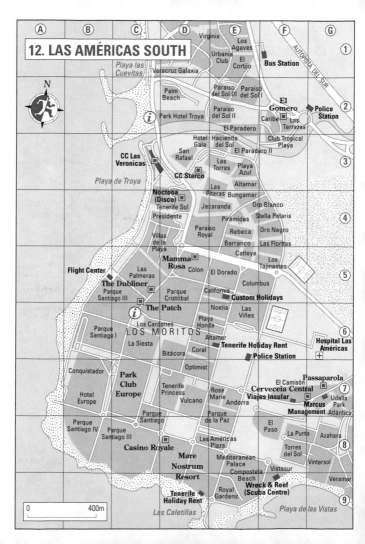

12. LAS AMÉRICAS SOUTH

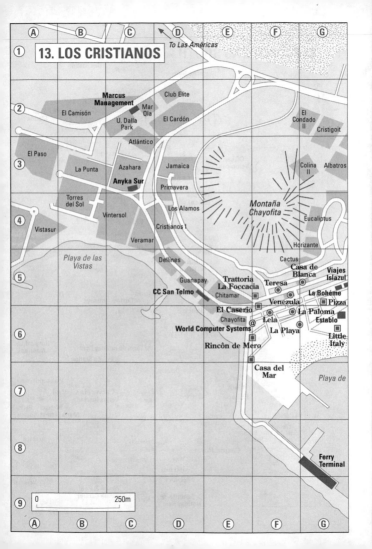

13. LOS CRISTIANOS

To Las Américas

Marcus Management
Club Elite
El Camisón
Mar Ola
U. Dalla Park
El Cardón
El Condado II
Cristigoit
Atlántico
El Paso
Azahara
Jamaica
Colina II
Albatros
La Punta
Anyka Sur
Primavera
Montaña Chayofita
Torres del Sol
Vintersol
Los Alamos
Eucaliptus
Vistasur
Veramar
Cristianos 1
Horizante
Playa de las Vistas
Delines
Cactus
Casa de Blanca
Viajes Islazul
Guanapay
Trattoria La Foccacia
Teresa
CC San Telmo
Chitamar
Venezula
La Bohéme
Pizza
El Caserio
Lela
La Paloma
Chayofita
Establo
World Computer Systems
La Playa
Little Italy
Rincôn de Mero
Casa del Mar
Playa de
Ferry Terminal

0   250m

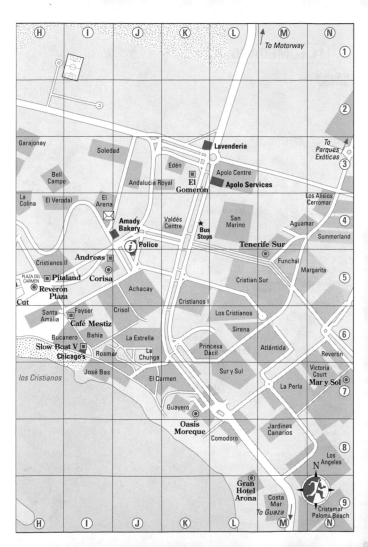

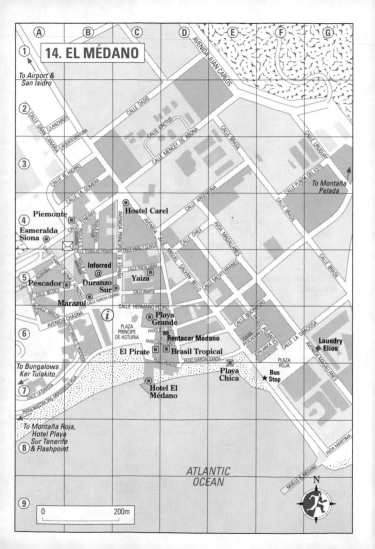

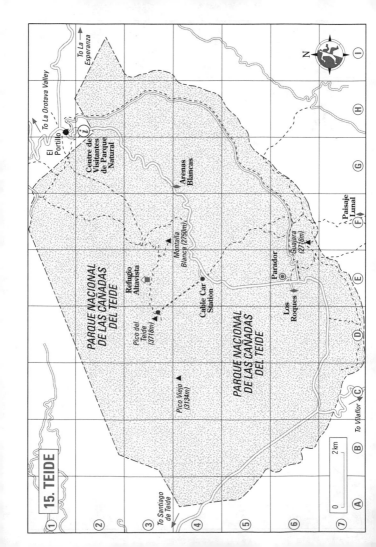

15. TEIDE

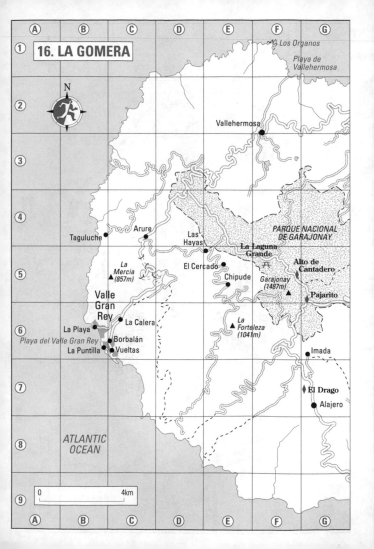

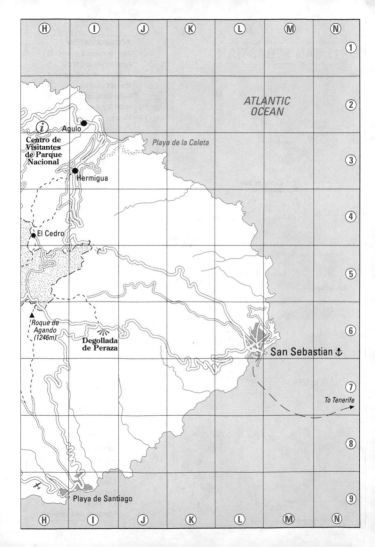

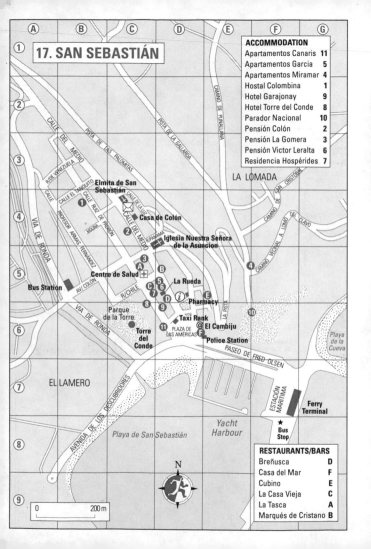

17. SAN SEBASTIÁN

ACCOMMODATION

Apartamentos Canaris	11
Apartamentos Garcia	5
Apartamentos Miramar	4
Hostal Colombina	1
Hotel Garajonay	9
Hotel Torre del Conde	8
Parador Nacional	10
Pensión Colón	2
Pensión La Gomera	3
Pensión Victor Leralta	6
Residencia Hospérides	7

RESTAURANTS/BARS

Breñusca	D
Casa del Mar	F
Cubino	E
La Casa Vieja	C
La Tasca	A
Marqués de Cristano	B

LA LOMADA

EL LAMERO

Elmita de San Sebastián

Casa de Colón

Iglesia Nuestra Señora de la Asuncion

Centro de Salud

La Rueda

Pharmacy

Taxi Rank

El Cambiju

Police Station

Parque de la Torre

Torre del Conde

Bus Station

PLAZA DE LAS AMÉRICAS

PASEO DE FRED OLSEN

Playa de la Cueva

ESTACIÓN MARÍTIMA

Ferry Terminal

Bus Stop

Yacht Harbour

Playa de San Sebastián

N

0   200 m

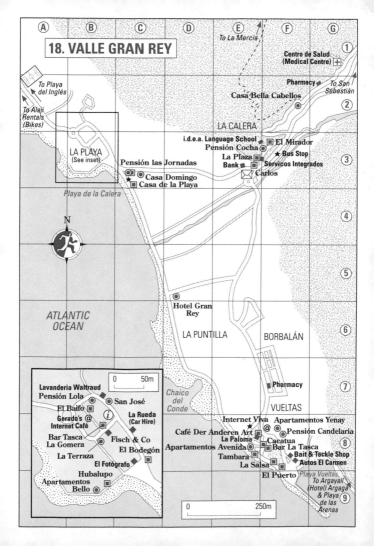

18. VALLE GRAN REY

A B C D E F G

1

To La Mercia

Centro de Salud
(Medical Centre)

To Playa
del Inglés

Pharmacy

To San
Sebastián

Casa Bella Cabellos

2

To Alají
Rentals
(Bikes)

LA CALERA

LA PLAYA
(See inset)

i.d.e.a. Language School
Pensión Cocha
Pensión las Jornadas

El Mirador
Bus Stop
La Plaza
Bank
Carlos
Servicos Integrados

3

Casa Domingo
Casa de la Playa

Playa de la Calera

4

N

5

ATLANTIC
OCEAN

Hotel Gran
Rey

6

LA PUNTILLA

BORBALÁN

Chaico
del
Conde

Pharmacy

7

VUELTAS

Inset (La Playa)

0   50m

Lavanderia Waltraud
Pensión Lola

San José

El Baifo

Gerado's @
Internet Café

La Rueda
(Car Hire)

Bar Tasca
La Gomera

Fisch & Co

El Bodegón

La Terraza

El Fotógrafo

Hubalupo
Apartamentos
Bello

Internet Viva
Apartamentos Yenay

Café Der Anderen Art
La Paloma
Apartamentos Avenida
Tambara
La Salsa

Pensión Candelaria
Cacatua
Bar La Tasca
Bait & Tackle Shop
Autos El Carmen

El Puerto

Playa Vueltas
To Argayall
(Hotel) Argaga
& Playa
de las
Arenas

8

9

0   250m